ASIAN
ART

ASIAN ART

Lark E. Mason

Antique Collectors' Club

For Erica, Melissa, Lark III and Joanna

British Library Cataloguing-in-Publication Data
A catalogue record for this book is available from the British Library

Printed in Italy
Published by the Antique Collectors' Club Ltd., Woodbridge, Suffolk

Frontispiece: Indian bronze figure of Shiva, The King of Dancers. See page 107.
Title page: Chinese silk military rank badge. See page 255.

The Antique Collectors' Club

The Antique Collectors' Club was formed in 1966 and quickly grew to a five figure membership spread throughout the world. It publishes the only independently run monthly antiques magazine, *Antique Collecting*, which caters for those collectors who are interested in widening their knowledge of antiques, both by greater awareness of quality and by discussion of the factors which influence the price that is likely to be asked. The Antique Collectors' Club pioneered the provision of information on prices for collectors and the magazine still leads in the provision of detailed articles on a variety of subjects.

It was in response to the enormous demand for information on 'what to pay' that the price guide series was introduced in 1968 with the first edition of *The Price Guide to Antique Furniture* (completely revised 1978 and 1989), a book which broke new ground by illustrating the more common types of antique furniture, the sort that collectors could buy in shops and at auctions rather than the rare museum pieces which had previously been used (and still to a large extent are used) to make up the limited amount of illustrations in books published by commercial publishers. Many other price guides have followed, all copiously illustrated, and greatly appreciated by collectors for the valuable information they contain, quite apart from prices. The Price Guide Series heralded the publication of many standard works of reference on art and antiques. *The Dictionary of British Art* (now in six volumes), *The Pictorial Dictionary of British 19th Century Furniture Design, Oak Furniture* and *Early English Clocks* were followed by many deeply researched reference works such as *The Directory of Gold and Silversmiths,* providing new information. Many of these books are now accepted as the standard work of reference on their subject.

The Antique Collectors' Club has widened its list to include books on gardens and architecture. All the Club's publications are available through bookshops world wide and a full catalogue of all these titles is available free of charge from the addresses below.

Club membership, open to all collectors, costs little. Members receive free of charge *Antique Collecting*, the Club's magazine (published ten times a year), which contains well-illustrated articles dealing with the practical aspects of collecting not normally dealt with by magazines. Prices, features of value, investment potential, fakes and forgeries are all given prominence in the magazine.

Among other facilities available to members are private buying and selling facilities and the opportunity to meet other collectors at their local antique collectors' clubs. There are over eighty in Britain and more than a dozen overseas. Members may also buy the Club's publications at special pre-publication prices.

As its motto implies, the Club is an organisation designed to help collectors get the most out of their hobby: it is informal and friendly and gives enormous enjoyment to all concerned.

For Collectors — By Collectors — About Collecting

Sandy Lane, Old Martlesham, Woodbridge, Suffolk, IP12 4SD, UK
Tel: 01394 389950   Fax: 01394 389999
Email: sales@antique-acc.com   Website: www.antique-acc.com
——————— *or* ———————
Market Street Industrial Park, Wappingers' Falls, NY 12590, USA
Tel: (845) 297 0003   Fax: (845) 297 0068
ORDERS: (800) 252 5231
Email: info@antiquecc.com   Website: www.antiquecc.com
Email: info@antiquecc.com   Website: www.antiquecc.com

Contents

Foreword

One of the greatest barriers to someone who is newly interested in Asian art has been the very nature of the field. It is vast, with divisions based upon geography, culture, media and language. Asia is a sprawling concept, bound together mostly by geography and trade. The study of Asian art is difficult and, even for experts, can be daunting and isolating, with many distinct specialities. There are countless books on specific aspects or cultures within Asia, yet very few which can inform someone who is either just starting out or someone who leapt in years ago and never looked around. I took a broad approach to what is Asian art, including examples from the Byzantine empire in addition to tribal cultures in Pacific Asia and the arts of Islam. Asia is a big, bustling, interesting place with variety, contradictions, and mystery. It cannot be stuffed into a convenient little package. If it is to be understood, it must be examined from all sides and a variety of perspectives. This book is just a first step for anyone beginning this journey.

This introduction to the arts of Asia covers the history of Asia, provides useful charts and maps, includes a glossary and, most importantly, a generous bibliography. It is not a work of original research. It is a distillation of information gathered from the work of skilled researchers, scholars, and art historians over many years accompanied by my own observations. I owe a huge debt to their efforts and, by including their works in the bibliography, I hope readers will delve into these specialised subjects.

My most and deepest thanks go to all my colleagues at Sotheby's, both in New York and London, who have generously provided counsel, advice and, most importantly, photographic images for this book. I am deeply indebted to them. Alison Price tirelessly tracked down transparencies, as did Hajni Elias. Edward Wilkinson and Sachiko Hori both offered a tremendous amount of sound advice and discernment in choosing which items to illustrate. Christine Lam was particularly helpful. Margi Schwartz, Max Rutherston, Regina Krahl, Susan Kloman, Tom Warren, Cindy Elden, Dick Keresey, Mary Jo Otsea, Lucille Lampton, Liz Mitchell, Jerry Fetzger, Thomas Del Mar, Nicholas Shaw, Sam Shum, and my colleagues in the Chinese department, Julian Thompson, Henry Howard-Sneyd, Alastair Gibson, Jason Tse, Jing Chen, Julian King, Nicolas Chow, Joe Yang, Edie Hu, Shu-Ping Shen, Mee Seen Loong, Sim Jones and Gail Clavel offered encouragement and support.

I have received generous support from many curators and scholars. It is impossible to list everyone, but special thanks to Matthew Welch, Bob Jacobsen and Erin Threlkeld at the Minneapolis Institute of Arts who provided not only many images but did so with grace and good humour. Many thanks to Woodie Woodward and Kate Lau at the Walters Museum of Art in Baltimore. Jan Stuart, Carol Huh and Rebecca Barker assisted me in the selection of works from both the Arthur M. Sackler Gallery and the Freer Museum of Art. Jim Robinson of the Indianapolis Museum of Art helped me make some critical early decisions. Hanni Forester of the Asian Art Museum of San Francisco was particularly helpful and responded almost immediately to my many email inquiries.

Thanks also to Michael Knight. Other contributors who deserve notice include: Laurie Barnes, The Detroit Institute of Arts; David Johnson, The Taft Museum; Ron Otsuka and Karen Ruthberg, The Denver Art Museum; Felice Fischer, The Philadelphia Museum of Art; Claudia Brown and Janet Baker, The Phoenix Art Museum; Martin Lorber and Penny Dante, The Asian Art Newspaper; Don Wood, The Birmingham Museum of Art; and John Finlay, the Norton Museum of Art.

The book would have been impossible without the assistance of my many friends and colleagues who own galleries and selected items to illustrate from their shelves, archives, and clients' collections. Roger Keverne; Linda Wrigglesworth; Katherine Martin, Scholten Japanese Art; Ben Janssens; Gerard Hawthorn; Carol Conover, Kaikodo; Jiyoung Koo; Deon Viljoen; and Leighton and Rosemary Longhi were extremely helpful. Those who were also generous with their help were: Martyn Gregory and Patrick Conner, Martyn Gregory Gallery; Benjamin Creutzfeldt, Degournay; Conor Mahony and Margi Gristina, The Chinese Porcelain Company; Andrew Kahane; Samina Khanyari; Tete Halle, Cora Ginsburg; Nick Grindley; Robert Kleiner; Colin Stair, Stair Galleries; James Godfrey; Ruby Chan; and Alan and Simone Hartman. Particular thanks to my colleagues on the Antiques Roadshow who offered their encouragement.

I also received generous support from several collectors. Notably these included John and Berthe Ford, who allowed me to choose from their many fine objects; Nancy and Anna Rosenblum, Marshall and Marilyn Wolf, Dora Wong, Robert H. Blumenfield; John C. Weber; and Edward C. Johnson, III.

Exceptional patience was displayed by my wife, Erica and my three children, Joanna, Lark and Melissa during this long process. My particular thanks to Dan Farrell, a friend and colleague whose patience with all of us on the Antiques Roadshow is only matched by his persistence in getting reluctant authors to publish. I also am appreciative to my publisher, Diana Steel, for her vision and clarity and Primrose Elliott for her unerring editorial skill and to the many others who worked on this project at the Antique Collectors' Club.

Lark E. Mason
September 2002

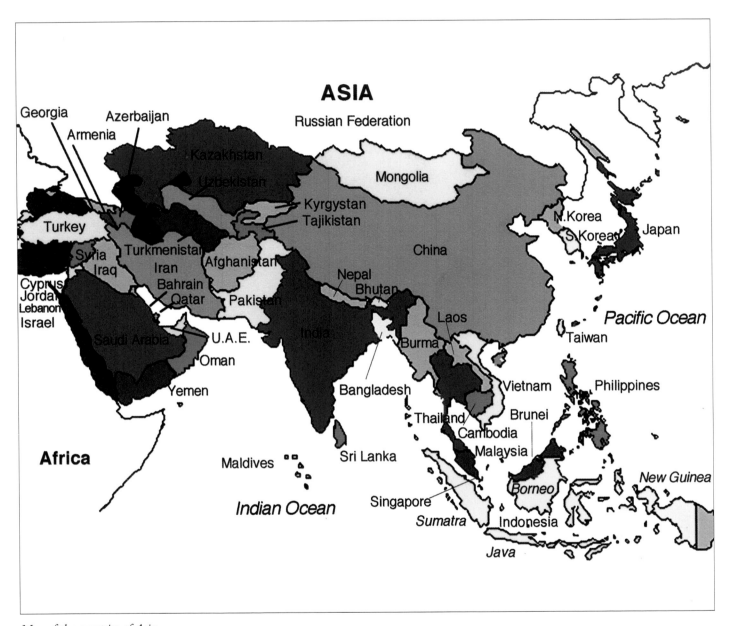

Map of the countries of Asia.

Introduction

Countries of Asia

Middle East

1. Armenia
2. Azcrbaijan
3. Bahrain
4. Cyprus
5. Georgia
6. Iran
7. Iraq
8. Israel
9. Jordan
10. Kuwait
11. Lebanon
12. Oman
13. Qatar
14. Saudi Arabia
15. Syria
16. Turkey
17. United Arab Emirates
18. Yemen

Central Asia

19. Afghanistan
20. Kazakhstan
21. Kyrgyzstan
22. Russian Federation
23. Tajikistan
24. Turkmenistan
25. Uzbekistan

South Central

26. Bangladesh
27. Bhutan
28. India
29. Maldives
30. Nepal
31. Sri Lanka
32. Pakistan

South-east

33. Brunei
34. Burma
35. Cambodia
36. Indonesia
37. Laos
38. Malaysia
39. Philippines
40. Singapore
41. Thailand
42. Vietnam

East Asia

43. China
44. Japan
45. North Korea
46. South Korea
47. Mongolia
48. Russian Federation
49. Taiwan

Many ancient, varied cultures lie within the vast reaches of the Asian land mass. Highland kingdoms of the Himalayan region juxtapose subtropical tribes of the Philippine archipelago. Within this diverse region, the cultures of Asia share many common features. Buddhism originated in Nepal, was nurtured in India and spread rapidly across east Asia through contact with Chinese traders and philosophers. In the same manner Islamic travellers brought goods in trade across the central Asian steppes, introducing the Islamic religion and, with it, Islamic culture to the Far East. Christianity was introduced to Asia in the 1st century and Byzantium, with its riches and highly skilled craftsmen, influenced western Asia for centuries. This cross-pollination of religions and culture continued over millennia, creating a variety of unique as well as similar art forms.

The production of ceramics in China began thousands of years ago and centred around the Chinese belief in the afterlife. Kilns supplied tomb models called mingqi and utilitarian wares to local markets throughout China. The innovations in ceramic manufacture made by the Chinese gradually filtered to Japan, Korea and other south-east Asian kingdoms. Islamic traders brought the bright blue mineral cobalt to Chinese potters and with it an introduction to the naturalistic designs preferred under Koranic law in Central Asia.

Metal casting began in Asia at an early date. Many of the earliest surviving metal objects are weapons: sword blades, arrows and axes were placed in tombs to protect the deceased. In China bronze ritual objects of fantastic form were created for ceremonial purposes. Buddhist, Hindu, and Confucian images were cast in bronze and sometimes embellished with gilded surfaces or even inlaid with semi-precious stones, gold or silver.

Furniture was used in varied ways throughout Asia. Elaborate ivory or pearl shell inlaid furniture derived from ancient Roman and Byzantine prototypes was popular in western and central Asia, but not with the nomadic tribes of the desert. Japanese furniture was mostly made for storage, as was lacquered Thai and painted Tibetan furniture. Seating furniture was virtually unknown in Japan or Korea until the late 19th century. Other Asian cultures such as China had a highly developed furniture tradition.

Among Asian cultures lacquer has played an important role. Secreted from the tree *Rhus vernicifera*, the sap solidifies only in conditions of extreme humidity and heat. When dry it becomes a durable, lustrous material which can be carved, polished and decorated. Lacquer bowls, furniture, boxes and other articles are found throughout the cultures of central and south-east Asia.

There is a strong tradition of carved stone monumental sculpture and other articles in most of Asia. Assyrian winged lions guard Babylonian palaces. In India, Hindu, Jain and Buddhist images carved in red sandstone embellish elaborate temples. Delicate jade vessels were made for Mughal princes. Jade, called the 'stone of heaven' by the Chinese, was believed to have special properties, facilitating communication with the spirit world. Marble, schist, sandstone and limestone were often the materials of choice for large religious sculptures and these are found throughout Cambodia, Thailand, Indonesia, and

Carved alabaster architectural relief depicting an image of 'winged genius' from the palace of King Ashurnasirpal at Nimrud. Assyrian (883-859 BCE). Height 93⅜in. (237.6cm).

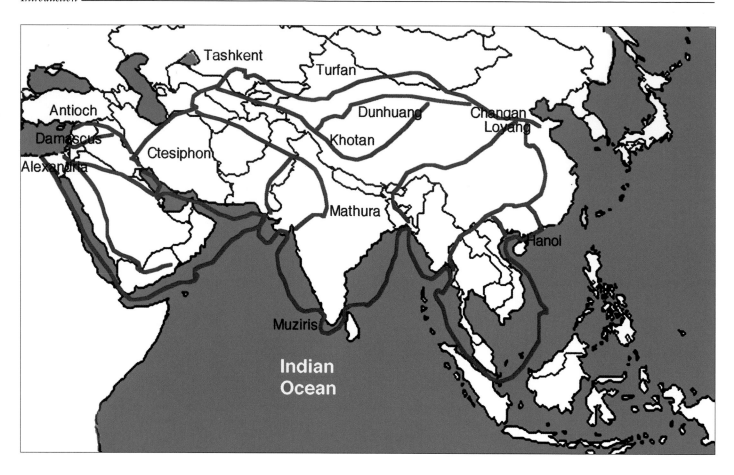

Map of Ancient Asian trade routes.

China in the remarkable architectural treasures of Angkor Wat and the caves of Dunhuang. However, it is the small carved stone, ivory or objects in other material that appear most frequently in Asian culture. Chinese, Persian, Turkish, Indian and Japanese artisans worked extensively with many media: ivory, horn, stone, wood, and even amber, to fashion precious objects.

The nomads of central Asia produced boldly woven rugs and carpets. The garden carpets of the Safavid dynasty are exquisite woven paintings. Further to the east in north-west China there also flourished a vibrant tradition of carpet weaving. Silk manufacture goes back thousands of years in Asia and finely woven garments incorporating gold threads were made in many cultures: Ottoman Turkey, Mughal India and China. In Indonesia and other parts of south-east Asia woodblock printed designs enlivened colourful batik cotton garments.

Chinese painting developed over thousands of years using the simple implements of brush, ink and paper to produce dramatic and inspiring images. Chinese, Japanese, Korean, and Islamic calligraphers used the written language in their often boldly expressive creations. The tradition of ink, silk and paper painting developed in China is similar to that of Japan, Korea and Vietnam. In India and Persia highly skilled painters specialised in the illustration of manuscript leaves or delicate miniatures. Jesuit missionaries introduced western oil painting techniques and perspectives to the Chinese court in the late 17th or early 18th century. Similar techniques emerged in Persia and India in the 18th century.

The tradition of printmaking is strongest in Japan where artists recorded in their prints an astounding variety of everyday scenes from Japanese life. These prints were made by using woodblocks which were carved and then applied with coloured inks. Many blocks could be required to complete a single image. Most of the best known artists date from the 19th and 20th centuries. Utagawa Hiroshige (1797-1858) and Kitagawa Hokusai (1760-1849) produced images which are masterworks of the printmaker's craft.

The folk arts and crafts of Asia are numerous and include Indonesian shadow puppets, Indian bronze pull toys, woven baskets of bamboo or reed, shop signs, bird and cricket cages and moulded gourds. The many minority tribes of island Asia are distinguished by their colourful costumes and local craft traditions.

The countries of Asia are linked by geography, religion and culture. Fine and decorative art objects define the differences between these countries and help us better understand their similarities. It is my hope that this text will provide a useful overview for anyone seeking better to understand the arts of Asia.

HISTORY AND CULTURE

Fifteen to eighteen thousand years ago, the end of the Ice Age inundated low-lying areas, submerging natural land bridges between geographic regions. The Asian land mass, which had been mostly contiguous, separated into islands and peninsulas. Peoples who once roamed freely in a nomadic existence across the slopes and plains now were confined by geography and began to assume regional identities. Over time these identities became the basis for the distinct cultures which we associate with Asia.

Ancient South-east Asia

The first organised Chinese state emerged around 1700 BCE in the fertile plains of the Yellow River valley. The state of Shang (1766-1045 BCE) survives in excavated art works taken from burial tombs. Noted chiefly for superb craftsmanship in bronze casting, the Shang were also skilled potters. The bronze forms and decorative repertoire continued to develop under the succeeding Zhou dynasty (1045-256 BCE). Painted lacquer wares and jade carvings reached a high level of creativity under the Zhou. Building of the Great Wall began in 214 BCE under the Chinese emperor, Chin Shi Huangdi, who also organised governmental functions, standardised the currency, built irrigation systems and unified the state against aggressors. The fertile plains of Japan were home to the ancient Jomon culture (10,500-646 BCE), active potters from the earliest time. China had a trading relationship with Korea during the Zhou dynasty, but in 108 BCE Chinese armies subjugated Korea to Chinese rule. The Dongsan dominated the other Indo-Chinese cultures living in present-day Vietnam, called Annam by the Chinese and stretching into parts of Indonesia. The Dongsan were a prolific bronze-making culture, surviving until Chinese conquest during the Han dynasty (206 BCE-220 CE). South-east Asia was home to innumerable tribes and these gradually fell under Indian cultural influence. Sanskrit became the primary means of written communication and tribes developed into kingdoms which assimilated aspects of both Indian and Chinese art, religions and culture.

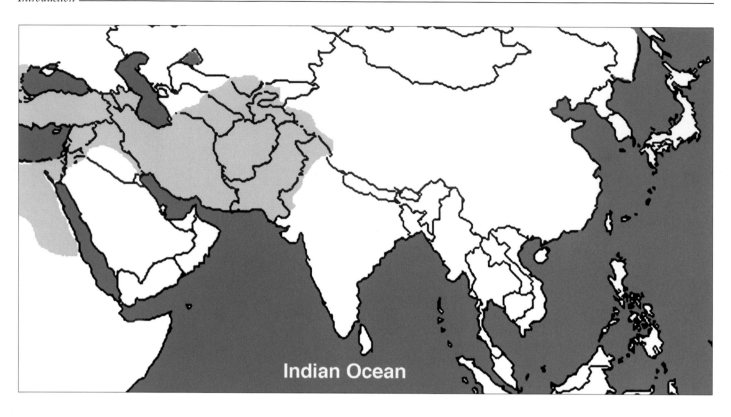

Indian Ocean

The Ancient Near East

Map showing the conquests of Alexander the Great, c.323 BCE.

Iraq, Iran and Syria were home to many ancient civilisations. Western Asian peoples established early agricultural settlements between 7000 and 4000 BCE in the fertile plains of Mesopotamia. Pottery was in widespread use by 7000 BCE. Urban centres, primarily in Mesopotamia but including such ancient cities as Jericho, were populated between 4300 and 3500 BCE. Earthenware painted vessels, carved pottery tablets and hardstone cylinder seals have been discovered from many archaeological sites.

Powerful city states emerged which eventually formed alliances. The two principal regions were Akkad and Sumer located in southern Mesopotamia. Kingship of cities in these regions was dependent upon the supremacy of a city state over other city states. The Akkadian and Sumerian city states were consolidated by Hittite and Assyrian rulers. Gradually Assyrians dominated the region, with control extending from the Mediterranean to the Persian Gulf. During the 7th century BCE insurrections toppled the Assyrian empire with control passing to the powerful city of Babylon. By 585 BCE the Babylonian army under Nebuchadnezzar had captured Jerusalem and removed the Jews into captivity, giving him control of an empire equal in size to that of the Assyrians. The Babylonian empire lasted until the rise of Persia under Cyrus the Great and his successor Darius, who extended the reach of Persia into Egypt and as far east as Gandhara and the Indus river valley. By 530 BCE Cyrus had conquered the whole of Asia Minor, making Persia the world's most powerful empire. Attempts to push the empire further west into Greece failed and set the stage for the eventual triumph of Alexander the Great. After the death of Cyrus a series of weak rulers caused Persian dominance to wane and Alexander conquered Persia in 327 BCE. In a few short years Alexander consolidated all western and central Asia under his control and that of his heirs, the Seleucids (312-247 BCE).

The Development of Indian Religion and Culture

The Indian subcontinent is a distinct geographical region bordered by towering mountains and water. The Aryans entered India in the 2nd millennium BCE and brought with them the Vedic religion, a belief system based on the elemental forces of nature. Gradually their culture was assimilated and this religion transmuted into Hinduism, with its many deities and complex iconography. With the Vedic religion, the Aryans also introduced the caste or varna system.

Buddhism originated in Nepal but flourished in India under the rule of Ashoka Maurya (269-232 BCE) who vigorously promoted the religion with vast numbers of buildings and monuments and official state sanction. Buddhism was introduced into China in 58 CE. During his brief reign, Alexander the Great established centres of Greek culture and influence as far east as Northern India in Gandhara. Traders and travellers passed through the region on the 'Silk Road' connecting the cities of China with the cosmopolitan city of Alexandria in the west. In Gandara Roman and Greek classical art and culture mixed freely with the arts and religions of the Far East, creating a unique hybrid artistic style incorporating Buddhist iconography in sculpture with western classical poses and clothing.

The Sassanians, a Zoroastrian state, established control over Mesopotamia, Iran, Afghanistan, Turkmenistan and as far west as Egypt, ruling from 226 to 651 CE. The capital city of Ctesiphon in Mesopotamia was a major cultural and trade centre at the heart of the silk trade route. It was along this trade route that Buddhism spread to China. In the 2nd century CE Indian traders travelled to the kingdom of Nepal and southward into the Indonesian archipelago, especially Java, introducing not only Buddhism but also Hinduism to cultures which mostly had animistic beliefs, such as the Dongsan peoples (600 BCE-100 CE) who had extensive trade relations throughout south-east Asia.

In 372 CE Chinese traders and monks brought Buddhism to Korea, followed by Japan in 552 and Tibet in the 7th century. Chinese written characters were introduced into Japan in 538 CE. Sects of Buddhist thought developed unique to the peoples and cultures in regions where it spread. Following the fall of the Han dynasty, China was in turmoil until reunited during the Sui (589-618) and Tang (618-906) dynasties. Tang China was a powerful state and immensely influential in both Korea and Japan.

Developing in relative isolation was the Khmer kingdom, founded by Jayavarman II (802-850). The Khmer dynasty was founded as a divine kingdom, expressed by the lingam, a phallic symbol representing the union of king and god. The cities built by Jayavarman II and his successors, the most notable being Angkor Wat, are monuments to the divine power of the kings of Angkor. Although visited by travellers and pilgrims, Angkor was not a centre of trade or commerce and the influence of the Khmer was not as pervasive as that of the Tang. The Tang capital, Changan, was a cosmopolitan centre of trade and culture, sending caravans of luxury goods throughout Asia and as far as the shores of the Mediterranean. Japanese emissaries travelled to the Tang court and brought back to Japan models of Chinese government and works of art. Many of these objects remain in the imperial Japanese repository, the Shosoin in Nara. Chinese hegemony extended along the coast and into Vietnam, called Annam, occupying it until 939 CE Much of Vietnam was dominated by the Champa, a powerful maritime kingdom trading throughout south-east Asia from the 4th to 14th centuries.

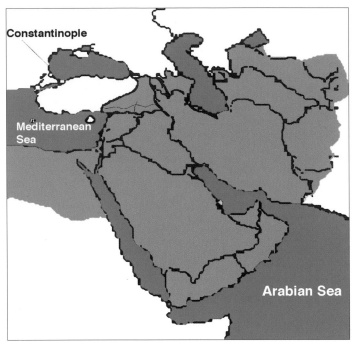

Map of the Abbasid Empire 749-1258.

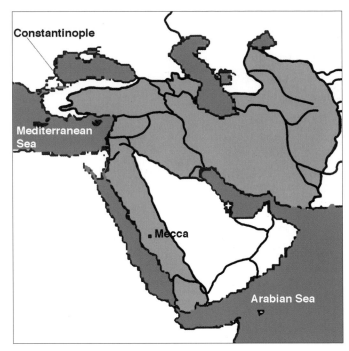

Map of the Seljuk Empire in 1090.

The Spread of Islam

The prophet Mohammed founded the Islamic religion in Arabia in 622 CE and it spread rapidly across central and western Asia, eventually reaching Egypt, Syria, Iran, and Iraq. Europe was in general decline during this period, a time known as the 'Dark Ages', but the Islamic world was flourishing, with creative leadership in the arts, literature and science. This cultural flowering was possible only because of the common threads that joined these very different regions. Islamic religion, law, the Arabic language and trade provided a bond that brought prosperity across the Islamic world. There were many regional Islamic powers. The Umayyad dynasty was centred in Damascus and through conquest extended Islamic influence into Spain and as far east as China, until faltering in 747. The Umayyads had captured territory formerly under Byzantine rule and artists and artisans continued working for their Islamic rulers in Byzantine styles. The Abbasids, ruling from Baghdad, Iraq, traded with Tang China and were great patrons of the arts. The Abbasid Empire (750-1258) was eventually challenged by the Fatamids (909-1171) who gained control over much of the Abbasid dominions. Of the Islamic states, the Fatamids were the most stable. Fatamid power centred in north Africa but extended to parts of Syria, Yemen and Palestine, remaining in power until the rise of the Ayyubids in the 12th century.

The nomadic cultures of central Asia in Turkey, Iran, Afghanistan, and north-west Pakistan, were subject to vast movements of peoples and became adept warriors. From this region rose the Seljuks, a Turkic tribe which united much of Muslim Asia from the 11th to 13th centuries. The Seljuk empire originated in Iran in the 10th century and included modern day Turkey, pressing against the geographical boundaries of the Byzantine Empire. The Seljuks supported the arts primarily through religious patronage and ruled from 1038 to 1194, eventually losing control of eastern Anatolia to the Artuqids (1102-1408) and the Zangids (1127-1174). When the crusaders threatened

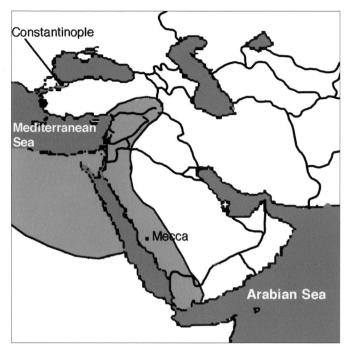

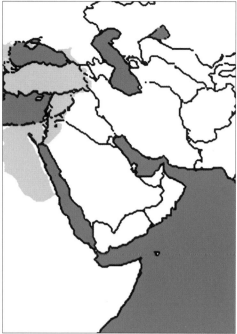

Map of the Ayyubid Empire in 1189.

Map of the Byzantine Empire in Asia between 527 and 566.

Islamic control of western Asia, the Zangids enlisted the support of Saladin, the founder of the Ayyubid dynasty (1171-1260) to travel to Egypt and repel their advances. He arrived in 1169, ousted the Fatamids and went on to rule over much of the Middle East, establishing Mosul as his capital and artistic centre. The arts and sciences flourished under Islamic rule, primarily because the foundation of Islamic civilisation was largely based on respect for Greek and Roman achievements in the arts and sciences. Arab scholars established centres of study in Babylon, Cairo, Damascus, and Isfahan.

The Byzantine Empire

Founded by the Roman Emperor, Constantine the Great in 330 CE, Constantinople was chosen as a centralised seat of Roman government, strategically positioned between Europe and Asia in the heart of the Roman empire. As the first Christian ruler of Rome, Constantine gave official recognition to the church which had become the state religion by the end of the 4th century. During the reign of Justinian (527-566) Byzantine lands encompassed modern Turkey, Syria and the Middle East, Egypt and north Africa. Control of these territories ensured prosperity.

Trade was the foundation of Byzantine power; silks, precious metals and stones, wheat and other foodstuffs, and luxury goods passed through Byzantine lands, enriching the local merchants and the capital, Constantinople. Control of the Asian trade routes and territories was compromised between 633 and 647 with the conquests of Islamic armies of north Africa and Syria. Although briefly regained, these losses presaged the gradual diminution of Byzantine control. In 1071 much of the eastern empire was lost to Islamic forces. Although these were regained, the empire gradually became centred on the capital, Constantinople. Crusader forces brought in to force back Islamic armies were successful, but at a huge cost.

Crusaders captured and occupied Constantinople from 1204 until 1261. The Byzantine government in exile returned and retook the city, briefly regaining some of the former glory until Ottoman forces surrounded it and laid siege, capturing and ending the empire in 1453.

The Spread of Buddhism and Hinduism

Relatively removed from the turbulence of Islamic conquest and Chinese influence were the south central Asian kingdoms of the Mon in Burma, the Khmer in Cambodia ruling from the 7th to 13th centuries, and the Sukhothai in Thailand. The art of Pre-Angkor and Angkor was entirely religious, influenced by Hinduism and then Buddhism introduced through Indian merchants. Magnificent temple complexes embodied a physical representation of the Buddhist universe. In Burma, the capital city of Pagan witnessed a vast building programme of temples and monuments between the 11th and 13th centuries. These and other remote kingdoms in Indonesia developed unique regional artistic styles from the mix of local religious traditions with Buddhism and Hinduism. Buddhism had begun to fade in India during the Gupta period (320-647 CE) and by the 12th century, under the onslaught of Muslim invaders, had been replaced by Hindu cults. Buddhist monasteries and universities in Northern India were abandoned, with monks and artisans fleeing to the neighbouring Himalayan mountain kingdoms of Tibet and Nepal. Many Indian Buddhist images created under the Pala, the last of the great Indian Buddhist states, were transported to Nepal and from there to Tibet, Mongolia, and China. Over the centuries, the original doctrines of Buddhist belief had become much more complex. Tantric thought introduced the concept of esoteric Buddhism with a pantheon of bodhisattvas and manifestations of the Buddha. Tibet received the influx of Buddhist monks and artisans and by the 13th century the various influences from India, Nepal and China had coalesced into a distinctive Tibetan Buddhist culture.

Tang power began to disintegrate in the 8th century and by the 840s the government sought to limit foreign access, foreigners being blamed for the decline. Buddhism was suppressed and over 4,600 monasteries were razed. Tibetan forces took advantage of Tang isolationism and reached out to secure trading routes in central Asia. The Tang dynasty finally collapsed in 906 and the new Song dynasty (960-1279) established trading relations with the many bordering kingdoms, buying accommodation with enormous payments in silks. The Song exerted considerable regional influence but did not dominate either Japan and Korea as during the Tang dynasty. The Song were unable to maintain overland trade routes and by the 10th century had lost control of the ancient silk trade route to the Uighur and Tangut states. To compensate for the loss of tax revenue, the Song embarked on a programme of maritime trade, building ships and exporting products throughout south-east Asia. The Koryo dynasty (936-1392) in Korea was a time of artistic experimentation and creativity, moving away from Chinese influences. Because of political instability in China during the Fujiwara period (897-1185), Japan suspended official missions to China, marking a divergence in Chinese and Japanese art. This independence allowed artistic patronage to grow in Japan during the Heian (794-1185) and Kamakura (1185-1333) periods. Between 1205 and 1227 Mongolian armies besieged and defeated the Tangut, beginning a domination that would overwhelm all Asia. Mongol armies overthrew the Song in northern China in 1126 and then in southern China in 1279, establishing the Mongol Yuan dynasty (1279-1368) with its court at Dadu, today called Beijing.

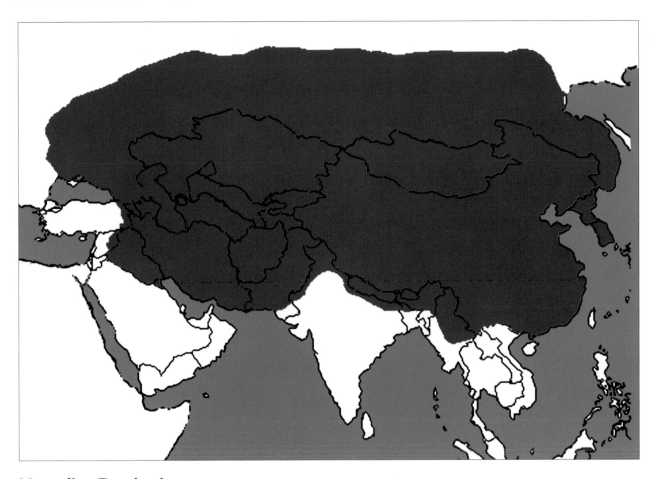

Mongolian Domination

It was during the reign of Kublai Khan that Marco Polo (1271-1292) and Europeans arrived in China for the first time. Hulagu, a grandson of Genghis Khan, brought the Mongolian invasion to the Middle East and in 1258 the Abbasid dynasty fell to the Mongols. Cities were depopulated and craftsmen sent back as slaves to Mongolia. Baghdad, the former Abbasid capital, became the Mongolian capital of the Il-khanid dynasty. In a few years the Mongol empire stretched from Korea to the Mediterranean. Mongolian armies pressed westward sacking the Ayyubid capital of Mosul, causing the artisans to flee to Damascus and Cairo. The Mongolian armies were finally defeated in 1260 in Palestine by the Mamluks. Even south-east Asia was not immune. The Mongols entered Burma, destroying the Mon capital of Pagan in 1287. The centre of the Mongol empire was Beijing with sub-states ruled by the Il-khanid. In Cambodia, the Khmer had risen to power under Jayavarman II (802-850 CE), whose achievements were followed by Indravarman (877-889). In the 11th century Jayavarman VI began construction of the most famous of the Khmer monuments, Angkor Wat, a massive Buddhist temple complex, probably based on the equally dramatic Javanese Buddhist temple complex of Borobudur begun in the 8th century but abandoned around 1000 CE. The Khmer expanded into neighbouring Thailand in the 11th century and into northern Malaysia, leaving southern Malaysia in control of the Shrivijaya empire in Sumatra until the 13th century. In south India, the Hindu Chola (9th to 13th centuries) and succeeding Vijayanagar (1300-1565) kingdoms resisted Islamic domination until finally succumbing in 1565, leaving many small Hindu states.

Map of the Mongol conquests in 1300.

Mughal and Ottoman Empires

Mongol domination secured the peace and greatly facilitated trade between Europe and China. The Mongols tolerated Christianity and Buddhism, and eventually embraced Islam in addition to their native shamanistic tradition. The Mongol ruler of the Il-khanids, Ghazan Khan (1295-1304), converted to Islam, established Tabriz as his capital, and promoted trade with the west. Central authority collapsed in 1336 leading to the creation of many smaller political entities in Iran and Iraq. Out of the confusion arose the Islamic conqueror, Tammerlane or Timur (1363-1405), who gained control of much of Iran, Iraq, India, Anatolia, and Syria. Tammerlane made his capital at Samarkand and depopulated cities throughout central Asia, massacring citizenry and sending artists and craftsmen back as slaves to his capital. The Timrud empire shrank on his death in 1405 until the rise of the Mongolian Babur, who pressed into India, founding the Mughal (or Mongol) empire in 1526. In Turkey Oman or Othman established the Ottoman Empire in the 14th century. The Ottomans survived the attacks of Tammerlane and conquered Constantinople in 1453 under the command of Sultan Mohammed II. In Egypt the Mamluks had risen to power following the Ayyubids (1171-1260) and fell under Ottoman power in 1517, giving Ottoman control to an empire stretching across western and central Asia. The secret of Ottoman success lay in their administrative genius. The empire was divided into small communal units which insured the regular collection of taxes and quick governmental action on local issues. The Ottomans were brilliant military leaders, establishing a professional army called Janissaries, recruited from all parts of the empire.

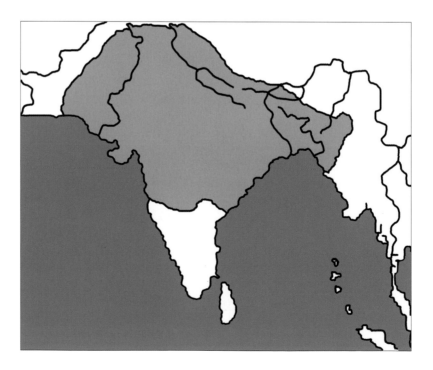

Map of the Mughal Empire in 1630.

The Ottomans under Suleiman the Magnificent (1520-1566) were thrusting westward and challenging the Timruds (1405-1500) and Safavids (1501-1736) in Persia. The Safavids rose from the fall of the Mongol sub-state of the Il-khanid and in 1501 established a Shiite Muslim political force. Although the Ottomans and Safavids were both Islamic, they were bitter enemies belonging to opposing Muslim sects. The Ottomans were Sunni Muslims and the Safavids Shiite Muslims. The Safavids under the rule of Shah Abbas I (1587-1629) continued Il-khanid support of European commerce and greatly expanded patronage of the arts and architecture. The capital city of Isfahan became a wealthy and cosmopolitan trading centre.

Decline of The Khmer

Hundreds of distinct tribal groups exist in south-east Asia, each with strong traditions and identities. These were influenced by the gradual introduction of Hinduism, Buddhism and then Islam. The last great Hindu-Buddhist dynasty in Indonesia was in Java, founded by Raden Wijaya (1293-1309), whose Majaphit dynasty ended in 1528. In Cambodia the weakened Khmer pulled back from neighbouring Thailand, enabling the Thai peoples to establish three centres of power: the Sukhothai in the north, flourishing between the 13th and 15th centuries, Lan Na with its capital of Chiangmai, and Ayuthia in the south, remaining strong from the 14th through the 18th centuries. The Thai kingdoms inter-mingled with the native Mon peoples and adopted from them Hinayana Buddhism, producing enormous numbers of distinctive religious images in bronze for Buddhist

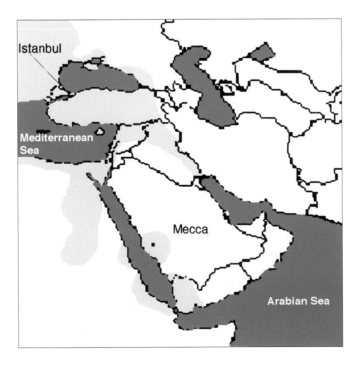

Map of the Ottoman Empire in 1683.

pilgrims and temples. Former Khmer strongholds in Thailand were abandoned as the Khmer faded from power. The enormous costs of building temple complexes eventually proved overwhelming for the Khmer, and they were unable to defend their borders. Thai armies sacked and burned Angkor Wat in 1353, 1385, and 1431. In 1453 Angkor Wat was abandoned and the long reign of the Khmer came to an end.

The Ming Dynasty

The Mongols were detested in China, finally overthrown in 1368 and Chinese rule re-established under the native Chinese Ming dynasty (1368-1644). The Ming set up a superb administrative system and created an effective civil service and trade links throughout south-east Asia, into the Philippines, Vietnam, Indonesia, Japan, Korea, India and as far west as Egypt. Tribute flowed into the Ming treasury from all over Asia, and many smaller south-east Asian kingdoms were under Chinese control. The Yongle emperor (1403-1425) sponsored a voyage of exploration, commerce, and diplomatic outreach under the eunuch admiral Zheng He. In 1405 the admiral began a series of seven voyages, the largest including over 300 ships and nearly 30,000 seamen throughout south-east Asia and into the Indian ocean. The last voyage ended in 1431 with the ascendancy of Confucian court administrators who sought to close China to outside influences. This decision eventually proved disastrous for China and opened the way for European control of Asian sea trade.

The Qing Dynasty

Although early Ming emperors were able administrators, those of the later Ming were not, and gradually the government deteriorated. Inefficiencies, peasant rebellions and foreign armies threatened government stability until finally opponents seized control of Beijing in 1644. Loyalist Ming forces continued to fight in southern provinces, but eventually the Ming were vanquished and the Manchu victors established the Qing dynasty (1662-1911). Under the able administration of both the Kangxi (1662-1723) and Qianlong (1736-1795) emperors peace was restored, the economy stabilised and the arts flourished.

European Explorers and the Foundation of European Trade

The long rule of the Ming came to an end in 1644 just as Europeans were establishing trading centres in the Far East. The Portuguese were first, setting up trading stations in Africa, India and Malacca and gained exclusive rights to trade in Bengal from the Mughal rulers, using this base to reach into Thailand, Burma, and Cambodia. European trading complemented existing trading patterns which had been long established. The Philippines, Indonesia and Malaysia all conducted active trade within south-east Asia, China and India. European contact also extended to remote island kingdoms: New Guinea was visited in 1526, Marquesas Islands in 1595, Tonga in 1615, Fiji and New Zealand in 1642 and Samoa in 1722.

A Portuguese ship arrived in Japan in 1542 in the midst of political upheaval and warfare, as the military sought to gain control over the government from the feudal lords.

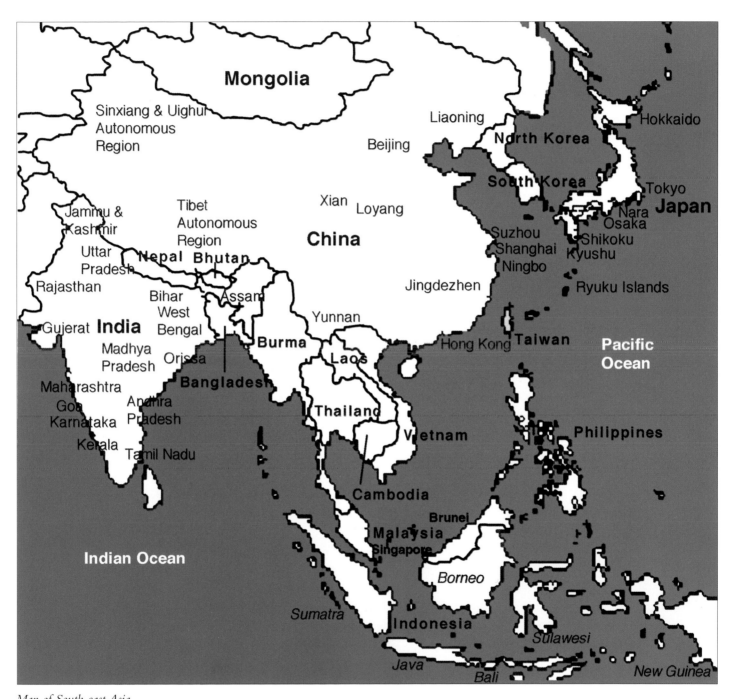

Map of South-east Asia.

Other western traders followed the Portuguese, whose influence rapidly declined. The Japanese were suspicious of western intentions and expelled westerners from Japan, leaving only the Dutch in a modest outpost on Dejima, an island in Nagasaki harbour. In China the Manchu rulers opened the Chinese mainland via the port of Canton to western trade. Spain wrested control of the Philippines from the Portuguese in 1680, establishing an important trading station in Asia. Much of the trade was based on an exchange of copper or silver for spices, silks, tea and ceramics. The Spanish treasury had ample access to gold and silver from mines in Mexico, Central and South America. Silver laden ships were sent by Spain to the Philippines where silver would be used as a medium of exchange for the commodities sought by western traders. The profits to be gained for the European traders were enormous; investors could expect a return of thirty times their original investment. Silver ingots and trade dollars from the new world financed the growing empires of European nations all across Asia.

Calcutta was established around Fort William in 1691 and became the major centre of British trade with the Mughal empire and the headquarters of the British East India Company in India. The Dutch secured Bali and Indonesia with Batavia as the headquarters of the Dutch East India Company. In India the British and other colonial powers traded with the Mughal rulers with the British eventually gaining administrative control, resulting in a drastic decline of Mughal court patronage and native Indian artistry. Delhi, the artistic centre of Mughal rule, was succeeded by Lucknow, which brought Islamic, Hindu, and European influences together in the arts.

Trade and Empire

Safavid rule collapsed in 1722 leaving Iran in chaos until order was restored under the Qajars (1787-1925). The Thai kingdom of Ayuthia finally succumbed to Burmese military aggression in 1767. The Burmese army pillaged, plundered and enslaved thousands of citizens in Ayuthia, effectively destroying the city. The Thai court moved to Bangkok founding the Chakri dynasty in 1782. The Muromachi period (1392-1573) in Japan had been riven with power struggles and warfare but was followed by a period of peace and stability during the Momoyama (1573-1615) and Edo periods (1615-1868). Following the installation of Meiji rule in 1868, Japan increasingly sought trade with the west, exporting traditional art works and embracing western culture.

Western trade with Asia first began with the establishment of trading ports, but gradually expanded these centres into areas of political influence. The profits from trade were substantial and, to secure safe and consistent access, western powers increasingly sought political control over the countries in which the trade was most valuable. In the 19th century China lost a series of wars with the western powers, ceded ports to western control and eventually was divided into spheres of western influence. Chinese merchants had always required payment for trade goods in silver, creating a trade imbalance with all countries except Spain where silver was in short supply. English, American and European traders found a substitute in furs and opium. Both commodities were eagerly sought by the Chinese merchants but were in violation of Chinese government policy. The Opium Wars (1840-1842) began when a Chinese commissioner in Canton attempted to force

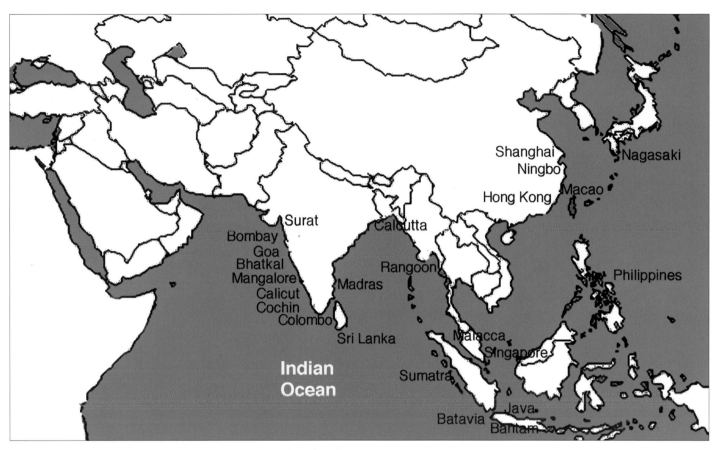

Map showing European trading centres in Asia in the 18th and 19th centuries.

the British to end the trade in opium which was ravaging the country. The Chinese were defeated and the terms of defeat included huge payments and the opening of additional ports to western trade.

In 1857 a rebellion among soldiers expanded in India into a protest against British rule. The British prevailed and the last Mughal emperor was sent into exile to Rangoon. In 1877 Queen Victoria was proclaimed 'Empress of India'. By the end of the 19th century western European nations had established control and areas of influence over much of central and south-east Asia, which only began to diminish in the 20th century when European conflicts made far-flung colonies difficult to administer. Long-lived Asian dynasties fell, led by the end of the Chinese Qing dynasty in 1911, leaving Ottoman Turkey as the most enduring of the major Asian empires. In the late 19th and early 20th century the Ottoman government grew increasingly ineffective and, although nominally in control of vast geographic areas, was widely known as the 'sick man of Europe'. It finally succumbed following World War I.

Chapter One

Asian Ceramics

The earliest fired ceramics manufactured in Asia were probably produced by accident. A simple sun-dried clay vessel placed near or in a fire was hardened by the heat, making it noticeably more durable. Innovations following this discovery over a period of thousands of years eventually culminated in the production of the fine, translucent material called porcelain.

How to Determine Quality, Condition and Authenticity

Most ceramic objects were made as multiples. As a matter of economy, kilns were designed to fire large quantities of wares at the same time. Potters worked with designs and forms which were standardised, making it convenient for the collector to compare objects of the same type, date and kiln source.

Quality

The overall design, form and material used in the potting are important determinants of quality. The object should be evenly formed and well proportioned. The decoration should be freely drawn with a spontaneity of expression that communicates the artisan's skill and intent. The material of which it is made should be free of unexpected imperfections in the clay, glaze and colouring agents. Finally, the skill of the kiln master is judged by the finished product. Colours should be bright and clear and the material without unsightly discolorations.

Condition

Cracks, chips or other losses of the ceramic material occur through use and can dramatically devalue the worth and usefulness of an object. Ceramic objects were often used daily and through repeated handling will often have a worn surface or edges. Objects with wear are generally less desirable than those without wear. Areas of wear can be redecorated by skilled restorers. Enamels which have flaked off are sometimes retouched and gilded or painted details re-applied. A careful comparison with similar decoration in

---

(Opposite). Chinese underglaze blue decorated porcelain dish, Yuan dynasty (1279-1368), diameter 16⁵⁄₁₆in. (41.4cm). Dishes such as this example were widely exported throughout Asia and were made specifically for the Middle Eastern market. Porcelain dishes were durable, retained their colourful brilliance, and were used for serving food. This example is both moulded and painted with cobalt pigments. It was created in the Chinese porcelain manufacturing city of Jingdezhen.

Chinese enamel decorated 'Kinrande' bowl, 16th century, diameter 7¼in. (18.5cm) Gold lacquer repairs of this type were favoured in Japan for use on prized ceramic objects which had been damaged.

adjacent areas will often reveal these repairs. Generally, repairs and damage to earthenware and stoneware articles are less serious than comparable damage to objects in porcelain.

Authenticity

Each specific type of ceramic has forgers who are actively seeking to make copies to deceive the collector. These can be avoided by following some basic guidelines. Regardless of the ceramic object, there should be consistency in how it was made. Ceramics made of porcelain in China were made primarily in Jingdezhen and the clay from that location is unique. A visual memory of the clay of a particular kiln site is an invaluable tool in identifying copies made at a later date. The glaze material is equally important. If glazed, the object should be glazed in a manner typical of other objects from that same site and period of time. It is helpful to reconstruct how the object was created. Put yourself in the position of the potter, glazer or decorator and go through the process. Imagine yourself painting meticulous designs over a glaze or dashing off images in cobalt under a glaze. Look for any signs of inconsistency or hesitation in the design.

Copies of earthenware can be detected by the hardness of the firing and, if wet, the tendency of the clay to absorb water at a different rate from parts of the object which have been restored. Often earthenware is 'reconstructed' using shards from the correct period to create an object that is essentially new, but made of old materials. A careful examination of the surface will sometimes reveal a thin coating of clay covering the many joined fragments. Some early glazed stonewares have been augmented at a later date with appendages to enhance their value. A careful, close examination with a bright light and magnifying glass will detect most forgeries of this type. A useful tool to date earthenware is the thermoluminescence or TL test. This test is done in a small number of laboratories and is only considered valid when handled by a person skilled in the process. While a useful tool, the TL test is not infallible. Often in years of examining ceramics I have been presented with TL tests which present an object as authentic, while other aspects reveal it clearly to be a copy. In the final analysis, the eye of a skilled expert is the best judge of authenticity.

Many copies of Asian porcelains were made by Samson, a French factory operating in the late 19th and 20th centuries. Most Samson wares were marked with an iron red overglaze mark on the underside of the object. Unfortunately, these marks are often rubbed off by unscrupulous individuals. Some of the more difficult to detect Samson and other copies were made in the late 19th century.

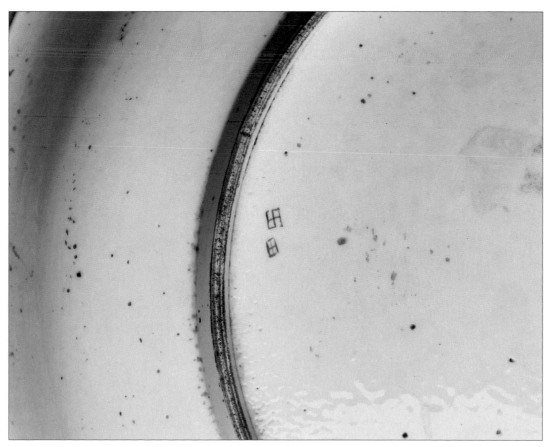

Detail showing the bone-white porcelain body of the Samson dish and the iron-red overglaze simulated Chinese character mark on the reverse. The pitted glaze is a feature not found on authentic Chinese Kangxi porcelain.

(Above). Detail of a Chinese famille verte vase dating from the Kangxi Period (1662-1723) showing the enamel decoration. The freely painted designs and colour of the porcelain differ substantially from that of the Samson copy.

(Left). French copy of a Chinese famille verte porcelain dish dating to the Kangxi Period (1662-1723) made during the early 20th century by the Samson factory in Paris. Note the indistinct landscape scenes in the reserved panels of the basket and the stiff pattern of the diaper design on the border.

Copies have been made of most porcelain types, either as forgeries designed to deceive or as copies made because of the popularity of a particular design or ware. Recently, fine quality porcelain articles have been made in China, imitating Ming and later wares, including objects for the export market. Generally, copies are commercially manufactured and easy to detect by a careful comparison with an authentic example. However, forgeries can be extremely difficult to detect and the best protection is experience.

A Tang Dynasty Horse

When cataloguing the estate of a well-known collector I was pleased to see a large, magnificently caparisoned Sancai glazed (see page 41) earthenware Tang dynasty horse. This horse had a rare green glazed simulated fur covered saddle and a short bristled mane. The ears were unusually large and mule-like and there was a gap between the saddle and the horse's body, implying that the saddle was added later. The straw glaze on the body extended under the saddle, a technique completely inconsistent with how Tang horses of this type were constructed. The straw glaze had the typical fine network of glaze cracks, but none appeared on the glazed saddle, tail, ears or short cropped mane. A forger had taken an authentic plain straw glazed Tang horse, added a mane, saddle and tail and resculpted the ears to make an elaborate and much more costly and desirable model. When it finally came up for sale, the additions were carefully noted and the price was substantially less than had been expected.

Chinese glazed earthenware horse, Tang Dynasty (618-906) showing a gap between the straw coloured glazed body and the dark green simulated fur saddle blanket. The gap and glaze inconsistencies between the saddle blanket and the body would not exist on an authentic example.

EARTHENWARE

The earliest and most common of all ceramics is earthenware. Earthenware is formed from clay which has been heated or 'fired' in a kiln to a temperature ranging from 600 to 1100 degrees centigrade, allowing the material to harden and retain its shape. There are various types of earthenware, but most are grey or reddish brown in colour, tinted by the natural presence of iron-oxide or other minerals found in the clay.

Early earthenware vessels were formed by hand, most often by stacking or coiling long strands of clay on top of each other, building up the sides of the vessel one layer at a time. As each layer was added, the potter would smooth and press the wet layers of clay together. Earthenware is generally porous and most earthenware vessels were utilitarian, used to hold dry materials, such as grains. The surface of earthenware can be enhanced with simple, natural pigments which are absorbed into the body, by impressed or carved designs, or by burnishing the surface with a smooth stone or hardened bit of leather, creating a dull sheen.

Firing Time

Earthenware can be either high fired or low fired, a reference to the temperature and length of time the object is in the kiln. Low fired objects are less durable than high fired objects. While in a kiln, water is driven from the clay between the temperatures of 400 and 600 degrees centigrade. Earthenware is porous and does not fuse or vitrify. The length of time an object is in the kiln and the type of clay determines the type of ware that results. Early kilns were heated with wood and the kiln master gauged the temperature and appropriate length of firing time by the colour of the flames, determined through years of experience and by trial and error.

Early Chinese Earthenware

The Chinese were master potters from a very early period, extending back at least 10,000 years. Among the most prolific and notable earthenwares are examples made in northern China by the Yangshao culture. Yangshao earthenware vessels have been excavated from hundreds of sites, including coarse utilitarian cord impressed vessels and finer quality simple shaped storage vessels, often boldly painted with ovals, concentric circles, or sawtooth patterns in burgundy or black, against a reddish brown

(Below). Chinese painted red earthenware jar, Neolithic Period, c.3000 BCE. Large numbers of earthenware vessels of this type were made by coiling lengths of clay on top of each other and then smoothing the coils together with a paddle.

(Opposite). Earthenware stag-form vessel, North-western Iran, Amlash, Marlik style, c.10th century BCE, height 11in., length 9½in. (27.5 x 23.7cm). There are two principal types of earthenware: red and grey. Often the strong natural colours of earthenware were muted by covering the surface with a thin layer of refined white clay, called a slip. This allowed the artisan to decorate the surface in colours which would appear uninfluenced by the bolder earthenware tones.

body. Large numbers of these vessels were produced and in recent years have been excavated from tomb burial sites throughout northern China. The best examples have striking, forceful designs and are skilfully potted with beautiful proportions. They appear in a range of sizes, from large jars to small ovoid containers. These early earthenware vessels are referred to as 'neolithic' and date c.5000-2000 BCE.

Early Japanese Earthenware

Japanese potters during the Jomon period (10,500-646 BCE) also made earthenware and funerary vessels modelled with mat and rope patterns and boldly applied elements. Jomon is translated literally as 'cord marked'. Following Jomon is a type of wheel turned ware called Yaoyi after the site of its discovery.

During the Kofun period (248-646 CE) potters experimented with glazes and earthenware funerary models. Kofun, literally translated as 'old mound', refers to the large number of burial mounds dating from this period. Haniwa are usually stylised cylindrical shaped human or animal forms punctured with simple geometric cut-outs placed above ground and set in rows encircling a grave tumulus mound to protect the entombed. A large tomb would have thousands of Haniwa. As with all earthenware models, Haniwa are often broken and repaired and, unless the repair is extreme or it is missing many elements, the restoration will not substantially affect the value.

Indian and South-east Asian Earthenware

In India the Harappan culture was discovered during railroad excavations near the city of Karachi in 1856. Harappan civilisation extended roughly from 2300 to 1750 BCE and produced earthenware food storage vessels and votive figures in a buff coloured clay decorated with geometric designs, animals and plants in coloured pigments of red and black.

Alexander the Great conquered most of western Asia by 323 BCE, along what was to become known as the 'Silk road'. Cities established by Alexander were centres of Greek influence for centuries. By the 1st century CE Gandhara in Afghanistan was home to classical Greek and Roman trained artisans who created sculpture and artworks mixing Asian and western iconography. Buddhist images in terracotta are depicted with classical western features. These terracotta and stone sculptures are often coated with a polished gypsum surface.

Ancient pottery dating from 3600 to 1000 BCE has been excavated from burial sites throughout Thailand, the most notable of which is called Banchiang. The finest examples are in a buff coloured earthenware, usually decorated with bold swirls of brick red

(Opposite). Japanese red earthenware Haniwa horse, Kofun Period (300-550), height 26in. (66cm). These cylindrical models of animals and people were constructed to be placed above ground on huge burial mounds. Burial ceramics were never intended to be handled, they were intended only for the tomb. When in a collection, care must be taken to avoid regular contact with the surface, particularly for those with an unglazed surface.

Three Banchiang vessels. Left: Early Period, c.3600-1000 BCE. Centre: Late Period, c.300 BCE to 200 CE. Right: Middle Period, 1000-300 BCE. The Banchiang culture was not identified until 1966; since that time many significant discoveries have been made.

pigments. Most vessels are large ovoid jars, included with burial artifacts. The Banchiang sites are divided into periods based on date, with the most sophisticated examples dating between 300 BCE and 200 CE. Huge quantities of small terracotta votive plaques were made for Buddhist pilgrims in Burma during the 12th and 13th centuries.

Han and Tang Dynasty Earthenware

Chinese earthenware reached an apex in sophistication during the period from the 2nd century BCE to the 9th century CE, a period incorporating the Chinese Han (206 BCE-220 CE) and Tang (618-906 CE) dynasties. Potters exploited earthenware to the fullest extent, with elaborately decorated figures and models, called mingqi, often covered in brilliant lead-based glazes in hues of green, ochre, brown, yellow and sometimes blue. There are two types of mingqi, miniaturised versions of full-scale objects and full-size wares used in real life. The earliest examples are monochromatic and later examples are glazed in a mix of several colours, referred to as 'Sancai' or three colour wares.

(Opposite). Chinese grey pottery figure of an entertainer, Eastern Han Dynasty (25-220 CE), Sichuan Province, height 22½in. (57cm). The lively composition is typical of figures which have been recovered from Sichuan tombs. It is not unusual for large size earthenware models to have been broken and restored. The underground tombs often collapsed, breaking the ceramic models inside.

The lead glazes used in the Han dynasty were monochromatic and the most popular colours were dark green and mustard. Jars, architectural models, animals and simple figures are usual subjects. The glazes will occasionally have an iridescent sheen resulting from the chemicals in the soil reacting to the lead glaze. In extreme cases the glaze will scale and flake, substantially affecting the value.

Tang dynasty pottery models were placed in tombs of the wealthy and aristocratic to accompany the deceased into the next world. These models were specifically made for burial in tombs, and glazed and unglazed examples were made. The best glazed models are proportionately formed, brightly coloured, have few if any repairs, and have detailed features. Among the more distinctive are the models of camels and horses. Both were symbols of wealth and power to the Tang people whose economy was based largely on trade with the Middle East. These powerfully modelled animals were made in moulds, allowed to dry to a leathery consistency, luted together, and applied with glaze prior to firing. Glazed models from the Tang typically have a white slip covering the reddish earthenware body. The glaze has an almost indiscernible fine network of cracks. Often damage occurs through the legs and neck of both camels and horses. Painted pigments and repairs can be identified by careful observations. The potters made an incredible range of models including: entertainers, domestic workers, mothers with children, aristocratic ladies, soldiers, farm animals, ritual objects, cosmetic boxes and utilitarian vessels.

(Left). Chinese green lead glazed pottery watch tower, Han Dynasty (206 BCE-220 CE). Architectural models were often made for inclusion in tombs. Watchtowers were made in separate sections and stacked on top of each other. Often the green lead glaze has an iridescent surface, resulting from the chemical action of water leaching into the tomb, leaving deposits on the lead glaze.

(Opposite). Chinese Sancai glazed pottery horse, Tang Dynasty (618-906). Elaborate and realistically modelled figures made for the tomb during the Tang Dynasty were often constructed in moulds. The applied glaze often drips in colourful patterns on to the surface, in contrast to the care taken to represent the form with precise naturalism. The use of three colour glazes is called Sancai.

Later Chinese Earthenware

The tradition of working in earthenware continued in China long after the introduction of stoneware and porcelain. In the Ming dynasty (1368-1644) brightly glazed tilework figures and models were in great demand as architectural elements and for furnishing tombs. The earliest glazed tilework roofs appear to date from the Northern Wei dynasty (386-535). It was during the Yuan dynasty (1279-1368) that the bright turquoise blue colour often associated with these tiles was introduced. The centre for tilework production was in Shanxi province, with numerous kilns providing a range of products. Large roof ends and other elements were created in moulds but finished by hand, with great attention to detail. During the late Qing dynasty the quality is substantially lessened.

Ming tombs were furnished with miniature models of soldiers, attendants, ceremonial tables laden with food offerings, and other ceramic furniture. These models differ substantially from the Han and Tang prototypes. The modelling is much less realistic and the high fired glazes are in a broader range of colours. The glaze does not have the finely crackled surface of Tang lead glazes.

Other non-funerary high fired earthenwares include the specialised Yixing pottery teawares. Yixing developed as a pottery making centre in the Ming dynasty and the teawares made in Yixing gained great renown. Prominent Ming potters such as Gongchun and Shi Dabin were among the first in a tradition in which master potters routinely signed their work. In addition to teawares, Yixing potters made snuff bottles, models of fruits and nuts

Set of Chinese glazed tilework figures, Ming Dynasty (1368-1644). Ming tilework figures with bright glazes are descendants of Tang tomb figures. These latter versions are generally less detailed, fired at a higher temperature, and were made for both the tomb and as architectural embellishments.

Chinese Yixing teapot, 17th century, with contemporary European gilt silver mounts, height 4in. (10.2cm) The Yixing potters created a wide variety of wares, including teapots, snuffbottles, models of fruit and articles for the scholar's desk.

and other vessels. By the early years of the 20th century workshops were producing large quantities of Yixing wares, mostly stamped with the workshop name and also the name of the carver or potter who worked on the object.

Central Asian Earthenware and Fritware

The cross currents of Asian culture were driven by nomadic traders who brought caravans of exotic goods from central Asia across northern India and into China. The earliest central Asian wares were generally utilitarian but through exposure to Tang ceramics central Asian potters from the 7th to 12th centuries developed a colourfully decorated ware with an opaque white ground painted with plants and foliate patterns in cobalt and green pigments. Other wares with incised sgraffito designs of plants, figures, swirls and geometric patterns were splashed in brilliant glazes of yellow, green, brown and blue. These ceramics were certainly influenced by

Large red earthenware jug, North-west Iran, c.1350-800 BCE, height 14¼in. (36.2cm). Early earthenware vessels such as this example often were either based upon metal shapes or were the inspiration for metal shapes.

Glazed clay bowl, Iran, Samanid Dynasty, 10th century, diameter 8⅝in. (21.8cm).

glazed and moulded wares made in Roman Syria and also by Chinese lead-glazed wares dating from the Tang dynasty. Unlike Chinese examples, these were utilitarian, not tomb wares. Chinese lead-glazed earthenwares made for the tomb were not suitable for daily use. Islamic potters sought to emulate the bright, colourful appearance but not the fragility of the Chinese polychrome wares. Tang white wares were much more durable, but lacked the colourful appeal.

Fritware glazed dish, Iran, 10th century BCE, diameter 15½in. (39.3cm). Fritware has a ceramic body with a very high silica content, making it almost glass-like.

Fritware

The emergence of an Islamic style of decoration began under the Abbasids (750–1258) at the capital city of Samarra around 850 CE with the introduction of coloured and lustred painting over a white glaze. In addition to vessels, Abbasid potters made architectural tiles.

Painting detailed images was difficult using lead glazes; the colours would run and mix together. Seljuk potters in Turkey found a solution in a new type of ceramic body called

Jar, Syria, Ayyubid Period, 13th century BCE, earthenware with manganese purple glaze, Raqqaware, height 17½in. (44.5cm).

fritware, a siliceous material essentially made of glass mixed with small amounts of clay and covered with an alkaline quartz glaze. Frit paste was made by pulverising a glass mixture into a fine powder, which could be moulded into appropriate shapes. Syria had long been a major glassmaking centre and techniques of glassmaking are at the core of the Islamic ceramic tradition. With its glassy surface and durable, transparent body, fritware was a close approximation of Chinese porcelain.

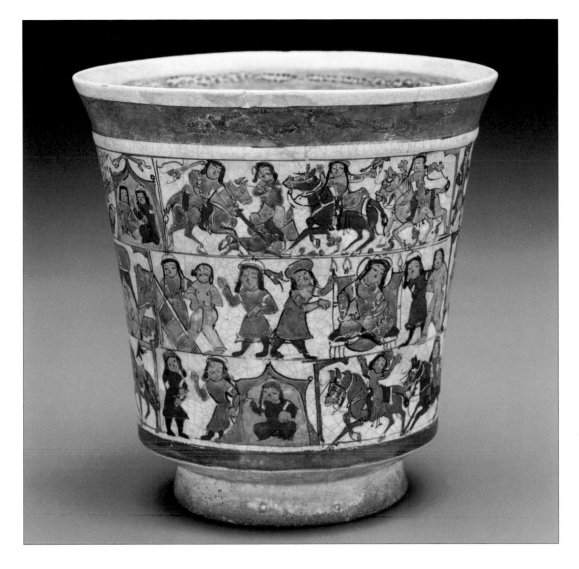

Beaker, Iran, early 13th century BCE, stone-paste painted overglaze with enamel, Minaiware. Delicately painted figural friezes are often found on Minaiware objects.

(Below). Bowl with inscribed poem, Iran, Qajar Dynasty, late 19th or 20th century. Glazed porcelain, diameter 4¼in. (10.8cm).

Two early types of fritware developed: enamelled Minaiware, which would be fired a second time and is identified by the often finely drawn images, and lustreware. Lustreware emerged from Egypt as potters left the collapsing Fatamid dynasty (ending in 1171). Early Persian lustreware of the 12th and 13th century is similar to Egyptian lustreware of slightly earlier date.

By the 12th century colourful glazed earthenwares were popular trade items. These wares incorporate plant and animal motifs amid swirls of calligraphy and were influential on later Chinese porcelain designs developed under the Mongols in the Yuan dynasty (1279-1368 CE). The Mongol Il-khanids in Iran manufactured ceramics at Kashan from approximately 1200-1330. Immense quantities of ceramic vessels and tiles were made for many building projects. Star and cross-shaped tiles in turquoise and cobalt blue were produced by Il-khanid potters in Kashan. By 1350 the ceramic production of Kashan was in decline.

Persian star-form lustred tile with combat scene, late 13th-14th century, diameter 8⅛in. (20.6cm). Tiles such as this example were made for public buildings. Those with enamel and underglaze decoration required several firings in the kiln.

Tiles

The regular use of glazed architectural tiles began in Persia under the Seljuks (1038-1194). Tammerlane or Timur (1370-1405), the founder of the Timrud dynasty, was a brutal warrior but also a patron of the arts. He built magnificent tile-covered buildings in his capital of Samarkand. Tiles used in Islamic buildings are derived from ancient sources. Byzantine mosaics were widely used in western Asia and undoubtedly contributed to the

Qajar polychrome decorated tile, Persia, 19th century, 16⅛ x 20¹⁄₁₆in. (41 x 51cm). Many Qajar tiles are moulded in relief and depict narrative, figural scenes.

use of tiles in architecture. Timrud ceramics are generally blue and white imitations of Chinese porcelain and tiles in brilliant colours and in a range of techniques. Following the fall of the Timruds, the Safavids (1501-1736) lavishly decorated buildings with tiles inside and out. Kubachi was a major ceramic centre in north-west Iran from the 15th to 17th century, making blue and white and polychrome wares. Blue and white wares dominate, inspired by imported Chinese porcelain. Shah Abbas I revived the ceramic industry in Persia, importing over three hundred Chinese potters and their families during the late 16th century. As in Turkey, architectural tiles were also manufactured in large numbers.

The Qajars (1779-1925) moved the capital to Tehran and potters during this period revived earlier styles and techniques. There were several centres manufacturing ceramics, with Shiraz and Tehran the major centres. These later tiles are often moulded in relief, naïvely painted and thickly glazed.

*Iznik bowl with floral
decoration, Turkey, c.1550,
diameter 13in. (32.5cm).
Iznik wares are among the
most beautiful of all Islamic
ceramics. A white slip is
applied over a white clay
body, which is then painted
with overglaze enamels.*

Iznik

In Syria and Turkey the Sunni Mamluks stopped Mongol advances and were great sea traders, receiving quantities of Chinese porcelain into their ports. The Mamluk potters imitated Chinese blue and white porcelain through the early 16th century. Similar advances took place in Turkey in the 13th century. Secular and religious buildings were decorated with colourful tiles in foliate and geometric patterns.

One of the great centres for ceramic production was Iznik, which rose to prominence in the 14th and 15th centuries. Iznik developed a blue and white fritware, very similar in appearance to Chinese porcelain. The most celebrated examples had a brilliant white body decorated with flowers and grasses in bold, bright colours. Ottoman potters produced colourfully decorated wares in greens, purple and grey. In the second half of the 16th century Iznik potters created a bright tomato red enamel which enlivened brilliant glazed hyacinths, tulips and carnations mixed with scrollwork and grasses. In addition to vessels, these was also a large output of brightly glazed ceramic tiles made to decorate mosques and palaces. The height of Ottoman ceramic production was during the reign of Suleiman the Magnificent (1520-1566) whose vast building projects required enormous numbers of glazed tiles. As high quality Chinese imports threatened the market, potters increased production and the court imposed restrictions on trade. By the early 17th century production at Iznik had ceased.

Kutahya

The earliest production at Kutahya began in the 16th century but most Kutahya wares date to the 18th century or later. Brightly glazed and decorated, these ceramics display some common stylistic characteristics with earlier Iznik wares. Many Kutahya forms are European. In the 19th century Kutahya produced imitations of Iznik. Kutahya potters also produced tiles.

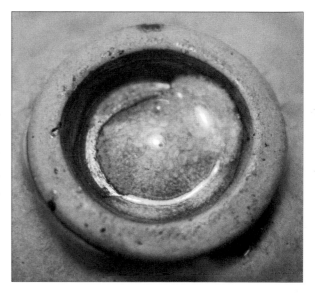

STONEWARE

Thousands of years passed between the creation of the first earthenware vessels and the introduction of stoneware. Potters discovered that at higher temperatures some clays would fuse more completely than others, producing a durable, much less porous material similar to stone. Stoneware vitrifies between 1200 and 1280 degrees centigrade and can be in a variety of colours, but most are earth toned. It can hold liquids, is much stronger than earthenware, and is sometimes 'glazed'.

Glazes

A glaze is a glassy, often colourful outer covering applied to the ceramic body which reduces the porosity of the vessel and often enhances the appearance. Glazes are usually applied in a liquid mixture prior to firing in the kiln. The glaze medium is either sprayed on to the surface by blowing through a reed or bamboo straw or the object is dipped into the glaze. The glaze mixture usually contains silica to which a flux (a material used to lower the firing temperature) is added. Lead is a common flux used in ceramics. When the vessel is fired in the kiln the glaze fuses to the exterior of the vessel, forming a hard, glassy coating.

Early glazes were accidentally produced by ash from the kiln alighting on the object, forming a thin, pale ash-glazed surface. Over time potters developed controlled glazes

The foot and glaze of a Jin Dynasty (1115-1234) Junyao stoneware bowl. Note the crystalline structure in the glassy glaze and the sharp, compact foot.

Detail showing the glaze on an Iznik animal style dish, Turkey, c.1570. The white body and glaze were attempts by the Iznik potters to create a ceramic body with the appearance of porcelain.

51

Chinese green ash glazed stoneware bottle vase, Western Han Dynasty, 2nd- 1st century BCE, height 10⁷⁄₁₆in. (26.5cm).

which were coloured by the addition of various minerals. The most common mineral additives used in glazes are cobalt, iron and copper. All will produce a range of colours depending upon the temperature in the kiln, the firing time and amount of oxygen present. An oxygen rich kiln with iron in the glaze mixture will produce a rich green glaze colour called celadon. An oxygen poor glaze using iron will be brown. Similarly, copper based glazes can range in colour from red to green.

When a vessel has been misfired because of imperfect kiln conditions, the glaze will often flake off or be discoloured. A poorly adhering glaze is said to have a poor 'fit'. Glazes which cool at a different rate from the ceramic body will develop a network of cracks. Skilled potters exploit this characteristic and incorporate crackled glazes into the design.

Chinese Stoneware

Stoneware developed at an early period at various kiln sites throughout China. Among the most notable of these early examples is a type with a pale thin green glaze resulting from falling ash, dating from the Han dynasty. Potters improved and perfected the technique and the rich, green glaze called celadon resulted. Sophisticated funerary vessels and figural models were made in large quantities and in many locations. These greenwares were popular throughout China.

Among the earliest of these greenwares is a type with a thin, finely crackled glaze called yueyao. Made at kiln sites in Zhejiang province from the Han to Song dynasties, yue wares most often were simple bronze vessel shapes, sometimes embellished with impressed or incised designs.

Song Dynasty

The ninth to twelfth centuries were times of great prosperity and innovation in China. In the Song dynasty (960–1279) potters experimented with stoneware glazes and thousands of kilns produced wares for local markets modelled after popular types created for the imperial household. A dazzling array of colours and shapes were created which had never before existed. These stonewares are associated with specific kiln sites in China and are identified not only by shape, design, firing techniques and colour, but also by the specific type of clay and glaze materials.

Kiln techniques differed. Some kilns fired objects set into sand, others in clay containers called saggars. Still other kilns used small platforms to hold the fired vessel aloft so the glaze would not adhere to an adjoining surface. These small stands would leave marks on the base or 'foot' of the vessel and these are called 'spur marks'. Collectors of Chinese ceramics develop a visual memory of these characteristics.

Provincial kilns produced utilitarian storage vessels which were sent throughout south-east Asia in trade, containing foods, oils and other commodities. Others were themselves sent abroad as storage vessels for neighbouring trading countries. These jars typically have loop handles on the shoulder which were used to secure the cover tightly to the body.

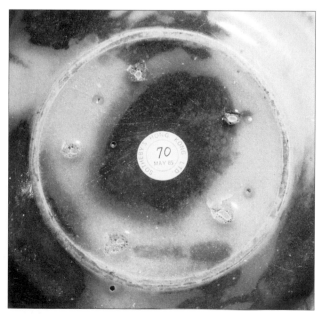

Chinese Junyao purple splash decorated stoneware dish, Jin Dynasty (1115-1234), diameter 7in. (18cm). Jun wares continued to be made, as were many other ceramic types, well beyond the Song dynasty. It is possible to date these pieces accurately by comparing broken pieces, called shards, recovered from the kiln refuse piles. As with all ceramics, the determination of the origin of an object depends not just on the outward appearance, but also the specific type of clay, glaze material, design, and how the object has been made. This example is particularly beautiful with a bold splash of colour and perfectly formed body, beneath a lustrous, thick glaze.

Detail showing the underside of the Junyao dish. The unglazed points in the centre of the foot are called spur marks. These resulted from the unfired object resting on ceramic supports so the glaze would not fuse to loose sand or other material in the kiln. The tag on the back refers to the auction number of this dish, providing information about its history of ownership. The provenance is often extremely important, establishing a chronology of ownership, records of exhibitions, and information about where the object has been published.

Two Henan stoneware teabowls, Song Dynasty, diameters 4⁵⁄₁₆ and 4⅞in. (12.5 and 12.4cm). Henan wares are noted for striking rust brown splashes against a black glassy surface. Many of these teabowls were prized in Japan for use in the tea ceremony.

Northern and Southern Song

Song ceramics are divided into northern wares and southern wares, based on the removal of the Song court in the face of Mongol advances to southern China in 1127. Junyao is a type of northern stoneware which most often has a bright blue and lavender splashed glazed surface. Ding vessels are among the most finely potted and accomplished of all Chinese ceramics. With a creamy ivory colour and typically unglazed rim, these wares are often skilfully carved or moulded with foliate or figural designs. Northern celadons have a grey body and dark olive green glaze and the best examples have deeply carved foliate or figural designs in which the olive glaze pools in the carved recesses. Cizhou wares are sgraffito carved or painted stonewares with a white or dark slip usually decorated with foliate designs or painted with scenes taken from domestic life or nature. Henan wares are usually dark, lustrous glazed and in black or brown. The

Northern Song greenware or celadon with carved decoration, c.12th century, height 9in. (22.9cm). One of the characteristics of Northern Song or Yaozhou stonewares is the pooling of dark green glaze in the sharply carved or moulded designs. The green colour results from iron in the glaze. Many other kiln sites in China produced greenwares, but those of the Yaozhou region are particularly prized.

Chinese stoneware jar with moulded dragon design and cover, Longquan ware, height 9¾in. (24.8cm).

finest of all northern wares is Ruyao. Extremely rare, Ru wares have a bluish green glaze and a finely crackled surface.

After the Song court fled south to Hangzhou in 1127, patronage was extended to a number of new kilns. A southern type of celadon was made in Zhejiang province called

Chinese 'oil spot' stoneware bowl, Northern Song Dynasty, diameter 8¼in. (21cm). The name 'oil spot' comes from the evenly spaced silvery graduated spots on the glassy glaze.

Chinese Northern Song Ding ware dish, c.12th century, diameter 10¾in. (27.2cm). Chinese ceramic dishes were both moulded and carved. This example is particularly finely carved in an elegant and crisp design of peony flowers.

Chinese Cizhou sgraffiato decorated vase, Northern Song Dynasty, 960-1126, height 16¼in. (41.1cm). Cizhou type objects were made in many locations and over a long period of time. Cizhou wares are decorated with carving, incisions or painting.

longquan. Longquan celadons have a thick, lustrous glaze in a rich bluish green shade. Yingqing wares are closely related to porcelain and have a pale bluish white glaze. Jian wares are usually of dark colour, streaked with brown and mostly of small size. Jizhou wares are also dark but imitate tortoiseshell and other materials. Both jian and jizhou wares were prized in Japan by practitioners of the tea ceremony.

Japanese stoneware jar with natural ash glaze, Tamba ware, 17th century, height 16in. (40.6cm). Jars such as this were designed to store tea leaves and are prized by collectors of tea ceremony objects.

Japanese Stoneware

It was during the Kofun period (4th-7th century CE) that Japanese potters first began making objects in stoneware. These early stoneware vessels are called Sue ware and were made to be placed in a tomb or used on an offering table. The shapes are closely related to forms made in Korea during the Silla period (57-668) CE. Often these conical or stylised forms have pierced cut-out designs. They are grey bodied, high fired, non-porous, and some even have a rudimentary ash glaze. Larger utilitarian ovoid jars were also made with a reddish brown body and rudimentary thickly streaked olive green ash glazes. Sue comes from 'to set or place', referring to the function of these vessels as funerary table offerings.

Trade with China and Korea brought potters and their wares from both countries to Japan. Kiln sites were established in Japan which drew on the fashionable designs from both cultures to supply high quality wares to the Japanese aristocracy. At the same time over eighty kiln sites operated throughout Japan which produced utilitarian storage and other vessels for the local market. Perhaps due to the preference among the wealthy classes for imported ceramics, local potters were unable to compete with the fine quality imported Chinese examples and instead established a strong tradition of more rustic looking stoneware.

Japanese stoneware storage jar, Ko-Seto ware, Kamakura Period, 14th century, height 10¼in. (26cm). Seto ware was produced in the village of Seto in Owari province beginning in the 12th century. With Asian ceramics, the ceramic name often refers to the kiln location.

Early Kiln Sites

During the Heian period in the 8th century, ash glazes were purposely applied to stoneware. Sueki kilns continued to produce ceramics into the Muromachi period (1392-1573). The kiln sites of Tamba, Seto, Bizen, Tokoname, Echizen and Shigaraki are among the most famous. Many of the wares produced in these kilns were made for the tea ceremony or for utilitarian purposes. Although produced in many localities, these wares are similar in their often rough, natural hued appearance. The hand of the potter is visible with purposely made markings and random faults formed in the kiln. The earliest examples have natural glazes formed from ash in the kiln alighting on to the surface, leaving a variety of thin, usually greenish toned glazes. By the beginning of the 16th century these early utilitarian vessels were sought by collectors and prized by practitioners of the tea ceremony, forming the basis of an aesthetic standard for later stoneware.

Shigaraki and Other Wares

Shigaraki stonewares include large storage jars and other utilitarian vessels collected by tea practitioners. These are often made of reddish brown clay and have rudimentary glazes. Tamba wares are rustic in appearance, often displaying natural impurities in the clay. Bizen wares are high fired and usually of a dark reddish brown colour, sometimes exhibiting a rudimentary ash glaze. Karatsu stonewares closely relate to Korean ceramics with a pale greyish green body and underglaze iron painted decoration. 17th century Kutani wares are striking in bright enamel colours of aubergine, golden yellow and dark green. Mino kilns were noted producers of small jars in a dark brown glaze for holding powdered tea. Seto wares are similar to those produced in the Mino kilns, usually in a dark, lustrous brown glaze and potted in simple functional forms.

(Above). Two Japanese Shigaraki jars, Muromachi Period, 15th-16th century, heights 15¾ and 17⅜in. (40 and 44cm). After firing, the white clay of Shigaraki turns a reddish brown colour. The ash in the kiln leaves a pale green glaze.

(Opposite). Storage jar, Japan, Muromachi Period, 15th century stoneware with natural ash glaze, Bizen kilns, height 20¹⁄₁₆in. (51cm).

(Left). Japanese tea bowl, Momoyama Period, 1585-1589, with a black Raku glaze, height 3⅜in. (8.5cm).

In response to imported colourful teawares, local potters developed a type of stoneware called Oribe with boldly decorated patterns reminiscent of textile designs. The dark green and brown glazed wares of Oribe appear in the Momoyama period (1553–1615). Often made in striking patterns and constructed from slabs of clay, the glazes pool in thick drops. Raku teawares are celebrated for their 'dry' glaze in dark brown or brownish black.

The use of contrasting slip colours against darker backgrounds and the emphasis of natural glazes gives many Japanese stonewares an immediacy and intimacy with the potter not found in any other Asian culture. Collectors of Japanese stoneware look not only for wares from specific kilns but also for those made by specific potters.

Japanese rectangular dish with flower, Momoyama Period, 9⁹⁄₁₆ x 8⅛in. (24.2 x 20.7cm), Shinoware, stoneware with paint and lacquer. The edge of this dish has been skilfully repaired with gold lacquer.

Korean prunus vase, Maebyong, stoneware with iron painted decoration under a Celadon glaze, 1100-1150 BCE, Koryo Dynasty, height 11in. (28.6cm). Painted Korean stoneware of this type is related to Chinese Cizhou wares of the Song Dynasty.

Korean Stoneware

In Korea potters had been active at least since 7000 BCE, first producing earthenware and then stoneware. Korean and Chinese potters were the first in the world to manufacture stoneware. Stoneware funerary vessels made during the Silla period (57 BCE-935 CE) are usually dark grey and of ovoid shape with unusual angular cut-outs. Silla potters probably emigrated to Japan and developed similar techniques there.

One of the most beautiful of all Korean stonewares is a rich olive or sea green celadon colour. Celadons or greenwares were made in both China and Korea. There was a rich cultural interplay between the Chinese, Japanese and Korean cultures which promulgated an exchange of ceramic innovations. Many ceramic shapes in Korea and Japan can be attributed to Chinese prototypes. Each culture took these shared ideas and shaped them to suit local taste.

During the Unified Silla dynasty (668-935 CE) trade and cultural exchange were common between the two cultures and this continued into the Koryo dynasty (936-1392 CE). The earliest Korean celadon wares were produced in direct response to innovations made by Chinese potters whose wares were sought by the Korean aristocracy. The most successful of these wares were inlaid celadon vessels, called sanggram, made during the Koryo dynasty. Inlaid celadons are produced by forming the vessel on a potter's wheel in wet clay, allowing it to air dry, and then carving out designs which are filled with coloured clays and fired under a clear glaze. Unlike Chinese celadons, many Korean examples are fired while raised on a small clay support which leaves 'spur marks' on the underside of the body in the glaze. The finest Korean celadons have clearly visible carved or impressed designs, are beautifully potted and have a clear unblemished glaze. With the Mongol invasion and eventual submission of the Korean court to Mongol rule in 1270, the production of inlaid celadons was dramatically curtailed.

Inspired by Chinese Cizhou wares, Korean potters during the Koryo dynasty adapted the Chinese style of Cizhou painted stonewares to their culture. These robustly decorated punchong vessels often have a white or grey slip and decoration in iron brown or white.

(Right). Korean stoneware footed bowl, Silla, 5th-6th century, height 9¼in. (23.5cm). Korean potters brought their skills to Japan, working in many early Japanese kiln sites.

(Opposite). Korean inlaid Celadon vase, Maebyong, Koryo Period, height 12³⁄₁₆in. (31cm). High shouldered vases of this shape are called Maebyong *in Korea and in China* Meiping.

Thai stoneware figure of a
Dvarapala, Sukhothai style,
Sawankhalok Region,
15th/16th century, height
36in. (91.4cm)

South-east Asian Stoneware

The Khmer kingdom spanned the modern-day countries of Thailand, Cambodia, Laos and Vietnam. The Khmer traded with China and other parts of south-east Asia and stonewares, both glazed and unglazed, were part of this trade. Vessels generally are glazed dark olive green to almost black over a white slip and are often decorated with incised geometric patterns. There is a limited range of shapes in Khmer stonewares, most forms being jars, bowls and small covered boxes. During the 11th and 12th centuries small dark brownish black glazed figural and animal form containers were made for the storage of lime used in making betel paste, a mild stimulant. Production of Khmer ceramics continued through the 14th century.

PORCELAIN

After the discovery of stoneware, potters continued to experiment with refined clays, searching for materials which had fewer impurities and which would fuse even more completely. Eventually this led to the discovery of porcelain. Porcelain clay, commonly called kaolin, is refined and mixed with a hard white stone called petunse or 'china stone', a type of feldspar. It fuses into a translucent body when fired to a temperature of at least 1250 degrees centigrade.

The white body of porcelain is strong, translucent and can be colourfully decorated. Most decoration on porcelain uses the mineral cobalt. When painted with a brush in a liquid mixture on to the unfired body, cobalt is dark grey. When fired, the grey brightens into blue.

Most porcelain is covered with a clear glaze. When the painted design is under the glaze it is referred to as 'underglaze decorated' and, when applied over the glaze, 'overglaze decorated'. Metallic oxides are often mixed together into a viscous substance which, when painted on to the glazed surface after firing and fired a second time, will harden into rich colours, called 'enamels'. When these metallic oxides are combined with the glaze, they produce a coloured glazed surface.

The underside of a Chinese underglaze blue decorated porcelain dish dating to the Yuan Dynasty (1279-1368). The porcelain clay of Jingdezhen is a creamy, white colour. Porcelain made in China, Japan, and other locations can often be identified by the colour and consistency of the porcelain clay. Often in firing the unglazed portion of a porcelain body will partially burn, turning a reddish-brown colour. The cut marks on the porcelain foot were formed by the potter as excess material was trimmed from the edge.

(Above). Detail showing a Xuande (1426-1435) reign mark on the edge of a porcelain bowl. The mark reads from right to left 'Da Ming Xuande Nian Zhi'.

(Right). Detail of underglaze cobalt blue Ming style design on an 18th century porcelain vase. Revivals of Ming designs were popular during the 18th century, but the painting technique differed from the Ming originals, with darker areas of colour achieved by concentrations of small points of colour. Early Ming concentrations of cobalt blue were often very dark from impurities in the cobalt, a feature referred to as 'heaped and piled'.

(Opposite). Chinese vase with dragon design, Xuande Period, 1426-1435, height 13½in. (34.3cm), porcelain with blue underglaze.

Chinese Porcelain

It was the Mongol conquest which spurred the development of underglaze blue decorated Chinese porcelain. Yuan dynasty (1279-1368) porcelain was often made for the Near Eastern market and included large dishes, bowls and pouring vessels of traditional central Asian metal form. The decoration usually incorporates flowers and vine scroll patterns, animals and mythical creatures. The dark blue cobalt was imported into China from the Near East and each source of this mineral contained a combination of impurities which affected the tonality of the colour. As supplies of cobalt were exhausted and new sources found, the variation in the colour produced from these impurities would change. Thus it is possible to date an object closely based on the tone and intensity of the blue colour. The earliest porcelain examples are extremely rare and were produced in the city of Jingdezhen, which is still the centre of porcelain manufacture in China.

Reign Marks

The innovations in design inspired by Mongol and Near Eastern taste were gradually adopted by the Chinese majority and other decorative elements added. Potters continued to experiment with firing techniques and coloured glazes. By the 15th century it was an established practice to identify porcelain articles made for the imperial court with a reign mark indicating the object was made in the official kilns of Jingdezhen. These reign marks are invaluable tools in establishing benchmarks for dating and each reign mark corresponds to the reign of a specific emperor. Porcelain vessels from the official kilns made in the Xuande (1426-1435) and Chenghua (1465-1487) periods of the Ming dynasty met particularly rigorous standards of quality.

Chinese Wucai enamel decorated dragon and phoenix bowl, Qianlong mark and Period (1736-1795), diameter 6in. (15.2cm). Wucai refers to a combination of enamel colours with overglaze iron red and underglaze blue.

Enamel Glazes

A wide variety of enamel glazes and techniques were introduced during the Ming dynasty. Doucai, translated as 'contrasting colours', refers to a design with underglaze blue and overglaze enamels. Wucai, literally 'five colours', refers to ceramics in underglaze blue and iron red overglaze enamels. Porcelain vessels were made for specific occasions and purposes: small cups for wine and tea, bowls for rice and large dishes exported to the Middle Eastern market for serving mutton. Underglaze copper red was introduced in the Yuan dynasty and later to great success in the Kangxi period (1662-1723).

(Opposite). Chinese Doucai enamel decorated vase, Yongzheng Period. Doucai refers to the combination of underglaze cobalt blue with overglaze enamels.

(Right). Chinese underglaze copper-red decorated porcelain bowl, Hongwu Period (1368-1398), diameter 16½in. (42cm), with a design of peony and chrysanthemum flowers. Copper produces a red colour in firing under optimum circumstances. If improperly fired, it turns a grey colour.

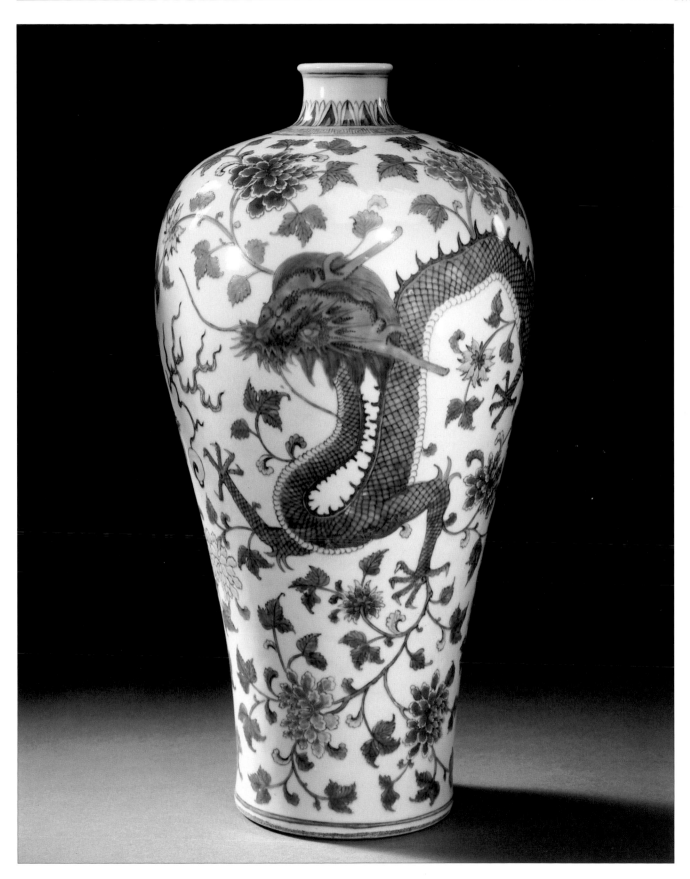

(Opposite). Chinese vase with peach design, height 19¾in. (50.3cm) porcelain with overglaze enamels. Qianlong Period (1736-1795).

(Right). Chinese famille verte rouleau vase, Kangxi reign, c.1700, height 18¼in. (46.3cm). Bold new patterns and designs were popularised during the early years of the Qing dynasty (1644-1911) in addition to imitations of early Ming designs.

Transitional Period

At the end of the Ming dynasty, in the late 16th and into the 17th century, the Chinese government became increasingly corrupt and impotent and the controls exerted by various guilds governing the quality of porcelain articles produced in the kilns relaxed. The resulting transitional wares are more freely drawn and in surprising shapes taken from contact with western traders.

During the succeeding Qing dynasty (1644-1911) controls were re-established, kilns rebuilt and porcelain production reached a high standard of excellence. Many objects

Chinese Blanc de Chine figure of the Daoist Immortal Cao Guojiu, 18th century, height 14⅛in. (36cm). One of the most talented modellers of the Dehua kilns was He Chauzong whose works, like those of other Dehua potters, are often stamped with the artist's seal.

were made for export to the west and those for domestic use often incorporated nostalgic designs from the early Ming period. The quality of 18th century official blue and white and enamel decorated porcelain was superb, particularly during the reigns of Yongzheng (1723-1735) and Qianlong (1736-1795).

Chinese export famille rose *armorial decorated figural tureen and stand with the arms of Astegvieta, Qianlong Period (1735-1795), c.1770, height of tureen 16in. (40.7cm), length of stand 19⅜in. (49.3cm).*

Export Porcelain

China was an important seafaring nation long experienced with trade throughout all of south-east Asia. Vast quantities of underglaze blue porcelain and celadon wares were exported in trade to the Philippines, Thailand, Vietnam, Malaysia and Indonesia. This trade was drastically reduced in the 15th century with an inward looking bureaucracy which curtailed maritime commerce.

In 1514 Portuguese merchants began trading in China and brought back large quantities of blue and white decorated porcelain, silks and spices to the west. Other western countries followed and established trading outposts. England, Holland, Spain, Sweden and later the United States were engaged in the porcelain trade. Popular export

Vietnamese export porcelain group from the Hoi An *cargo shipwreck, late 15th/early 16th century, diameter of largest 13¾in. (35.1cm). Many kilns were active in Vietnam from the 12th to 16th century, producing domestic as well as export wares. The* Hoi An *cargo was recovered from a sunken trading vessel off the coast of Vietnam in the late 1990s. Over 150,000 porcelain objects were found.*

patterns included mythological subjects, tobacco leaves, images taken from popular engravings, and monograms and heraldic emblems. When the Chinese emperor protested and attempted to restrict western access, a series of wars were fought which collectively are known as the 'Opium Wars'. These wars opened China in the 19th century to spheres of western influence which greatly increased western commerce and eroded Chinese sovereignty. *Famille rose* export porcelain, typically decorated with flowers, insects, butterflies, and figural subjects, was sent abroad, as was blue and white porcelain. During the 19th century a succession of weak rulers and lax oversight allowed for a gradual decline in porcelain quality mirrored by a rise in quantity, much produced for trade with western Europe and the United States.

(Opposite). Group of Chinese export famille rose *articles, first half 19th century. Also called Rose Medallion, this type of decorated porcelain was exported in huge quantities to the west from China throughout the 19th and early 20th centuries. The term* famille rose *refers to the dominant use of pink enamel.*

(Above left). Korean underglaze blue decorated porcelain dragon jar, 18th century, height 15¾in. (40cm).

(Above right). Vietnamese enamel decorated jar, c.1450, height 22½in. (57cm). Vietnamese potters drew extensively on Chinese shapes and design.

Korean Porcelain

Early Korean porcelain articles are drawn directly from Chinese and Korean stoneware shapes. The earliest Korean porcelains date from the Choson dynasty in the 15th century and are generally austerely decorated in accordance with the prevailing Confucian court taste. Korean potters were much more successful in using colourful underglaze copper red and iron brown than their Chinese counterparts. With the fall of the Ming dynasty in 1644 and subsequent military incursions by the Manchu, Korean intellectuals reassessed their relationship with China and new shapes and designs were introduced which substantially depart from contemporary Chinese examples. Pierced dragon decorated brushpots, animal form water droppers and large ovoid jars are among these new designs.

Japanese Porcelain and Later Earthenware

Porcelain was not made in Japan until hundreds of years after its introduction in both Korea and China. Japanese potters had been at a disadvantage because of the aristocratic preference for imported ceramics from China, stifling the nascent demand for locally produced porcelain wares.

Japanese underglaze blue decorated dish, Arita, 17th century, diameter 14¼in. (36.3cm). During the late 17th century the porcelain kilns in Jingdezhen were burned during fighting between the defeated Ming troops and the Manchu army. Japanese kilns met the demand from western traders and produced wares in Chinese styles for export to the west.

Arita and the Dutch East India Company

The earliest Japanese porcelain wares were made in the 17th century near the city of Arita. Porcelain kilns, probably under the tutelage of Korean and Chinese potters, were built at Arita because of huge local supplies of kaolin. Discoveries at early kiln sites in Arita have produced shards which show a direct foreign influence. The cobalt used by Arita potters is distinctly different from that used at the same time in either China or Korea. The impurities in the cobalt mixture give the blue a dark, inky violet hue.

Porcelain was made for the domestic and export markets and, as demand grew from western European traders, production increased to meet that demand. In the early 17th century the Dutch East India Company, Vereenigde Oostindische Compagnie, commonly abbreviated VOC, was the only authorised European trading company in Japan and monopolised the market. With governmental functions severely disrupted from the fall of the Ming dynasty in 1644, porcelain production in China decreased and the Dutch increased their purchases of Japanese wares, giving a dramatic boost to the Arita potters. Japanese porcelain was first exported in 1659 after the disruption of production from the Chinese kilns at Jingdezhen from the fall of the Ming. The shipments of exportware were directed through the port city of Imari, a name which later became associated with a particular type of decorated porcelain.

Pair of Japanese Imari porcelain jars, 17th century, height 23¼in. (59.3cm). Large jars of this type were sent back to Europe to furnish princely houses. One of the greatest collectors of Chinese and Japanese porcelain was Augustus the Strong, Elector of Saxony.

Imari

Imari generally refers to underglaze blue decorated porcelain with iron-red and other overglaze enamel colours. Many early objects of this type were sent abroad and sold in western Europe. Augustus the Strong, Elector of Saxony (1694-1733), was a passionate collector of Japanese and Chinese export porcelain and filled entire palaces with dome covered jars and large dishes called chargers.

Kakiemon

Enamel overglaze colours in red and shades of blue and green applied over a creamy glaze in spare naturalistic designs of great delicacy characterise a distinguished type of Japanese porcelain called Kakiemon. Named after the family who specialised in this type of decoration, Kakiemon porcelain was hugely popular in Europe, and Meissen and other European factories imitated Kakiemon designs.

(Opposite). Japanese enamel decorated porcelain jar, Kakiemon, c.1670-1690, height 21in. (53.3cm). The delicate colourful enamels of Kakiemon inspired European potters to imitate these designs throughout the 18th century. Ironically, the design on this jar was taken from a Dutch design inspired by a Chinese original.

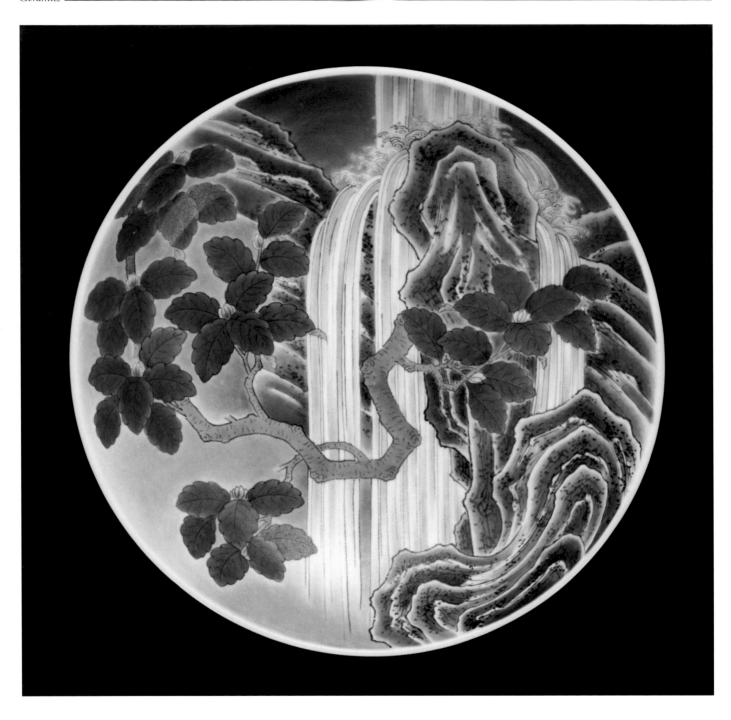

Japanese enamel decorated
porcelain dish, Nabeshima,
early 18th century, diameter
11⅞in. (30.2cm).
Nabeshima porcelain articles
have a characteristic comb
pattern encircling the foot.

Nabeshima

Nabeshima, the third major type of Arita porcelain, was produced for wealthy merchants and aristocrats. It has a high footrim usually painted with an underglaze blue comb pattern and with delicately drawn naturalistic designs, often in underglaze blue but high-lighted with iron-red overglaze or other enamel colours. Nabeshima designs are created on paper which is then transferred on to the unfired clay body, allowing for the production of exact sets. Often Nabeshima wares were decorated by two artists, the master creating the front and the apprentice the underside.

Kutani, Imari and Satsuma

During the 19th century Kutani, Imari and Satsuma wares were produced in vast quantities to meet foreign demand. Satsuma kilns date to the invasion of Korea in the 16th century and the subsequent removal of Korean potters to Japan. The Satsuma kiln was sponsored by the Shimazu family and the cream coloured enamel decorated ware we associate with Satsuma dates to the end of the 18th century. It is a Kyoto style ware and is often confused with works in a similar style produced by the master decorator and potter Yabu Meizan (1853-1934). Satsuma is low fired and the finely crackled ivory toned

Japanese glazed porcelain figural group, Hirado, Edo Period, height 11¾in. (30cm). Hirado kilns mostly produced vessels of various forms; sculptural groups are unusual.

Japanese enamel decorated porcelain dish, Ko-Kutani, 17th century, diameter 13⅜in. (34.1cm).

glaze is the result of an uneven contraction between the glaze and body during cooling. It is usually decorated with minutely drawn landscapes, flowers or figural subjects.

The popularity of Satsuma wares spread with international renown achieved from European exhibitions and fairs and by the end of the 19th century many kilns were working in the style, most producing wares of uneven quality. In the early 20th century huge quantities of Satsuma were being exported to the west in garish designs of hybrid forms taken from both European and Asian sources. Among the finest of the late 19th century artists is Yabu Meizan working in Osaka. Typically artists signed their work and accompanied the signature with a self-effacing eulogy, sometimes including comments about the length of time an object took to create.

Similarly, Kutani wares, originally inspired from Wucai enamel decorated Ming designs of the 16th or 17th centuries, were also produced in large quantities. By the late 19th century Kutani porcelain bears little resemblance to the earlier examples, mostly being moulded teasets or dishes decorated with printed designs in either underglaze blue or in overglaze iron-red.

Brightly enamelled Imari vases and chargers were produced in large numbers in the late 19th century for the export market. These large decorative dishes and vases were popularised in many international expositions and trade fairs in the late 19th century. It was the commercialisation of the Japanese ceramic industry during the late 19th and early 20th century which led to a revival of traditional techniques and the revitalisation of the potter's art.

Group of Japanese earthenware vessels, Satsuma, by Yabu Meizan (1853-1934), heights 3¾ to 7¼ in. (9.5 to 18.4cm). Satsuma vessels are often noted for detailed scenes populated by minute figures.

20th Century Asian Ceramics

The most prolific centres for ceramic manufacture in Asia during the 20th century were China and Japan. Both countries have a strong ceramic culture and many ceramics manufactured there in the past century were based upon earlier designs. Exceptions include large quantities of paper-thin porcelain made in China during the early part of the 20th century immediately after the end of the Qing dynasty in 1911 and continuing through the end of the 1920s. During this period Yuan Shi Kai, a military leader, sought to establish a new dynasty. Ultimately he failed, but ceramics were made during this period which were created for his reign. Some of these are finely made and are sought by collectors. Other ceramics were made using earlier reign marks, particularly in the style of ceramics made in the Qianlong period.

Aside from these copies, large numbers of stoneware figures and monochrome wares were made in southern China. These figures are sometimes referred to as 'mud figures' and are roughly sculpted with thick colourful glazes. The majority of the late monochrome wares are deep red in colour and bear a superficial resemblance to monochrome wares of the Qing dynasty.

(Above). Japanese enamel and underglaze blue decorated bowl and charger, Imari, late 19th century. Large bowls and dishes, called chargers, were made in substantial quantities during the late 19th and early 20th century for export to the west. The finest examples are hand decorated; those of lesser quality are often decorated with stencils.

(Opposite). Japanese yellow ground porcelain jar, Makuzu Kozan, Meiji Period, height 23in. (58.4cm). Makuzu Kozan was a major innovator in ceramics, creating striking, modern designs using traditional techniques.

Japanese Sumidagawa vase, c.1900. Sumidagawa wares are identified by the colourful glazes and high relief sculptural modelling.

The majority of 20th century Japanese wares are extremely roughly made earthenware vases and other forms created for sale in the west during the first thirty years of the 20th century. These are often called 'satsuma' but bear little resemblance to the fine quality satsuma wares made in the late 19th century. Most are western forms with thick enamels and sketchily drawn scenes with figures or nature subjects. Fine Satsuma was produced alongside these commercial wares, with such artists as Yabu Meizan (1853-1934) consistently winning acclaim for his wares. Sumidagawa is another popular ware, identified by the high relief modelling, irregular shapes and bright enamel colours in unusual combinations, frequently including orange and red pigments. Other frequently seen Japanese ceramics are large porcelain dinner sets or tea services boldly decorated with dragons in high relief enamels. Many of these teasets have lithophane images at the

Japanese earthenware vase made for the western market, c.1900. Objects of this type were made in huge quantities for the Western export market. They are usually sketchily decorated with moulded decoration.

base of the teacups. The model for these sets remained virtually unchanged from the early 20th century until the 1950s.

Japan developed a strong tradition of studio pottery during the 20th century and many artists produced notable ceramic works based both on traditional forms and in completely new designs. Itaya Hazan (1872-1963) was the first among many studio artists in Japan. A strong collectors' market exists for these wares both in Japan and abroad.

The majority of the ceramic output from central Asia has continued using motifs established during the high points of the Ottoman, Safavid or Qajar periods. Among the more unusual objects made from the 18th through the early 20th century are beehive covers. These small circular covers were created to secure the ends of Persian beehives, which are cylindrical wicker objects covered with mud and having openings at either end.

Chapter Two

Metalwork

*M*any examples of Asian metalwork are made of bronze, an alloy of copper, tin and lead. The raw materials are crushed from rock and heated until molten, with the impurities rising to the top of the mixture as slag. The slag is skimmed from the surface, leaving the molten metal which is further refined in preparation for combination with other metals and pouring into moulds.

Bronze Casting Techniques

There are two principal types of bronze casting: the piece mould and lost wax processes.

The piece mould process begins with the creation of a model of the object to be cast. Wet clay impressions are taken from the designs on the model. These are allowed to dry and are joined together to form a mould. The original clay or wood model is shaved down in size and encased by the clay moulds. Small spacers are placed between the clay core and exterior mould to ensure an even thickness. Molten metal is poured into apertures cut into the mould, allowed to cool, and the bronze object removed. The cooled bronze will have rough areas and other imperfections which are removed in a finishing process. Unless several impressions are taken of the original model, each bronze cast in the mould will be unique.

The lost wax method is similar. A clay core is covered in wax and the wax surface is carved with a design. The wax coated object is then covered with wet clay which takes an impression of the carved wax model. The clay is allowed to dry and joined to form a mould. Metal wires or rods are inserted through the sides to ensure stability. Molten metal is then poured into apertures, the wax melts, and molten bronze fills the gap. The object is removed when cool, and the surface is cleaned and finished with files and chisels.

Gilding

Bronze or silver objects are often gilded. Mercury gilding is a process using a mixture of gold and mercury applied to the metal which is heated until the mercury evaporates, leaving the gold residue behind, which is then burnished. Other objects were gilded with a mixture of translucent lacquer over gold or other metal foils.

(Opposite). Chinese bronze ritual vessel (Fang Yi), c.1000 BCE, height 13⅞in. (35.3cm). Bronze ritual vessels held great significance in early Chinese society. Shang and Zhou Dynasty examples often are decorated with stylised animals and mythical creatures. The shapes and decoration form the basis for many later Chinese objects.

Patina

Bronze objects have an accidentally created or purposely applied surface called a patina. Usually the patina is dark greenish brown and is formed by a careful application of corrosive agents to the surface. Other patinas are formed naturally, particularly those on ancient bronze vessels interred in tombs which reacted to acids leaching from the soil on to the surface causing a chemical reaction. Bronze also accumulates a patina by being handled, from the mildly corrosive effects of the oils in our skin.

Specialised Metalworking Techniques

The working of patterns on metal by hammering is called chasing. Gold is more easily worked than silver which can split. Specialised tools are used to produce designs in relief, called repoussé, and engraved details are achieved by cutting away metal with a sharp, pointed instrument. Designs are hammered into the surface background using punches.

Asian metalworkers also worked in iron, copper, brass and many alloys. Most iron objects are cast and prepared in much the same way as bronze objects. Iron in Asia often came from meteors, adding a mystical element to the finished product. Metal objects were sometimes inlaid with other metals such as gold, silver or copper. A process called damascening, named after the city of Damascus, the supposed source of this technique, involved filing the surface of the metal object to produce narrow rows of upright ridges into which gold or silver wires would be hammered, flattening the filed ridges to produce an inlaid effect.

How to Determine Quality, Condition and Authenticity

There are a variety of techniques for working metal. All involve hammering or casting. Metalworking is a time-consuming specialised process. A metalworker develops his skill through practice and apprenticeship, working with a skilled master to learn techniques and processes perfected by others. Unlike some other crafts, the raw materials used by metalworkers must be refined prior to use. This additional expense makes any object worked by the metalworker more costly than a comparable object in most other materials. In addition, some metals such as silver and gold have always been considered precious, making an object made of these materials even more valuable.

Quality

When evaluating a metal object comparisons are best made with other similar objects from the same culture and time. Within this context, evaluations can be made of the proportions, scale, fineness of the details, finishing, and overall stylistic impression. The finest bronze figures were made as objects of veneration and should be well finished, having sharp, crisp details and probably a gilded surface. Rougher, utilitarian items such as iron tools were not as well finished. Iron rusts and the surface of an iron object is frequently pitted.

When evaluating a metal object, consider its use and the audience for whom it was intended. The wear should be consistent with the purpose for which it was made. Cast bronze vessels with surface decoration should be sharp, well defined and easily read.

Smudging of lines or indistinct images may indicate that an object is a later version or recast from a mould of an original. Metal objects are often worn from handling. This kind of damage is expected, aids in determining age and authenticity and, if not too severe, can actually increase the value if it has an attractively patinated surface.

Condition

Because bronze is an alloy, sometimes the chemical processes which bind together the several metals can break down. A condition called 'bronze disease' results and, while the exterior remains visually the same, at least in the beginning stages, as time passes the metal becomes granular and weak, eventually disintegrating. There are techniques which can stabilise bronze disease but it cannot be reversed. Rust and other corrosions affect a metal surface and if severe will reduce the value of an object. Gold is mostly unaffected by corrosion but silver reacts harshly to many acids and can be damaged if left untreated. Islamic metal objects are often inlaid with other materials. These inlays should be expected to become loose and fall out. Rarely does an inlaid metal object retain all of the inlay. Many Islamic objects are covered in a thin tin wash. This surface rapidly wears away and can deceive anyone not familiar with this characteristic into believing the object to be of greater age than is actually the case.

Detail of corrosion on a Chinese archaic bronze vessel dating from the Western Zhou period. The bright green and brown deposits result from the chemical interaction of the metals in the bronze alloy with elements in the ground water or soil in the tomb.

Authenticity

Many of the most sophisticated bronze copies are made in China but skilled forgers have also been active in the Middle East and south-east Asia. Among the more ambitious copies are bronze figures, often enhanced with gilding. The best copies often are beautifully cast with incised and well-finished details, unlike lesser examples with sharply cut, stiff and lifeless decoration. The forgers usually fail in their attempts to replicate an authentic, early patina, creating dark brown smudgy surfaces instead of the rich golden brown expected from a patina accumulated over several hundred years. The interior of the casting typically is filled with clay and applied with accumulated grit in an attempt to cover the raw, recently cast metal.

The patina on an ancient bronze is actually in the metal, not on the surface. Often copies will have a surface patination which simulates the effect of thousands of years of burial. The surface patination on a copy can usually be removed by pressure from a fingernail, leaving bright smooth metal showing beneath the patina. A patina also develops from years of handling. Mild acid in human skin transfers to the metal surface and causes corrosion. This corrosion accumulates and if left unchecked will eventually damage the object. Vessels for holding liquids, jars for grains and other utilitarian objects all should exhibit areas of wear consistent with the use of the object. Wear should be particularly noticeable on areas of greatest exposure. Skilled forgers are aware of these characteristics but in their efforts to replicate hundreds or thousands of years of wear often leave a subtle pattern which identifies the object as a forgery.

A Group of Forged Ancient Bronzes

I once examined a group of bronze objects which had been recovered from a sunken ship dating to the Ming dynasty. The objects were covered in marine growth and, although difficult to see, the cast decoration which was visible was smudged and ill defined. When some of the surface accretions were removed, the metal surface was bright and clean with no corrosion. Forgers had concocted an elaborate scheme where an authentic shipwreck dating to the Ming dynasty was salted with recently made bronze copies which had been disguised under a cloak of marine growth.

Early Chinese Metalwork

Sophisticated bronze casting techniques emerged in China much earlier than in any other Asian culture. In the Shang Dynasty (1766-1045 BCE) the Chinese produced large scale elaborately cast bronze ritual vessels. These often incorporated zoomorphic or ritual mask designs. Early bronze vessels in China were cast using the piece-mould method. Movable handles or elaborate elements were sometimes added after the initial casting by 'casting on' using small moulds.

(Opposite). Chinese bronze ritual vessel, Gui, Early Western Zhou Dynasty (1050-211 BCE), width 10⅝in. (27cm). Boldly cast masks and designs appear on many early Chinese ritual bronzes. The masks gradually become more distinct during the Western Zhou period, birds and other motifs are incorporated, and finally by the Warring States Period disappear in preference for inlays of gold, silver, and precious stones.

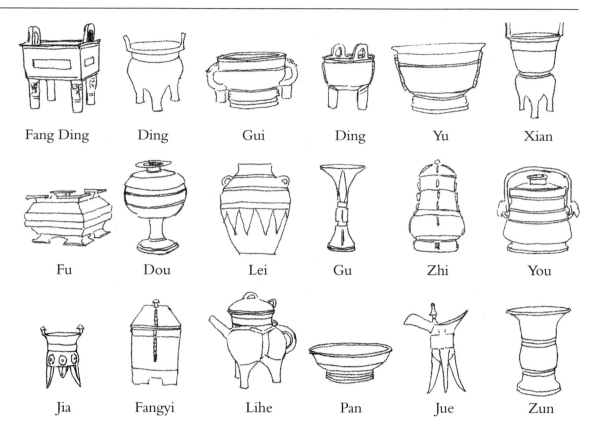

Fang Ding   Ding   Gui   Ding   Yu   Xian

Fu   Dou   Lei   Gu   Zhi   You

Jia   Fangyi   Lihe   Pan   Jue   Zun

*Drawings of Ancient
Chinese bronze shapes.*

Shapes and Decoration

Shapes include food containers, wine vessels and storage jars. The jue is a tripod pouring vessel with a narrow spout on three blade-form legs. Often the background design is a pattern of small coils called leiwen, with stylised birds and dragons separated by low flanges. The gu is a trumpet-shaped vase with a flared mouth. A ding is an ovoid tripod vessel on circular section legs. Shapes such as the you often had movable handles and covers which were separately cast. The most elaborate of these vessels had animal-form legs or large bold masks called taotie cast in high relief. Gold, silver, turquoise and other inlays were sometimes added and sumptuous vessels dating from the Warring States and Han period occasionally have human figural designs. The shapes of vessels were sometimes influenced by the casting process, using legs or other elements as pouring channels. By the 2nd century CE the ritual significance of these bronzes had diminished and bronze was supplanted in importance as a symbol of wealth by other materials, notably lacquer.

Mirrors and Belt hooks

Chinese bronze mirrors generally have a high tin content and were made in large quantities and date from all periods. They are generally small circular shapes cast with elaborate concentric bands of design including mythological animals and figures from the zodiac. The cast design is only on one side; the other is highly polished to produce a reflective silvery surface. Other bronze articles include chariot fittings, lighting devices, tools, weapons, mounts on crossbows, staff finials, and braces and brackets on furniture.

The Chinese also worked in gold and silver and used both materials to embellish bronze articles. Small belt buckles called 'belt hooks' were often of stylised animal or dragon form and inlaid with gold, silver or turquoise.

(Left). Chinese bronze ritual bell, 6th to 5th century BCE, height 24⅝in. (62.6cm). Large sets of graduated size ritual bells were sometimes included in a burial chamber.

(Below). Chinese bronze lion and grapevine mirror, Tang Dynasty, diameter 6¼in. (15.9cm). Mirrors in this pattern are identified by the band of decoration including lions with grapevines. Other patterns on mirrors include birds, astronomical signs and mythical creatures. The reflecting surface on the reverse was polished to a bright silvery sheen. The quality of a mirror is based on the rarity of the design, condition and crispness of the casting.

Chinese gilt bronze seated bodhisattva sculpture, Song Dynasty, 10th century, with traces of paint, stand a later addition. Height 9in. (22.9cm) with base.

Later Chinese Metalwork

During the Tang dynasty (618-906 CE) metalworkers excelled in the production of luxury goods for the wealthy aristocratic and merchant families. Silver inlaid lacquer mirrors and other sumptuous articles in gold or silver were often included in a tomb, as were articles for personal adornment. Funeral masks and jewellery in the Liao Dynasty (907-1125 CE) were made of thin sheets of gold.

Religious Images

In the Tang, Yuan, and Ming dynasties large numbers of bronze and gilded bronze Buddhist and other images were made for devotional purposes. These figures range in size from just a few inches to many feet in height. The images vary greatly in quality and were kept in temples, household altars and monasteries. The best examples are crisply cast, gilded, and well finished. Early Ming and Qianlong (1736-1795) examples sometimes have dated inscriptions, chiselled into the metal surface, usually on the front of the base, after the casting was complete and prior to gilding. The metalworker would take a newly cast bronze figure and file away encrusted bits of metal left at the joins of the mould. Gaps from air bubbles would be plugged with metal inserts and filed down. The rough edges would be filed away and small castings made to replace the missing elements. Once finished, a gilded surface would be applied. Average bronzes would not merit this extra work and would be covered in a thick transparent lacquer which would obscure the defects.

Revivals of Ancient Bronzes

In the Ming dynasty there was a revival of interest in ancient Chinese ritual bronze vessels. Copies were made and new forms created which were inspired from the antique originals. Many of these copies were commissioned for temples or to satisfy demand by the merchant class for furnishings suitable for their grand multi-courtyard homes. These forms included censers to burn incense, vases and bronze representations of mythical animals.

Hu Wen Ming was one of the most celebrated of late Ming bronze workers. He lived in the region near Suzhou and worked between 1560 and 1620. Objects from his workshop are often gilded or inlaid and are based on ancient bronze forms. These differ

Chinese gilt decorated copper censer, 16/17th century, signed Hu Wen Ming, height 4¾in. (12cm). Hu Wen Ming was a celebrated bronze worker in the Ming dynasty whose output was considerable and is characterised by fine quality casting often heightened by gilding. Bronze articles made with the signature of Hu Wen Ming continued to be made into the Qing dynasty.

from the originals in the misinterpretation of the original shape and often disproportionate perspective of the taotie mask or other designs.

The fashion for revivals continues into the Qing dynasty and includes forms often cast with apocryphal six character Xuande (1426-1435) marks on the bases. Among the finest examples are the 'gold splash bronze' vessels. These are usually of archaic form but have irregular spaced gold splashes on the patinated bronze surface. The finest examples actually have thick gold splashes and those of lesser quality, or made as recent imitations, will have thin gold leaf applications.

Baitong and Other Metals

The Chinese developed an alloy of copper with a high zinc content which is referred to as baitong or paktong, translated as 'white metal'. In the 17th and 18th century this metal was used for the manufacture of domestic and western export items, but more often for fittings on furniture, small desk articles, trays or hand warmers. Occasionally baitong is inlaid with copper. If not regularly polished, baitong develops a thick encrustation which eventually will damage the metal. Pewter was popular in the Qing dynasty for table settings, fanciful candlesticks for the altar, fruit-form serving dishes, trays and boxes. A specialised group of iron vessels popular in the Qing dynasty are set with sword furniture mounts. These vessels are also often inlaid with gold or silver wires.

Silver

Chinese silver dating earlier than the Qing dynasty is very rare. Wonderful engraved small silver and silver gilt vessels were made in the Tang dynasty as well as personal articles, but post-Tang silver is extremely scarce. There are very few examples of Chinese export silver made for the western market in the 17th and early 18th century. Large quantities were produced in the 19th century and a variety of forms were made in western shapes for export to western markets.

Silver arrived in China from mines in Yunnan province and from western traders who used it as a medium of exchange. Chinese merchants required western traders to pay for commodities in silver. Much of the silver was mined originally in Mexico, Central or South America. The first silver articles purchased by westerners were flatware and table articles made for use while stationed in the trading ports. Consequently, most items made before 1840 are copies of western forms. As additional treaty ports opened there were hundreds of silver workshops responding to the demand. Most designs from this later period incorporate traditional Chinese motifs, such as dragons and landscapes crowded with figures, executed on objects of western form such as graduated mugs, teasets, hot water kettles, trays of various sizes and decorative bowls and vases. 20th century wares are generally more commercial.

(Opposite page). Chinese export Portuguese market baitong pitcher and basin, mid-18th century. Baitong, literally translated as white metal, was used primarily for domestic Chinese articles, but examples were also made for export to the west. Portuguese traders had been active in China from an early period and retained a presence in China in Macao until the late 20th century.

(Left). Chinese gilt silver dish, Tang Dynasty, width 9¾in. (24.8cm).

(Below). Chinese ewer and basin, Qing dynasty, late 17th or early 18th century, height of ewer 9in. (23cm), diameter of basin 7⅛in. (18cm). Early examples of Chinese export silver are extremely rare. This example is an unrecorded example of a European mannerist form, replicated by a Chinese artisan, most likely from an engraving, accounting for the unusually small size.

Islamic Metalwork

Early Persian metalwork is drawn from many sources. Ancient Greek and Roman traditions continued in central Asia long after both empires had waned in influence. Magnificent silver and gold articles were created in Byzantine workshops, usually incorporating classical elements or Christian motifs. Originating from this region are ancient Achaemenid (559–330 BCE) and Sassanian (226–651 CE) silver and gold vessels. With the fall of Sassanian rule to Arab invaders in 651 CE, Islam replaced Zoroastrianism. Very few works of art survived this turbulent period and gradually the Islamic and native Persian cultures mingled.

The earliest Islamic inlaid metal objects date to the 9th or 10th centuries and are utilitarian vessels from Afghanistan. The inlay technique spread to western Asia with centres of production in Mosul and Damascus. Mosul had been established in 1169 as a major metalworking and artistic centre by Saladin, the founder of the Ayyubid dynasty. When Mosul fell to Mongolian armies in 1260, the metalworkers and artisans fled in panic to Cairo and Damascus, promulgating the spread of these techniques and styles of decoration and workmanship throughout the Islamic world. As a result, much Islamic metalwork is similar in style regardless of the city of manufacture.

(Above). Islamic silver and gold inlaid copper bowl, Fars, South-west Persia, 14th century, diameter 9⅝in. (23cm). Islamic inlaid vessels were made in centres throughout western Asia and the Middle East.

(Opposite). Sassanian silver gilt bowl, 4th to 5th century BCE, diameter 7½in. (19.1cm.).

Much of the work produced in Damascus from the 13th to 16th centuries was sent abroad in trade to Venice. Designs were cut into the metal surface and then sheets of gold or silver were hammered into place and often finished with fine engraving. Gold was augmented with techniques of inlay using silver, copper, or niello. Early examples are very scarce. Brass, bronze, copper, silver and gold inlaid vessels were decorated with elaborate interlacing foliage, calligraphy, and arabesque strap work. Writing boxes for scribes, large vases, serving implements and vessels, mosque lamps, torch stands, candlesticks, animal form censers and other personal articles were made throughout Islamic

Silver beaker, Marlik Civilisation, c.800 BCE, height 6¼in. (15.9cm). The Marlik people inhabited an area in North-west Iran.

(Right). Islamic ewer, Syrian, dated 1232, Ayyubid Dynasty, brass with silver inlay, height 14⁷⁄₁₆in. (36.7cm).

(Opposite). Two damascened steel animals, Qajar, Persia, 19th century, heights 9¾in. (25.3cm). A lively metalworking tradition exists throughout central and western Asia.

western and central Asia. The technique rapidly spread to Iran, Baghdad, Aleppo, and Egypt. The Mongol conquest of China and Persia increased trade and cultural exchanges between the Yuan and Persian courts, influencing the cultural styles of both countries.

Production declined during the 17th and 18th centuries, reviving again in the late 19th century as European demand for Asian decorative arts increased. Objects made for the west included large trays, ewers, Koran boxes, containers of various sizes, and military accessories such as swords, helmets, and shields.

Indian Metalwork

Buddhism was established as a state religion in India by the emperor Ashoka Maurya (269-232 BCE) and lasted until the Turkish invasion of the 12th century, only remaining in the Himalayan strongholds of Tibet and Nepal. With the decline of Buddhism there was a concurrent rise in Hinduism. The last of the great Indian Buddhist kingdoms, the Pala, in the 9th century witnessed the introduction of a variant of Mahayana Buddhism known as Vajrayana or Esoteric Buddhism. Esoteric Buddhism greatly expanded the number of manifestations of the Buddha and bodhisattvas, even bringing Hindu deities into the Buddhist pantheon. The basis of the movement was centred in the remaining Buddhist monasteries in Northern India of Nalanda, Bodh Gaya and Sarnath. As these centres fell to advancing Islamic forces, monks and scholars brought the esoteric teachings and images to Nepal, Tibet and other parts of south-east Asia.

The Chola

In South India the Chola from the 10th to 12th century produced fine quality graceful solid cast bronze images using the lost wax method. These bronze figures were made to exacting, religiously established standards. Among the most graceful of these images are depictions of Shiva, as lord of the dance, and his consort Parvati. The Chola were followed by the kingdom of Vijayanagar (1336-1565) which finally fell to Muslim forces and then split into small Hindu kingdoms. There is an ancient tradition of folk bronzes in central and eastern India which usually incorporates Hindu imagery. These were made by itinerant craftsmen and include bronze pull toys, animal forms and utilitarian objects.

(Left). Bronze figure of bodhisattva Maitreya, Kashmir, 10th century, height 14⅞in. (37.8cm).

(Opposite). Indian bronze figure of Shiva, The King of Dancers, Chola, 12th century, height 36⅞in. (93.7cm). This image of Shiva is as Nataraja, the King of Dancers, who dances the universe into and out of existence as all time passes through the circle of flames.

Group of Indian bronze vessels, 16th/17th century or later, height of largest 12¾in. (32.5cm). Bronze, copper, and brass vessels were made by travelling metalworkers throughout Asia.

Mughal Metalwork

Mughal domination of Northern India was consolidated under Akbar (1556-1605). The Mughal empire produced a variety of richly fabricated gold jewellery, jade and hardstone encrusted swords, and a type of silver or brass inlay set into a copper, zinc and lead alloy, called bidriware. The contrast between the bright silver or brass inlay was often accentuated by darkening the metal ground. Bidriware developed in the 17th century

Indian bidri ware ewer, Mughal, c.1700, height 13⅞in. (35.2cm). Bidri is a type of inlaid metalwork found only in India; it is an alloy of zinc, lead, copper and tin.

and most examples are huqqa bases, spice containers, bottles, cups, or betel nut boxes. In addition to gold jewellery, the Deccan was a noted centre for gold decorated iron jewellery. A strong tradition of silver working was developed in India during the late 18th and 19th centuries, particularly creating objects for the British market. These objects were created in the latest styles popular in England and were intended both as trade items and for the British subjects stationed in India.

(Right). A pair of large Turkish brass mosque candlesticks, 16th century, height 30¼in. (77cm).

(Below). Turkish silver scribe's pen box (divit), Ottoman, inscribed 'The Tughra of Ahmed III' (1703-1730), length 11in. (28cm). Scribes performed an important function in the Islamic world. Pen boxes are usually made of brass or bronze, with the finest examples in silver or gold.

Ottoman Metalwork

In Turkey under Ottoman rule (c.14th century-1918) silver ecclesiastical lamps, reliquaries, and other objects were made for the Christian minority. Christianity had long been established in Asia, and in areas under Byzantine control silver articles for religious worship were common.

A vibrant market also existed for metalwork incorporating traditional Islamic motifs. Many of these early items were very similar to Islamic metalwork made in other centres. Scribe cases, made with small ink pots attached to rectangular containers, were made in silver and bronze. Bowls, beakers and other silver vessels often have engraved details heightened with a black ground in a technique called niello.

During the late 19th century the Ottoman court increasingly imported European silver and other metalwork for the local market. These wares are usually in rococo or baroque styles and sometimes incorporate enamelwork.

South-east Asian Metalwork

Most south-east Asian cultures were centred around large temple religious complexes such as Angkor Wat of the Khmer or Borobudur in Java. The identification of metal and stone sculpture from these cultures is based upon archaeological finds and comparisons, when possible, with sculpture which remains at the original location. Collectors and scholars identify metal and stone sculpture not only by culture but by the style associated with a specific temple complex.

Dongsan bronze drum, 16th century or earlier, height 28in. (71cm), diameter 47¼in. (120cm). Bronze 'rain' drums were made from ancient times up until the present. The early examples retain an old patinated surface and other signs of wear. Newer examples are often artificially patinated.

Javanese gold and silver figure of Tara, c.9th century, height 3⅝in. (9.2cm).

Vietnam

The Dongsan culture flourished in the region around present-day Vietnam (Annam) during the 3rd and 4th centuries BCE. The Dongsan tribes created a variety of bronze objects but are particularly noted for large cylindrical bronze drums. Although produced up to the present day, the design of the drums has remained relatively unchanged. A large star centres the striking surface which is surrounded by radiating bands of geometric decoration and small crouching relief cast animals perched on the edge. Similar bronze drums are found in Indonesia and Thailand.

Indonesia

Indonesian bronze objects include religious images based on Chinese Buddhist or Indian Hindu prototypes as well as a variety of smaller decorative bronze items, such as blade-form finials and, at a later date, animal form bronze weight measures. Hinduism and Buddhism flourished in the region from the 5th through the 15th centuries until the arrival of Islam in the 16th century. The central Javanese temple complex of Borobudur in the 8th and 9th centuries produced extraordinary bronze objects and many small bronze Buddhist and Hindu images were created in Java. Esoteric Buddhism overwhelmed the earlier tradition of Hindu-Buddhist images by the 13th century and bronze meditative aids are produced, such as vajras, bells and other articles. Temples constructed in Indonesia from the 8th to 15th centuries often mix Buddhist and Hindu iconography reflecting the varied influences from India and China.

Betel Nut Containers and Accessories

Inlaid bronze betel nut containers and accessories are found in Indonesia and the Philippines as well as Malaysia. The boxes are often inlaid in simple geometric patterns and hold an addictive stimulant mixture made from areca nut pieces, betel leaves and powdered lime. When chewed it produces a mild narcotic effect and red saliva.

Javanese Gold

Java was a rich source of gold from early times and many burial sites dating from the 8th to 18th centuries contain gold vessels and jewellery. Among these are delicate gold filigree and granulated ground necklaces and earrings. The Hindu Javanese period ended in the 16th century with the introduction of Islam and with it the demand for cast bronze and gold objects. Javanese bronze figures from this late period have a gentleness and sweet expression that typify the best examples of Buddhist art.

Cambodia

In Cambodia, the Kingdom of Angkor Wat created bronze images derived from Indian and Chinese prototypes brought from Indonesia. The earliest of these scarce images dates from the 8th to 15th centuries. The sculpture of the Khmer focused on representations of divine concepts of perfection, not attempts accurately to portray the human figure. The most often seen figures are of the singha (lion), naga (serpent or cobra figures), garuda (mythical bird and enemy of the naga), Ganesha (Hindu elephant-headed god), makara (mythical water creature with features of a crocodile, elephant and serpent), and the aspara (a winged heavenly creature).

Burma
In Burma Buddhism flourished alongside the ancient native animistic worship of the Nats. Nat deities representing almost all aspects of nature were incorporated into the Buddhist pantheon. The golden age of Burmese Buddhism extended from the 11th to the 13th centuries, a period when many of the most important temples were constructed. Small bronze devotional figures of Buddhist and Hindu dcities were produced in large numbers.

A tradition of working in silver existed from early times in both Burma and Cambodia but most surviving examples date to the late 19th or 20th centuries. These are mostly bowls, usually worked in high relief with a complex frieze of figures in a lush landscape.

Sri Lanka
Sri Lanka was also a centre of Buddhism from the 6th to 14th centuries, producing many small votive images.

Lotus-shaped bowl, Cambodia, 12th century, metal alloy with gold, diameter 8½in. (21.6cm).

Bronze figure of Buddha, Northern Thailand, Lan Na School, 15th/16th century, height 28⅝in. (72.7cm).

Thailand

Thailand has had several centres of political power over the centuries. The Thai kingdom of Sukhothai flourished in north central Thailand between the 13th and 15th centuries, the kingdom of Lan Na had its capital at Chiangmai and Ayuthia remained powerful from the 14th to the 18th centuries. Much artistic production of bronze religious imagery centred in Angkor controlled areas, especially Lopburi. Bronzes created in Lopburi greatly influenced those produced in other centres, especially Ayuthia. Each of these kingdoms produced bronze images associated with a specific style.

As Khmer influence waned, other styles developed. Hinayana Buddhism, prevalent in Thailand, promoted the idea that the original artistic representations of the Buddha taken from India were to be copied as faithfully as possible. This tradition resulted in a repetition of earlier established patterns. Thai bronze figures continue the Gupta tradition of sculpture from India, with images having serene expressions and elongated features. Bronze working centres created huge quantities of images for temples and private worship.

Nepalese gilt copper, lapis lazuli, coral and turquoise mounted figure of Bhairava with a goddess, 18th century, height 9¹⁵⁄₁₆in. (25.3cm). Bhairava is the angry manifestation of Shiva and is also called Mahakala. Metal sculptures from Nepal and Tibet frequently are embellished with semi-precious hardstones.

Nepal, Tibet and Mongolia

The transmission of Buddhist imagery to the Himalayan kingdoms took place over hundreds of years. Bronze images created in Indian Pala workshops were transmitted to this region during the 8th and 9th centuries. A further transmission of styles took place in the 11th century, introducing a new range of complex iconography which greatly affected the direction of Himalayan Buddhism. Early Nepalese and Tibetan bronzes dating from the 7th to 12th centuries bear a close stylistic relationship to Indian bronze forms. These often incorporate Hindu iconography and are cast with a high copper content with turquoise, coral and other embellishments. Many images were cast in silver. Newari craftsmen from Nepal were known as superb metalworkers.

During the early Ming dynasty in the Yongle and Xuande reigns, Tibetan and Nepalese bronze workers were brought to the Chinese imperial workshops in Beijing, bringing with them their highly developed skills. The high quality work produced by these artisans were imperial commissions created as gifts for the many Buddhist monasteries in China,

115

Nepal figure of White Tara, gilt bronze with inlay of precious stones, 15th-16th century, height 21¼in. (53.7cm).

Tibet and Nepal. Bronze work during this period set a standard for later Ming and Qing dynasty bronze images. A large number of these works are identified by a short imperial reign mark across the front of the lotus base. Bronze images created after the 11th century are much less reliant on early designs and introduce a broad range of deities with complex iconography. Many bronze figures had sealed bases which contained consecrated materials, usually prayers.

Tibetan bronzes are similar in style to those from Nepal and in addition to the many figural images include ceremonial objects such as vajra, bells, ewers, lamps and a ritual dagger called a purba. In addition to bronze, Tibetan ironwork belt buckles, boxes, ritual objects and weapons inlaid with gold or silver were produced at the metalworking centre of Derge. Later Himalayan bronzes continue the tradition established in the early Ming dynasty. Many of these bronzes were created in the 17th and 18th centuries, usually with sumptuous gilded surfaces.

Mongolian silver is in the same tradition as both Nepalese and Tibetan. Silver and gold vessels were produced for ritual and practical purposes and gifts of ritual objects in precious metals were received from the Chinese imperial court. Close relationships between these cultures greatly influenced artistic styles. Silver ewers, lamps and other similar objects are often inset with turquoise and coral and have bold foliate and mask decoration. In addition to these forms silver mounted boxes, usually of circular shape, were used as food containers during the 19th century. Tsampa containers were made to hold a thick barley porridge and are made of wood, often with silver and hardstone mounts. Most surviving Mongolian, Nepalese and Tibetan silver dates to the late 19th or 20th century.

Tibetan silver ritual box, 18th century, height 12in. (30.5cm), width 12in. (30.5cm), depth 6in. (15.2cm). This box is replete with imagery designed to repel malevolent spirits. Skulls, bones, tantric symbols, and spirits were protective images guarding the precious contents.

Korean Metalwork

Korean gilt bronze standing Buddha, Unified Silla Period, 8th century, height 18⅝in. (47.3cm).

Korean bronze pouring vessel, Kundika, Koryo Dynasty.

Korean metalworkers developed distinctive bronze shapes at an early date. Korean bronze vessels and Buddhist images from the 6th to 10th century borrow extensively from Chinese and Indian prototypes. As emissaries and travellers brought Buddhist texts to the Korean mainland, Buddhist images were also transported, influencing the bronze and other figures made by Korean metalworkers.

Many of these forms, such as slender vases, bells, alms bowls and pouring vessels, were made as Buddhist ritual objects. Burial sites in Korea have divulged a rich treasure of gold jewellery. Crowns, earrings and other thinly hammered gold objects were included in the tomb with the deceased. The close relationship between Korea and China influenced bronze images and many Korean figural bronzes are very similar stylistically to Chinese examples. In addition to bronze Buddhist images, later Korean metalwork of the 18th and 19th century includes iron censers, boxes, brushpots, and other forms, some with hammered silver wire inlay.

Japanese ritual bell (Dotaku) Yayoi Period, 2nd/3rd century CE, bronze, height 24¼in. (61.7cm).

Japanese Metalwork

Advanced metallurgy began in Japan in the 3rd century BCE. Many of the earliest examples of Japanese metalwork are directly inspired by Chinese originals, brought to Japan in trade or by governmental emissaries, beginning with the introduction of Buddhism in the 6th century CE. These include bronze Buddhist images, mirrors, bells and other articles. The use of bronze with sacred images created a strong link between bronze and Buddhism.

Japanese mirror with Matsukuizuru motif, Heian Period, 11th/12th century CE, bronze, diameter 3¹⁄₁₆in. (7.9cm). The popular motif of flying cranes is called Matsukuizuru. Bronze mirrors were introduced into Japan from China in the Kofun Period (248–646 CE).

Mirrors

Mirrors hold special significance in Japan. Mirrors were considered as a repository of the soul and were used as votive offerings, tossed into bodies of water. Japanese bronze mirrors were originally based on Chinese mirrors and early examples are faithful to the Chinese repertoire of shape and design.

Over time, the distinctions between Japanese and Chinese design grew more noticeable. Japanese mirrors, based on early Chinese bronze examples with formulaic borders, retained the basic shape and style of the Chinese original, but with different decorative details incorporating auspicious symbols and natural images. An inner raised band found on Chinese mirrors eventually is ignored as a decorative device in the Kamakura period and by the Edo period the circular inner field has spread and obscured the inner band. Later Japanese mirrors depart substantially from Chinese examples with the introduction of an entirely new form having an attached rectangular handle, a form called an ekagami.

*Japanese bronze vase,
18th/19th century, height
36in. (91.5cm).*

Flower Bronzes

Japanese bronze vessels were often modelled on Chinese archaic bronze examples. Tea
and Zen Buddhism were both introduced into Japan from China in the 12th century,
resulting in a popularity for all things of Chinese origin. As a consequence, bronzes in
the Muromachi period (1392-1573) are closely related to imported Chinese examples.
Vases made specifically to contain flowers were very popular, based on the Zen concept
of bringing nature indoors. Not many of these early Japanese bronze vessels survive, but
there are many later versions dating to the 18th and 19th century. The patina, or surface,
of these bronze vessels was an important part of their appeal. Bronze workers purposely
created decorative surfaces for bronze articles and bronzes which retain the original
surface are significantly more valued than those which do not.

Mixed Metal Inlays

During the 19th century a range of elegant, fanciful bronze shapes were introduced which were drawn from Chinese forms. In the Meiji period international exposure for traditional Japanese crafts was gained through expositions in Vienna in 1873, Nuremberg in 1885, and at many other sites in Europe and America.

The use of mixed metals on bronze greatly increased, based on traditional techniques used by metalworkers working on Japanese sword guards called tsuba. Inlays and overlays of gold, silver and copper or alloys containing these and other materials were combined in naturalistic designs on vases or other vessels. Murata Seimin (born 1769) was a bronze worker of considerable skill whose workshops specialised in these techniques. In the late 19th century, following the ban on sword manufacture, tsuba and other metalworkers sought new mediums to work their crafts. Large figural bronzes of great technical virtuosity were created. Early Meiji sculpture was based on western methods introduced by the Italian sculptor, Vincenzo Ragusa (1841-1928).

Large Japanese silver punchbowl, c. 1900, Arthur & Bond, Yokohama. Boldly decorated silver table objects were made in both Japan and China during the late 19th and early 20th century. Among the best known of the Japanese silversmiths was Arthur & Bond.

Pair of Japanese inlaid iron vases, signed Nihon (no) kuni Saikyo (no) ju Komai sei, late 19th century, height 8in. (20.3cm). Komai was a noted metalworker active in the late 19th century.

Iron, Silver and Gold

Cast iron tea kettles, called tetsubin, were first made for use in the tea ceremony in Japan during the 16th century. After the initial casting the pot would be reheated and decorated. Bells, gongs, candlesticks, censers and temple lanterns were created in iron and bronze. These and other wares were produced in large quantities following the Meiji restoration.

Early use of silver and gold in Japan was primarily for decorative inlay or use in alloys such as shakado, made from copper, gold and silver. Solid gold sword fittings were popular luxury items in the 17th century. Silver was used extensively as decorative inlay during the Edo and Meiji periods, particularly on bronze objects. The majority of silver articles created in Japan date to the very late 19th century or early 20th century. Some of these forms are similar to elegant bronze vessels, while others adhere to popular western shapes and were intended for the export market, embellished with dragons or naturalistic subjects. Among the most celebrated of Meiji period silversmiths was the British owned firm Arthur & Bond, located in Yokohama. Apparently the company, like so many others, ceased operation after the great earthquake of 1923. Other noted late Meiji silversmiths were Katsu Miyamoto and Takata and Company.

Detail. Chinese cloisonné enamel dish. Cloisonné enamel is made from crushed mineral pigments suspended in a glassy mixture which is separated by thin wires called cloisons.

ENAMEL

Enamelling refers to the use of vitreous substances such as glass which have been coloured and fired to another surface, forming a decorative design. Enamels can be applied to metal, ceramics or glass. Among the earliest enamels are those produced for the Byzantine aristocracy in Constantinople. Roman artisans working in various centres produced cloisonné enamels as early as the 3rd century.

Types of Enamelling

There are three major types of enamelling on metal found in Asian arts: cloisonné, painted and champlevé.

Cloisonné enamels are identified by the use of small metal wires called cloisons which are formed into decorative shapes and attached to the metal ground of the object which is to be enamelled. A powdered glass paste fills the cells which are then heated in a kiln and the glass paste fuses, forming a colourful pattern. To completely fill the design the process can be repeated several times with the excess polished down and the wire dividers gilded.

Painted enamels are formed using minerals in a mixture which is then fired and fused into a glassy surface, fixing them to the metal ground.

Champlevé is a process where recesses cut into the metal ground are then filled with enamel paste and fired. The surface is polished smooth, typically showing expanses of enamelwork against a metal patinated surface.

Byzantine cloisonné enamel and silver gilt reliquary of the True Cross, c.1000-1050, height 3in. (7.55cm), width 2¼in. (5.63cm). Byzantine enamelwork developed from Roman cloisonné techniques. The cross on which Christ was crucified was said to have been discovered early in the 4th century and fragments were distributed as gifts, presented in elaborate containers.

Chinese Enamels

Chinese cloisonné enamel censer, early 15th century, width 8in. (20.2cm). The colours and design of this censer are typical of early Ming cloisonné. Later versions are much more controlled and exact in the separation of colours and have thinner wire cloisons.

Some of the principal colours used in Chinese cloisonné enamelwork are red, green, white, yellow, dark and bright blue. Although enamelled metal articles date from ancient times in China, the first cloisonné objects date from the 15th century. Cloisonné enamel dating from the Ming dynasty typically is decorated with repeating foliate patterns, mythical animals and occasionally landscape scenes. Forms and designs follow those found on ceramics of the same period.

Cloisonné Enamels

Cloisonné was probably introduced into China by the Mongols. Byzantine enamels were widely admired in Central Asia and probably provided the inspiration for Chinese cloisonné. Ming decoration usually incorporates dragons, lotus scrolls, leafy vines, landscapes and flowers. Most Ming cloisonné enamels are unmarked but Jingtai marked examples (1450-1457) are an exception. The Jingtai mark is usually honorific and objects with it usually date from later periods.

During the Qianlong period cloisonné techniques became increasingly sophisticated with finely drawn patterns of delicate inlays. The patterns lack the robustness and vitality of the early Ming examples, but reach a new standard in technical execution. Typical vessels include sets of censers, candlesticks and vases made as garnitures for temples and vessels which are inspired by ancient bronze forms. These pieces are often accentuated with gilded bronze surfaces. The repertoire of shapes includes small models of animals, mythological creatures and large vases and other vessels.

Cloisonné continued to be made in large quantities during the 19th and 20th centuries, but much of this output recapitulates earlier forms and, possibly due to the larger quantities manufactured, often has a lifeless, stiff appearance.

Chinese cloisonné enamel vase, Qianlong Period (1736-1795), height approximately 18in. (45.7cm). Cloisonné vessels were often created in forms derived from ancient Chinese bronzes.

Chinese painted enamel dish, Canton, 18th century, diameter 13½in. (34.2cm). Painted enamelwork was done in both Canton and Beijing. The colours and design of this example are typical of the Canton workshops. Large size enamel articles are rarely in perfect condition, as any bending of the metal structure will cause the enamelled surface to crack and flake.

Painted Enamels

The other major type of Chinese enamelling is painted. Painted enamels on metal were introduced to the Chinese by Jesuit missionaries in Beijing during the 17th century. During the Kangxi period (1662-1723) the Chinese perfected the technique and a variety of opaque colours, including pink, were introduced. By the mid-18th century enamel wares began incorporating images of western scenes or western figures.

Japanese wireless cloisonné enamel tray, signed Kai (Namikawa Sosuke), late 19th or early 20th century, width 11¾in. (30cm). Wireless cloisonné is a technically difficult process and the finest examples are highly prized. Some enamel objects use a combination of both cloisonné and wireless techniques.

The major centres for the manufacture of painted enamels were Canton, Suzhou and the imperial factory in Beijing. Many of the Cantonese produced enamels depict western subjects or are western shapes. While the majority of these objects were made for export to the west, many were made for the Chinese market. The imperial factory in Beijing produced painted enamels of extremely fine quality, usually noted by a special mark or inscription on the base.

Japanese Enamels

The Japanese also produced cloisonné enamels. Unlike those made in China, most Japanese examples date no earlier than the mid-19th century when the process was perfected with the aid of a German engineer, Gottfried von Wagner (1831-1891), and Tsukamoto Kaisuke, who together developed a refined enamel paste with brighter colours. In 1879 Namikawa Yasuyuki and Wagner created a black enamel ground. The technique of wireless cloisonné was developed in 1889. The largest and most successful of the many cloisonné manufacturers was Ando Jubei, whose Ando company was founded in 1880.

The immense production of cloisonné continued into the 20th century with most items sent abroad for export. Many were poor quality, eventually crippling the industry.

Wireless Cloisonné

Japanese cloisonné of the late 19th century is generally of finer technical quality than Chinese examples of the same date. The techniques also differed. The Japanese used sulphuric acid to etch recesses into the metal surface into which coloured glass paste would be pressed, allowing for the formation of designs without the use of metal wire cloisons. Once fired, the enamel would be polished by progressively finer powders until the surface was flawless. Most cloisonné is done using a copper base, but the finest Japanese cloisonné enamel wares are on a silver ground and are sometimes signed by the master craftsman. Among the many artisans who worked in this technique is Namikawa Sosuke (1847-1910) who specialised in nature subjects.

Japanese cloisonné jar with silver wire inlay and silver mounts, Kyoto Namikawa, Yasuyuki, late 19th century, height 3½in. (8.9cm).

Silver Enamel Ware

Nagoya was a major centre for the production of silver enamel ware and enamellers who specialised in this technique include Kawaguchi Bunzaemon, Kawade Shibataro, Yashida, Suzuki and others who worked for the Ando company. Kumeno Teitaro and Tomiki Shobei both created superb examples of enamelled silver. The finest examples were produced between 1883 when the use of silver was first adopted and 1915 when large scale manufacturing eliminated most demand for the best quality examples.

Kyoto Ware

An important early centre for Japanese enamelwork is Kyoto, a type of cloisonné enamelling developed in Kyoto in the first half of the 19th century which is technically superior to any enamelwork. The decoration covers the entire surface with a fine network of cloisonné cells in a beautiful array of colours. The wires separating the enamel cells are usually gilded, as are other non-enamelled surfaces. The artistry of the Kyoto enamellers greatly influenced enamel workers in Tokyo and Nagoya who worked in landscape and pictorial techniques.

Islamic Enamelwork

Small painted enamelwork items were produced for the Qajar court and wealthy classes. Other enamel items were made for the Ottoman market, both in Europe to Turkish taste and in Istanbul. During the 19th century imported items included small cups called zarfs, often in gold or silver, sherbet spoon holders, flywhisks, mirrors, trays, decorative clocks, pocket watches and cutlery sets. European style enamel wares were produced in Istanbul at workshops next to the Suleymaniye Mosque. The centres for Indian enamelwork, which embellishes much Mughal jewellery, were at Jaipur, Delhi, Lucknow and Alwar.

20TH CENTURY METALWORK IN ASIA

The Islamic countries of Asia were major metalwork producers in the 20th century. Much of this production was made for the local market but many items were also made for export. The majority of these wares share some basic characteristics. Most are either brass or copper and those which are copper generally have a tin wash. Trays, bowls and jars constitute the most popular forms and almost all are clearly handworked. The most recognisable items are large trays with concentric bands of figural, calligraphic and foliate decoration made either for wall display or as a low tables.

Japanese and Chinese metalworkers crafted items in copper and brass, but generally better quality examples are in baitong, bronze or bronze with enamelwork. Vases and jars are the most common forms created in the early 20th century and are loosely based on ancient Chinese bronze prototypes. Often these objects are decorated with champlevé enamel.

India was a major producer of brass during the 20th century. Large numbers of bowls, candlesticks, trays and other forms were made for export. Generally these are very roughly incised with sketchy figural or natural scenes.

Mughal enamel box, 17th century, width 4in. (10.2cm).

Chapter Three

Furniture, Woodwork and Lacquer

*T*he Chinese have a long and distinguished history of furniture manufacture far exceeding that of other Asian cultures. In addition to furniture commissioned by the aristocracy, furniture in Asia was created for religious, governmental and domestic use. Large populations and crowded cities restricted the ownership of most furniture to wealthy or aristocratic families. Temples and religious centres used furniture for storage. In rural areas furniture was constructed of locally available materials, often bamboo, reeds or woven grasses. Central Asian nomadic cultures eschewed furniture almost entirely while other cultures, such as Japan, emphasised the use of furniture for storage.

The preferred cabinet woods of Asia include both soft- and hardwoods. Pine, elm, cypress, cedar, varieties of rosewood and many tropical hardwoods were used in the construction of furniture. Furniture was also constructed of rare and costly materials: ivory, bronze and stone. The tradition of working in costly materials originated from ancient Rome and continued under Byzantine rule. Finely worked inlays of ivory and bone in geometric patterns and delicate tracery carving, which characterise much Islamic woodwork, are traceable to Byzantine prototypes. Wood was also used for crafting small utilitarian or decorative objects. Some of these were functional, others were created as works of art.

At an early date it was discovered that lacquer, a protective sap, could improve the durability of objects created from wood. When tinted with pigments, lacquer would enhance the appearance and protect the object. Over time lacquer artisans developed a broad range of techniques for working lacquer, allowing lacquerwork to become an independent art form.

How to Determine Quality, Condition and Authenticity

Quality

The most essential determinant of quality in furniture is design and it is the most easily observable. Generally, the form should reflect the intended use. A successful chair will provide a functional seating surface and a successful table will safely support and display objects set on the top. The success of a design often is a signal of the overall skill of the cabinetmaker. The proportions, scale and quality of the carved or decorative elements and type of material directly influence the usability of furniture. Hardwoods should be used as the principal cabinet wood for furniture forms which undergo extensive stress. Softwoods can be used safely in non-weight bearing areas.

(Opposite). Detail of a Chinese huanghuali carved apron, 17th century. One of the major hardwoods used in Chinese furniture is huanghuali, a tropical hardwood with a vibrant grain ideal for carving.

Typical Lacquer Damages

Lacquer is an extremely durable material and most lacquer objects are damaged as a result of exposing the underlying wooden carcass material to air. A chip or crack in a lacquer object will allow changes in humidity to expand or contract the core material causing further cracks and loosening of the lacquer surface. These additional cracks increase the exposure and, if left unchecked, the object can become severely damaged with surface flaking and losses. It is important to address the damaged area as soon as possible and ensure that the level of humidity and heat remains constant until the repair is finished. Lacquer objects which are worn, chipped or cracked are much less desirable than those in perfect condition.

Authenticity

Furniture copies are often difficult to detect. Sophisticated cabinetmakers create furniture forms using original techniques and old woods. Signs of consistent wear must be present where the greatest amount of use has taken place. Table legs, drawer linings and exposed surfaces should show appropriate amounts of wear. Stains, scratches and burn marks are common on furniture and damage which is present on one member should also be present on the adjoining member.

As a general guide, furniture which has been over zealously cleaned or had the surface scraped or sandpapered has been seriously compromised. Furniture with recut joinery

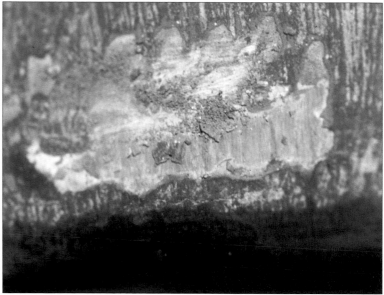

(Above). Modern forgery of a lacquer surface. Forgers will often attempt to duplicate the appearance of early lacquer surfaces. These later lacquer surfaces are usually thin, flake easily, and when removed reveal a bright, clean wooden surface.

(Left). An early lacquer surface applied underneath an Asian table. Lacquer was often used to seal the underside of furniture, providing additional protection against insect and water damage.

and sanded surfaces has lost an integral part of the appeal and becomes essentially the same as a newly constructed object in an early style. All evidence of age has been removed and the clues to the object's authenticity are no longer present. Although old surfaces can be replicated, it is difficult convincingly to replicate the surface and all other aspects of an object that identify it as being of an early date.

The most sophisticated lacquer copies are those made in both Japan and China and are generally copies of Chinese carved Yuan or early Ming lacquer objects. These can be very difficult to detect. The most problematic items are lacquer objects which have undergone repair, making it difficult to determine what is original and what is a later repair. The most often seen copies are Chinese late 19th or early 20th century carved red lacquer copies of Qianlong objects. These generally have a metal core and the base is set with a cast metal plate containing a six-character reign mark. Even more common are copies in cast plastic, identifiable by minute burst bubbles or broken lines in the carved decoration.

Chinese carved huanghuali couch, late 17th century. The finest examples of Chinese furniture will incorporate beautifully executed carving, choice material and superb proportions.

A Huanghuali Bed

In the late 1980s I was called to examine a large Chinese huanghuali daybed (lohan chuang). It was magnificent, constructed of extremely fine, strongly grained timber with a rich, worn polished surface. The high relief carved and pierced back and arms showed birds among seasonal flowers; unexpectedly, the carving was exquisitely finished on the front and reverse. The beaded gently scrolling aprons joined seamlessly to the robustly carved legs, perfectly complementing the overall design. It could not have been improved upon. Every aspect was ideal. The wax surface was old and lustrous, damages minimal and the oxidation on the exposed raw wood underneath untouched. The bed was sold a few months later for a record sum.

A Late Ming Carved Red Lacquer Dish

Early in my career I saw a rectangular red carved lacquer dish of a type found in the Palace Museum in Taipei. This particular example had well-carved details but was exceptionally heavy for its small size, measuring only ten inches (25.4 centimetres) in length. While the design and overall appearance was exactly what one would expect of a late Ming dish, the weight was too heavy for a wooden core, the appropriate material for a Ming lacquer dish. Visually it looked great, even having a network of age and expansion cracks from the buckled lacquer on the base.

We arranged to have it X-rayed and found that the core was indeed metal. This surprising discovery led to further examinations which confirmed that the dish was an exact replica of the example in the museum. Knowing this to be highly unlikely, we discovered that in the 1950s there had been a few highly exact copies made of some lacquer dishes in the Palace Museum collection. This example was one of these.

CHINESE FURNITURE

The Chinese furniture tradition extends back thousands of years. The principal cabinetmaking materials in China include hardwoods, softwoods, bamboo, lacquer, stone and metal. Because furniture made of pine or other softwoods is easily scratched or scarred and susceptible to damage by water or insects, it is often protected by a lacquer surface. Most lacquered furniture in China is burgundy coloured, bright red or black.

Wood Types

Furniture constructed of denser, more durable hardwoods and softwoods such as pine often had lacquer surfaces, particularly if the grain pattern was uninteresting or very open. Wood with a striking grain pattern was most often unlacquered, allowing the natural beauty of the wood to enhance the overall appearance of the object. The principal cabinet woods of China are: elm (jumu), cedar (nanmu), burl (huamu), cypress (nanbai), camphor (zhang), oak (zuo), pine (song), fir (shang), linden (duan), hongmu, tielimu, ebony (wu), jichimu, huanghuali, and zitan.

The best known of these tropical hardwoods is huanghuali. It has a rich reddish brown distinctive grain pattern suffused with dark flecks incorporating small tight knots. It is dense, oily and an ideal cabinetmaking wood. Zitan, a dark, purplish-black wood. is especially prized for its subtle grain of dense tight whorls and knots, often with a feathered appearance. Imperial edicts restricted the use of zitan and much imperial furniture was constructed of this material during the late 18th century.

Construction

The tradition of Chinese cabinetry is closely allied with that of architecture. Chinese architecture relies on mortise and tenon and post and beam construction and smaller scaled but similar techniques are used in the construction of Chinese furniture. Cabinet-makers and builders shared the same guild.

The crest rail of the Chinese chair is supported by two stiles in the same manner as a building with a pair of posts supporting a horizontal beam. A Chinese table is constructed in a similar manner. The table top acts as a beam with the legs as the supporting posts. Uniting these elements is a variety of mortise and tenon, dovetail and other joinery techniques created for very specific purposes. Tops of tables, sides of cabinets and cabinet doors are usually formed by a framework of four boards enclosing a panel of wood. The panel fits within grooves cut into the inner edge of the framework and is secured underneath by narrow boards joining two sides of the framework across a dovetailed cut-out housing in the underside of the central panel. This arrangement allows the centre panel to expand and contract with seasonal changes in heat and humidity, keeping the wood from splintering. This ingenious system of joinery is replicated in most Chinese furniture.

Chinese furniture is constructed like an interlocking jigsaw puzzle. The assembly and disassembly follow exact steps and each element reinforces the stability of the adjoining member. With the fall of the Ming dynasty in 1644, Ming design was gradually supplanted by designs which found favour in the Qing court. In provincial regions Ming designs continued in popularity and in many locations are still produced today.

Huanghuali table top showing the typical marks associated with wear. Furniture without signs of wear is often either a reproduction or has been over-restored with all indications of age removed. In either case, the value and desirability of the object will be diminished.

Furniture Types

The majority of Chinese furniture types are standard forms familiar to most people. Chairs, tables, cabinets and beds are easily recognisable forms. Other less familiar forms include garment racks, designed for holding long robes; document and other boxes; weiqi containers; games tables with reversible game boards; footstools; braziers; lantern stands; and a variety of circular and rectangular pedestals. In addition, there was a rich regional furniture tradition which often included forms only found in particular geographic areas.

Ming Design

Two major furniture styles developed in the Ming (1368-1644) and Qing (1644-1911) dynasties. Generally Ming furniture has simple, often straight lines enhanced by shaped and beaded borders. There is usually minimal carved decoration which incorporates flowers, flowering vines, leafy tendrils, dragons, beaded edges and shaped mouldings. Overall, Ming furniture has an economy of line. The finest Ming furniture designs are strong, linear forms enhanced by either a rich lacquer surface or composed of beautiful wood. The bold simplicity of the design becomes a vehicle for displaying the decorative elements.

(Left) Huanghuali brushpot, 17th century. Small wooden articles were created by the Chinese artisan for domestic and other purposes. Brushpots were used to hold artist's brushes.

(Opposite page). Chinese huanghuali painting table, 17th century, height 31in. (78.7cm), length 78in. (198.2cm). Large wide tables were used by artists as painting surfaces. During the 20th century tables of this type were brought to the west, mistaken for dining tables, and were reduced in height to accommodate sitters. The plain, straight lines are typical of Ming design.

(Above). Pair of huanghuali horseshoe-back armchairs, 17th century. Chairs with a U-shape back are derived from furniture constructed of bamboo or rush. Most Chinese furniture changed very little over hundreds of years. Slight differences in proportion, material, and carved details distinguish average from fine examples.

Qing Design

Qing design generally emphasises the decorated surface. Canton was a major furniture manufacturing centre during the Qing dynasty and furniture made in Canton is characterised by angular forms and the use of the cabinet wood hongmu. Much of the decorative repertoire of Qing furniture looks back to motifs found on ancient bronze vessels. To give legitimacy to their rule, the Qing court adopted well-established Ming and earlier historical designs. These included repeating key-fret patterns, stylised masks and zoomorphic images executed in carving; inlays of ivory, mother-of-pearl, and shell; and engraved metal mounts.

During the 19th century the two furniture traditions were influenced by trade with the west. By the end of the 19th century Chinese furniture often incorporated elements from both Ming and Qing design to form awkward hybrids.

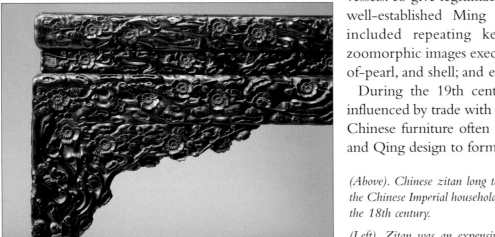

(Above). Chinese zitan long table, 18th century. Zitan was a wood favoured by the Chinese Imperial household and was restricted for use by imperial decree during the 18th century.

(Left). Zitan was an expensive material and surfaces were carved by the most talented artisans. Zitan is identified by the tight, dark grain, often with feather patterning. This extraordinarily fine quality table was probably a product of the Imperial Furniture Workshops.

Chinese export slant-front desk, mid-18th century. height 41¼in. (104.5cm), width 40⅛in. (102cm), depth 24in. (61cm). The serpentine front relates to Dutch 18th century desks of much the same form. Canton was a major cabinet making centre during the 18th and 19th century, creating furniture for both domestic and foreign markets.

Export Furniture

In addition to the tradition of Ming and Qing domestic furniture designs, Chinese cabinetmakers in the western trading port of Canton and other centres produced western furniture forms for export. Made of huanghuali and other Asian hardwoods, this furniture was commissioned by western traders during the 18th and 19th centuries and brought back to the west for sale or as private property. Apart from the construction and the wood, these pieces are often stylistically indistinguishable from examples made in the west which they copied. Chairs, cabinets, tables and chests are the most often found forms.

KOREAN FURNITURE

Korea has an ancient furniture tradition extending back over one thousand years. Many of the basic forms are little changed from examples dating to the 17th century. Most Korean furniture dates from the late 19th or 20th centuries. The principal cabinet woods are pine, gingko, paulownia, bamboo, persimmon, limewood and elm. Often Korean furniture is enhanced with either black or red lacquer. Most furniture was made for storage and a variety of storage cabinets were made, some small and compact with rows of drawers and others larger with sets of matching doors secured by decorative brass or iron hardware. Surfaces are generally undecorated and have minimal carving, mostly limited to beaded edges. The more elaborate examples have inset burl wood or lacquered panels.

In addition to wooden furniture, Korean craftsmen also produced many handsomely decorated mother-of-pearl inlaid storage chests and low tables and furniture with painted oxhorn and sharkskin veneers.

(Left). Korean book cabinet, 19th century, height 60⅝in. (154cm), width 24⅜in. (62cm).

(Opposite above). Korean mother-of-pearl inlaid cabinet, 19th century, height 14in. (36cm), width 37in. (94cm). Cabinets of this shape were used to store personal articles on heated brick couches in both China and Korea.

(Opposite below). Korean ox horn veneered box, 18th century, Choson Dynasty, length 20¾in. (52.5cm). The lack of tropical hardwoods restricted the Korean cabinetmaker to using softer timbers which were ideal for lacquer or veneered surfaces.

JAPANESE FURNITURE

Large tansu or storage cabinets were common in Japan. These cabinets were used for clothing storage and for the storage of personal or household articles. Most are made of pine, elm, or cryptomeria and have large, decorative iron mounts. Other woods common to Japanese cabinetmakers are hinoki cypress, yew, paulownia, mulberry, chestnut and a variety of imported Asian tropical hardwoods.

Often furniture was designed for several functions. Space was limited in most houses and often storage cabinets were built into an interior wall and covered by beautifully painted large sliding panels. Free standing cabinets set on large wooden wheels with sliding doors were made for storage and even movable stairs would be fitted with drawers underneath each rise. Other practical furniture included food service trays and storage containers, large kitchen cabinets with sliding doors, lacquered basins, towel and clothing racks, writing and cosmetic boxes, low tables, braziers called hibachi, lanterns and other lighting devices, and shelves of various size and type.

In the late 19th century Japan underwent an industrial expansion and many traditional crafts, including furniture making, made objects for export to the western markets. International expositions and world fairs provided a venue for the display and sale of the latest and most advanced products. Many of these items use traditional Japanese techniques but are executed in a western form. Small table cabinets are beautifully inlaid with parquetry patterns and large cabinets with designs executed in ivory, mother-of-pearl or other hardstones on wooden panels. In the late 19th century large, deeply carved sets of furniture with dragon-form arms and tall backs were popular in the west.

(Above). Japanese storage cabinet, Mizuya, 19th century, height 71¼in. (181cm), width 68¼in. (173.5cm). Constructed of cypress, zelkova (elm), and crytomeria. Very few examples of Japanese furniture date earlier than the 19th century.

(Opposite). Japanese storage cabinet, Chobako Funa-Dansu, early 19th century, height 21¹⁄₁₆in. (53.5cm), width 18¾in. (47.5cm). The elaborate metal mounts served not only as protective surfaces for the easily damaged edges but also as decoration.

CENTRAL AND SOUTH-EAST ASIAN FURNITURE

Elevated furniture was little used in India prior to the 17th century. Small chests and table articles were made of wood, often inlaid with foliate patterns in contrasting woods or ivory. Increased European contact came first through the Portuguese in the 1530s and then later the Dutch and English. Eventually England gained a monopolistic concession with the Mughal rulers which eventually came at the expense of Mughal political control.

The long Dutch and English presence in India created a demand for western inspired furniture for use in India and for export. This furniture typically follows a western form but is constructed of dense, fine quality hardwoods such as teak, ebony, and rosewood. Tables, cabinets and other furniture forms were made in large quantities beginning in the 18th century and continuing throughout the 19th. Among the most notable of these pieces are ivory veneered or solid ivory furniture and silver sheathed furniture. The majority of ivory furniture was made in special centres, principally Vishakhapatnam and Orissa.

Portuguese and Dutch Cabinetmakers

The Portuguese during the 16th century were the first to establish furniture workshops in Asia. By the 17th century Dutch traders had set up large scale furniture workshops in south-east Andhra Pradesh and northern Tamil Nadu, and the Portuguese were isolated in Goa and along the Malabar coast. The Dutch workshops were highly organised and employed thousands of woodworkers, operating until the Dutch left India in the late 18th century. When the Dutch departed, the workshops and skilled craftsmen were brought to Batavia, Ceylon and Indonesia. The earliest objects were made for the Netherlands market, but, as demand grew, furniture was produced for local use. Chests, cabinets, cupboards, chairs and boxes of all sizes were made of inlaid and carved amboyna, calamander, ebony and satinwood. Many of the finest examples have silver mounts.

As the Dutch influence waned, Portuguese merchants re-established some Indian furniture workshops, creating items for the export and ecclesiastical market. Sofas, portable furniture called 'camp' furniture, ivory and silver inlaid cabinets and boxes, cupboards, chairs and other forms were sold both locally and abroad. Portuguese market furniture often has a lavish use of ivory and ebony inlay.

The Dutch eventually secured trading ports in Malacca and Indonesia, where the Asian headquarters of the Dutch East India Company was established in Batavia, now Jakarta. By the 18th century both locations had established furniture making traditions, chiefly based on western forms. Chinese immigration expanded the repertoire of furniture designs in the 19th century to include Chinese forms.

The Dutch extended their influence to the Thai court at Ayuthia, trading with the local Japanese population. In 1688 Thailand closed to the western powers, not to reopen for trade with the west until over one hundred years later. The late 18th and 19th century Thai court favoured French architectural designs and imported French furniture.

Spanish Colonial Furniture

The Portuguese lost control of the Philippines in 1680 to Spain. In the 18th and 19th century the Philippines developed a strong furniture making industry, based on a hybrid of Spanish colonial and Portuguese designs made by Chinese cabinetmakers. Many early

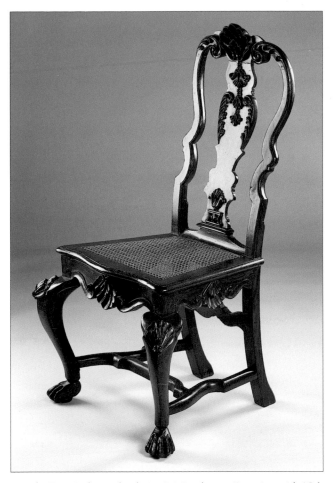

Dutch East Indies side chair, Sri Lanka or Batavia, mid 18th century. The design of this chair is modelled on the popular Queen Anne style of the first half of the 18th century. Often export furniture is indistinguishable from furniture made in Europe except for the construction and the material.

One of a set of six Anglo-Indian rosewood armchairs, Bengal, c. 1810. Variations of this chair design were made in western cabinetmaking centres in India, Ceylon, Java and Canton.

examples of Philippine furniture made in Batangas or Bulacan are inlaid with bone, ivory, or mother-of-pearl. The principal early furniture making centres in the Philippines were located in coastal Spanish settlements, such as Cebu and Manila.

BRITISH FURNITURE IN INDIA

British furniture making began in India during the 18th century. Many of the finest examples were made in Vishakhapatnam, a centre for ivory furniture production. These were mostly ivory veneered with black heightened foliate and figural decoration, dating to the late 18th and early 19th century. Vishakhapatnam became a noted ivory centre because of its convenient port and accessibility to hardwood from the forested Andhra Pradesh. Continuing the Dutch tradition, English style furniture was made in large quantities in Sri Lanka beginning in 1802 after English control was established. English furniture styles were produced in Sri Lanka throughout the 19th and into the 20th century.

(Above). Turkish painted and carved wood turban stand, 18th century, Ottoman, height 49½in. (126cm). The proximity of Turkey to Europe made European fashion popular in the Ottoman Empire. This turban stand is exuberantly carved and painted in a rococo style.

(Left). Pair of Persian applewood, painted, lacquered, and gilded doors, Safavid Dynasty, early 17th century, height 6ft.6in. (200cm).

OTTOMAN FURNITURE

Syria was a centre for the manufacture of small wood crafts inlaid in complex geometric patterns in light and dark exotic woods, mother-of-pearl, and ivory or bone. Intarsia is a furniture inlay of geometric patterns using mother-of-pearl, bone, ivory, and light and dark contrasting woods. Its origins are ancient, extending back to Grecian and Roman cabinetwork, and are derived from mosaics. Byzantine craftsmen excelled in mosaic work as well as delicate tracery carving. Under Islamic rule, these techniques were adopted by Islamic craftsmen and formed the basis for the elaborate geometric inlays popular throughout the

Syrian mother-of-pearl inlaid chair, 19th century. Inlaid mother-of-pearl furniture was popular throughout western Asia.

Islamic world. This style was popular in Syria, Egypt and as far east as India. The few traditional Syrian furniture forms include book stands of X-form, boxes and storage chests. In the late 19th century a strong export market developed to Europe of chairs, tables and small stands composed of small pierced panels, turned elements and intarsia work.

Late 19th century Turkish Ottoman taste brought imported European furniture to the homes of merchants and the aristocracy. Much of this furniture is French and in revivals of Louis XV and XVI styles.

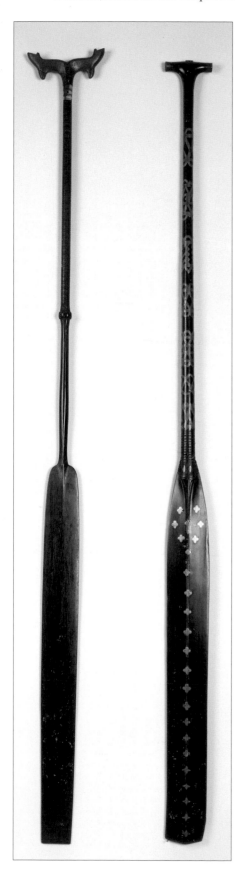

TRIBAL ISLAND AND MOUNTAIN PEOPLES

The Philippines, Malaysia and Indonesia all conducted an active trade with other south-east Asian countries. Although connected by trade and exposed to the west since the 16th century, many of the thousands of islands and inner mountainous areas are extremely remote and isolated. The tribal art of these regions is a separate tradition of the many independent cultures. Common among them is a belief in spirits and forces with supernatural powers controlling fertility, birth and death. These spirits are also believed to offer protection. Art was a means of joining the spirit and island worlds.

Borneo was first visited by the Portuguese in the 16th century and later the Dutch and British established trading centres on the island, but the island interior was largely inaccessible until the 19th century, due to tribal warfare. The Dayak on Borneo built communal long houses set with wooden guardian figures called hampatong, which housed the spirit of the deceased person represented. The long houses were symbolic of the interaction of humans with the spirit world. Religious ceremonies reinforce the relationship between the two worlds. Among the most important are fertility rites with male and female symbolism. The role of the male is warfare and trophies taken in battle and displayed in the long house would bring vitality and prosperity to the group. Ceremonial masks and wooden images were important parts of the culture.

On Borneo, the Iban people carved measuring rods with figural finials called tun tun to determine the location of pig trap pits set with sharpened bamboo spikes. Masks were worn in harvest dance ceremonies called the Hudoq. The Iban women carried infants in baskets called hawats with beadwork, fabric and shell decoration. These served as marks of status and good omens for the new born; the more beautiful the basket the more likely it was believed to attract benevolent spirits to the infant.

In Sumatra figural carved roof and door posts offered protection from spirits. The Batak culture used wooden puppets in a ceremonial dance to induce the spirit of a departed family member to leave the world of the living and travel to the spirit world. The Nias, like the Dayak in Borneo, carved figural images which were believed to be inhabited by the spirit of the deceased, offering protection to the family and the village.

A slightly different practice existed among the Tonaja people of Sulawesi whose life-size images called tau tau were created as portraits of the deceased, intended to memorialise the person's life. On Sumba island young women enter puberty wearing elaborate tortoiseshell combs and spinning wheels with spokes carved as figural images. In the remote Assam region at the north-east border with India the Naga tribes identify each tribal group with distinctive shell necklaces and ornaments. The Paiwan inhabit the mountainous region of Taiwan and embellish the noble families' houses with carved panels. The many tribes of the Luzon in the Philippines carve wooden rice spoons and scoops.

(Opposite page). Two Dayak ceremonial paddles, length 44in. (112cm). Tribes in Island Asia frequently carved wooden articles as auspicious emblems or symbols.

(Left). Nias ancestor figure, height 22in. (55.9cm). Ancestor figures were created as protective devices and kept in the houses of the nobility. Few images of this type have survived because of insect and weather damage

Chinese Lacquer of the Ming and Qing Dynasties

A variety of lacquer techniques were in use during the Ming dynasty. Some were earlier innovations, others were reintroduced or developed at this time.

Gold Incised Lacquer

Gold incised (qiangjin) lacquer was first produced in the Tang dynasty and records indicate many objects in this technique were sent abroad to Japan. Song and Yuan sutra covers from Tibet are often decorated in incised lacquer. Finely incised lines were cut into the surface into the desired design and then thin sheets of gold foil were pressed into the incisions with the wastage removed from the surface. The remaining gold in the incised areas brightly highlighted the design against the monochromatic ground.

Painted Lacquer

Painted lacquer developed in China in the Warring States period (481-221 BCE) in the southern China state of Chu. Painted lacquer vessels, musical instruments and tomb models of animals are generally in black or red pigments, often painted with swirl patterns or zoomorphic images. Painted lacquer continues through the Song dynasty but declines in importance, to be revived in the 16th century when gold in a lacquer mixture was painted on to a lacquer surface.

The earliest examples of furniture in this technique are almost all products of the Ming official workshops and are identified by the high quality of the workmanship, the presence of regnal inscriptions and the subject matter of the decoration. Polychrome painted woven boxes incorporating lacquer panels decorated with oil pigments were popular in the 17th century. The gold lacquer technique continued into the 18th and 19th centuries and was often used for export furniture and small boxes made in Canton. Variations of this technique were used in Japan, Burma, and other parts of Asia.

Chinese rectangular box with painted lacquer, Ming Dynasty, early 17th century, wood and woven bamboo, height 4¼in. (10.8cm), length 19in. (48.3cm). The beautifully painted scene on the cover is done with coloured pigments mixed with lacquer. During the 17th century many craftsmen employed in the imperial workshops lost their positions as the government spiralled out of control. These artisans found employment creating exquisite objects for the merchant and official classes.

Chinese three colour carved lacquer box, Ming Dynasty, Jiajing mark and Period, diameter 13⅞in. (35.4cm).
Many imperial workshop lacquer objects incorporate images of dragons or other symbols of imperial power. Others,
such as this example, depict domestic scenes or landscapes. The 'knicknack' seller was a popular subject during the
Ming Dynasty, but rarely represented in lacquer.

Carved Lacquer

Dishes and small boxes dating from the Song through early Ming dynasty attest to the
vitality of this type of lacquer decoration. Yuan dishes often have barbed outlines similar
to central Asian metal forms, reflecting the direct Mongol influence. Carved scenes
usually depict birds or flowers or landscapes with figures. Tixi is a type of carved lacquer
with pommel scroll patterns over the entire surface. By the early 15th century a standard
repertoire of designs was beginning to form, using official symbols such as the phoenix
or dragon. Carved lacquerware production was curtailed in the early 17th century and
did not resume again until the reign of Qianlong (1736-1795).

Carved lacquer is created over a wooden core covered with multiple thin layers of red
lacquer, occasionally with intervals of layers in yellow or green lacquer as markers for the
carver. The red colour was produced by the pigment mercuric sulphide creating what is
commonly referred to as cinnabar lacquer. The few examples of carved lacquer dating from the

Mother-of-pearl inlaid tiered box, 14th century, height 12in. (30.5cm). Inlays with mother-of-pearl were created by inserting the finely cut shell fragments in patterns into the still wet lacquer surface and then spreading a thin layer of lacquer over the top. This uppermost layer was then polished away to reveal the design.

Inlaid Lacquer

Inlaid lacquers were made using a range of materials and techniques. Although developed by the Chinese, Japanese lacquer craftsmen excelled in the technique of delicate and fine inlays using crushed shell and other materials. This type of inlay is referred to as makie, literally 'sprinkled picture'. Gold, silver or other powdered materials were sprinkled on to a wet lacquer surface and then polished. Inlaid coloured (tianqi) lacquer is primarily a Chinese technique often used for furniture. Coats of lacquer are applied to a well-prepared ground and, when the desired thickness is reached, designs are cut away and lacquer of a different colour is pressed into the recesses. Colours include yellow, red, brown, black, blue and green. Once the inlay process is complete, the entire surface is polished back and incised details added around the area cut out, which are often heightened by gilding.

This is a slow process and a quicker method uses shallow incisions into which a design would be thinly painted in the appropriate colour. The former technique retains the distinct coloration longer; the latter, when worn, will become monochromatic, matching the background colour. Inlaid coloured lacquer was in use into the 18th century but shortly afterwards fell into disfavour.

The most complex lacquer inlay is probably mother-of-pearl with metal foil highlights. Early mother-of-pearl inlay objects are known at least from the Tang dynasty and continue the tradition of inlays used in lacquer in the Han dynasty.

There are at least two major categories of mother-of-pearl inlay and both were in use in Korea and China. One is formed by small mosaic-like shell chips, often incorporating gold foil highlights, added colour tints and a scattered ground of ground shell. The other type is formed by large shell chips which generally have broad designs of flowers and vines which often are incised with detailed features.

Tiered boxes, trays and furniture were made in these techniques during the early Ming dynasty. The craftsmanship reaches a height of sophistication in the Kangxi period (1662–1723). Closely related are objects, often furniture, inlaid with various materials including hardstones, made in the Ming and Qing dynasties but much copied and imitated in the 20th century.

SOUTH-EAST ASIAN LACQUER

In Burma boxes of various shapes, headdresses, bowls and other vessels were created during the 18th and 19th centuries in a red, black or gold ground often incised with line drawings, paste or glass inlays, or with a built-up relief-carved surface. Both Burmese and Thai lacquer comes from *Melanorrhea usitata*, a different source from Chinese or Japanese lacquer. Generally these objects had a bamboo core supplemented with woven horsehair covered with a sawdust lacquer mixture which was then polished and covered with additional lacquer layers. The built-up decoration was moulded by hand and attached to the surface and usually gilded or supplemented with glass inlay. Incised designs were created with finely pointed cutting tools and the incision was then rubbed with a coloured pigment.

Dry lacquer Buddhist images are produced by constructing a clay figure which is covered with a layer of ash, straw and clay and then wrapped in lacquer soaked cloth. Additional coats are applied which are polished and painted or inlaid with details. Usually the interior clay core is removed to produce a light-weight sculpture.

Thai lacquered footed bowl with mother-of-pearl inlay, 19th century.

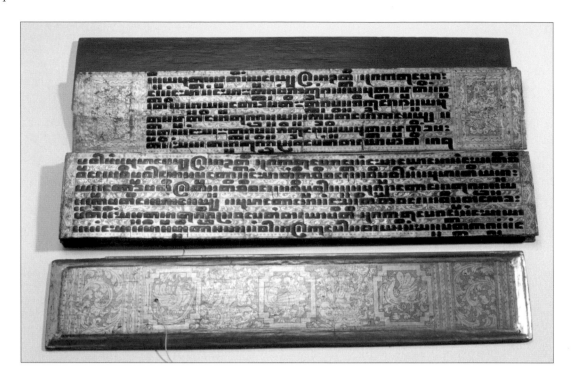

(Right). Burmese lacquer prayer sheets, 19th century.

(Below). Tibetan or Nepalese prayer book cover, 14th century, length 28½in. (72.4cm). Although most book covers were created for Buddhist texts, they were also made for the native Bon religion of Tibet which shares many iconographic similarities with Buddhism. Book covers protected the sacred texts within and were stored by stacking on shelves in monasteries.

Tapered lacquer storage cabinets were used in Thailand in the 18th and 19th centuries to store gilded lacquer coated bamboo prayer leaves. These cabinets usually have a black lacquer ground with elaborate gilded foliate or figural designs. The earliest examples rest on a carved base with wide apron; later versions have tall animal claw cabriole legs. Generally the 19th or 20th century cabinets are fully gilded while those of an earlier date will have a larger black ground area. The finest Thai lacquered wares were gilded and produced for the court at Ayuthia.

Tibetan scriptures are of two types: the Tanjur or sacred books and the Kanjur which are commentaries. The Tanjur comprises about 100 volumes, each having approximately 1,000 pages. The Kanjur has 225 volumes with a total of 4,569 texts. Books are considered as sacred embodiments of the Buddha's speech and are protected by wooden

lacquered and often gilded book covers. They are stored by stacking. Because they are sacred, the covers are exquisitely carved, incised and decorated depicting images which guard the texts contained within. Many of the finest of these book covers were created from the 12th to 14th centuries.

Painted lacquer on leather storage chests have been used in Tibet for centuries. Those from the 12th and 13th century are particularly lavishly decorated with gilt iron or brass mounts. These boxes were made in China for the Mongolian and Tibetan markets, intended for use in monasteries. Although the earliest examples seem to date to the Yuan dynasty (1279-1368) similar examples were made through the Ming and into the Qing dynasties.

CENTRAL ASIAN LACQUER

There is a long tradition of lacquer work in the Middle East. In India pen cases, book covers and other objects were finely painted in the region of Kashmir. These colourful objects often depict scenes identical to those found on Kashmir textiles. Indian lacquerwork was probably introduced from Persia, perhaps via Kashmir in the 17th century, and was centred in the Deccan. It was used for luxury items such as book covers, pen boxes, mirror cases and other small articles. Lacquerware continued to be produced in India throughout the 19th century.

A lacquer pen box made for Mirza Mohammed Ali Zabete-Nevis, signed by Haji muhammad Ibrahim, Persia, dated 1673.

Korean inlaid box, Choson Dynasty, 16th-17th century, wood with black lacquer and mother-of-pearl and tortoise-shell inlay, height 8⅛in. (20.6cm), width 8½in. (21.6cm), length 13in. (32.9cm). Mother-of-pearl inlays into lacquer are particularly susceptible to damage; care must be taken to avoid extremes of humidity or temperature.

Persian lacquer artists were active as early as the 15th century. The earliest examples are mostly book covers, decorated in the style of miniature paintings. Often designs were painted in gouache or oils on to a lacquer ground and then sealed beneath a protective transparent lacquer covering.

The majority of lacquer objects were created during the Qajar (1787-1925) period, a time of peace and prosperity. The three principal centres for lacquer production were Isfahan, Tehran and Shiraz. Probably the finest painter of this time was Muhammed Isma'il. He painted using western conventions and western themes reserved with portrait and landscape vignettes in shaped panels. Western designs dominate throughout the 19th century, with brilliantly painted pen cases, book covers, mirror cases, architectural elements and other forms made in a variety of painted lacquer techniques.

In Turkey lacquerwares produced from the 17th to 19th centuries for the Ottoman court included doors, ceilings and wall panels in addition to more intimate pen boxes, book covers and smaller articles.

KOREAN LACQUER

The earliest Korean lacquer objects date from the Chinese Han dynasty, a period of Chinese dominion of the Korean mainland. These early objects are essentially Chinese in design and very few examples have survived. During the Tang dynasty the technique of inlay using bits of shell was introduced to Korea and it came to dominate lacquer decoration.

Japanese lacquer storage box, Ogawa Haritsu, 1663-1747, height 10in. (25.4cm), width 14¼in. (36.2cm). Japanese lacquerwork is extraordinarily well crafted and was usually highly prized and stored in specially made boxes, wrapped in cloth. There is a premium placed on examples which are in perfect condition.

Korean craftsmen were probably the conduit for the introduction of lacquer to Japan, and it is in Japan that the finest early Korean lacquer objects are preserved. During this early period a technique of inlay using silver or brass wires was introduced which is unique to Korea. It is considered likely that the use of shell inlay inspired the famous inlaid celadon ceramic wares of the Koryo and early Choson dynasties. Korean lacquer often incorporates shell fragments and tortoiseshell depicting landscape scenes, foliage or figures, sometimes within a mosaic or patterned ground. Most of the earliest examples are boxes which are based on Chinese designs. Of square, circular, or rectangular outline, these black lacquer boxes are boldly decorative.

During the late 16th century Japanese invaders devastated the economy and Korean lacquer artisans were brought back to Japan, considerably advancing the Japanese lacquer industry. 19th and 20th century lacquerware includes shell inlaid bright red and black furniture and dragon decorated low tables. Often these are supplemented by tortoiseshell veneers, mother-of-pearl, sharkskin and twisted wire inlay.

JAPANESE LACQUER

Lacquerwork of Japan, although influenced by China, is distinctively Japanese. The Japanese artisan excelled with colourful, detailed inlays set amid powdered grounds creating jewel-like objects. Lacquer workers delighted in using odd combinations of materials, mixing powdered gold and silver with basketry or sections of shell or ivory set against a colourful lacquer ground.

(Above). Japanese Namban mother-of-pearl inlaid chest, 17th century, height 12in. (30.5cm), length 18in. (45.7cm). The bold mother-of-pearl inlay and metal corner mounts are typical of Namban wares. This style enjoyed a revival during the late 19th century when Japanese design was so popular in the west.

(Opposite). Japanese lacquer double incense box, Koami School, 19th century, height 3⅜in. (8.6cm). The finest examples of Japanese lacquerware employ a variety of techniques and depict well-thought-out compositions.

Namban Lacquer

In the 16th century European contact with Japan was made by the Portuguese, Dutch and Spanish. Setting up trading centres in the port city of Nagasaki, these traders brought Christianity to Japan and with it an introduction to western furniture forms. Namban lacquer was created for the western market and these lacquer objects are identified by shell inlays and gilt decoration with Christian themes or western forms.

The Japanese lacquer industry reached its zenith during the Edo period. In the 17th century a number of individual schools of lacquer artists were producing significant quantities of objects. Among these are Honami Koetsu (1558-1637) and Ogata Korin (1658-1716). Both excelled in bold uses of lacquer with inlays and applications of metal foils and shell. During the 18th and 19th century the range of lacquerwares

Chapter Four

The Artisan and Craftsman

Skilled craftsmen worked throughout Asia with specialties as diverse as basketry and sword making. Some of these artisans produced wares for a local market, others created objects for the wealthy merchant and official classes. In some cultures craftsmen worked exclusively under official court patronage, such as in China. The skills practised by these workers often passed from father to son and it is not unusual to find entire families employed in the same pursuit for generations.

How to Determine Quality, Condition and Authenticity

Quality

Much depends on the scale of the item, the culture of the creator, the material and the period in which that object was created. In general, the best quality objects are finely crafted for a particular purpose and, when decorated, display a lively spontaneity in the overall appearance with internally consistent proportional elements. They have a timeless, inspired vitality which transcends place and time of origin. The beautiful line, mass and attention to detail make the viewer marvel at the creator's genius.

Condition

Objects created by a skilled craftsman are intimate, personal possessions intended for close inspection and regular use. Details are important. The carver who created the object was influenced in untold ways by his environment. These influences will be evident in the object he created. The object is a microcosm of who he was, his experiences, his training, his motivations, his world.

Made to be handled and used, it also becomes part of the world of the original owner and everyone else who has used or touched it. Those who handle it experience and react to the original vision of the creator. How it is held and where it is touched accumulate in a pattern of wear and use which is unique to that object. Handling an object over hundreds of years creates a very different pattern of wear from weathering by rain, snow and wind. Damage or repairs which are incidental to the function of the object in general are not as serious as those which compromise the use for which the object was created.

(Opposite). The 'Rubens Vase', early Byzantine, Constantinople (?), 4th century CE, agate and gold, height 7½in. (19cm). The vase is named after the Flemish painter Peter Paul Rubens (1577-1640) who purchased it in 1619. Believed to have been created for a Byzantine emperor, it is an example of the fine quality objects created in Constantinople which influenced Asian and European artisans.

Authenticity

Skilled copies have been made of virtually every type of object. Some are easy to detect while others are more difficult. Copies of small Chinese jade carvings can be particularly difficult to identify and, as a result, the history of ownership or provenance of these ancient jades has become extremely useful and almost essential for a collector. Unfortunately most objects do not come with a provenance so it is particularly helpful to understand how an object was used when evaluating whether it is authentic. Patterns of use show up in wear. A forger must replicate these patterns and in order to do so convincingly must have a good understanding of how the object was made and how it was used. Small carvings are perhaps the easiest to replicate but it is extremely difficult to duplicate the years of accumulated wear from use or handling. When evaluating an object, the details are important.

A Bamboo Mountain in Hawaii

When visiting a collector in Hawaii I chanced upon an unusual small bamboo carving. It was a miniature mountain, only about eight inches high, carved with several peaks, rugged outcrops and covered in twisted pine, bamboo and brush. Winding up the side was a narrow trail bordered by small huts and heavily laden travellers with mules. The bamboo surface was dry, dirty and bleached by the sun. Even with these problems it clearly was exceptional. It was beautifully carved and a rare subject. I took it back to New York, cleaned away the dust with cotton swabs and carefully began working a wax polish into the dry material. The warm, rich colour of old bamboo reappeared and we sold it successfully for the client.

ARMS AND ARMOUR

Most of the earliest weapons created in Asia were of stone or bronze. In China jade axes and short blades were sometimes fitted with bronze hilts. Early bronze blades, crossbow fittings and arrow points dating from the Han dynasty were placed in tombs. Some of these were elaborately inlaid with gold or silver in a similar manner to ceremonial bronze vessels. Aside from these ancient discoveries, most armament from Asia dates to a much more recent period.

Islamic Armament

Firearms were introduced into India in the 16th century by the Portuguese. The early examples were wheellocks or matchlocks, often inlaid with bone or ivory, with gold or silver inlaid metal barrels and fittings, and fired with a lighted cloth fuse. Guns with inlaid ivory and bone stocks and silver inlaid metalwork are found throughout Islamic Asia. These are generally differentiated by the shape of the stock. Turkish and Persian stocks are usually straight while those of western Asia are often shaped and curved.

Firearms were supplemented with many varieties of cutting weapons: kards, talwars and katars were prized both for usefulness and beauty. The Turkish yataghan is distinguished by

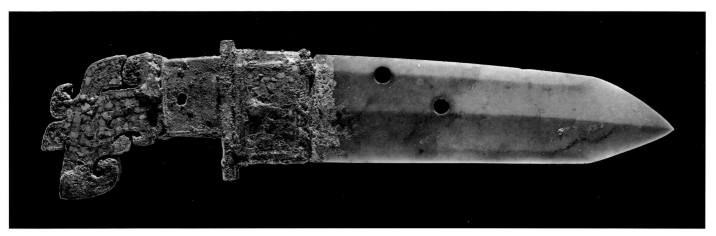

Chinese bronze dagger ax (ko), 16th-11th century BCE. *Ceremonial weapons were often included as part of the furnishings of a tomb burial. Some weapons were apparently intended for actual use, others were ceremonial with elaborate jade or precious stone inlays.*

the lack of a crossguard, the shamshir has a long, curved blade and the kilij blade is wider at the tip than at the hilt. Watered blades were usually hammered from slabs of steel formed from meteoric or mined iron and embellished with jade grips and hardstone and gold inlays. The finest examples were made for the Mughal court and are identified by sumptuous workmanship and precious materials. These daggers (jambiya) have evenly coloured jade handles, discreetly set with a few small precious stones, and animal head terminals. The metal blades are sometimes patterned, slightly curved and incised, or inlaid with gold. Those with a double edge are called a khanjar. Long curved swords are generally referred to as talwars in India. A chakram was a circular disc with a cutting edge used in battle by the Sikhs. The Naga tribesmen use a thick bladed sword with a squared tip called a dao.

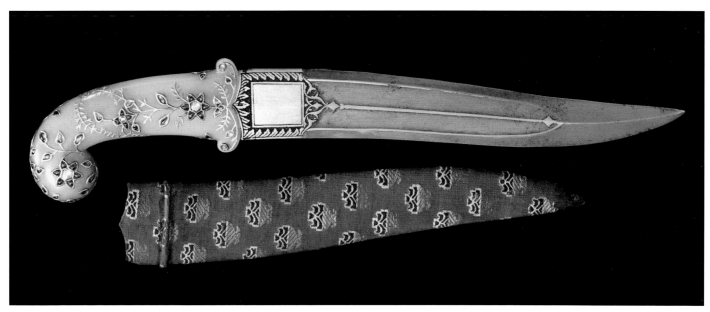

Indian diamond, ruby, and emerald set jade handled dagger, 18th century, length 15in. (38cm). Jewelled daggers were worn as much for decoration as use in Mughal India.

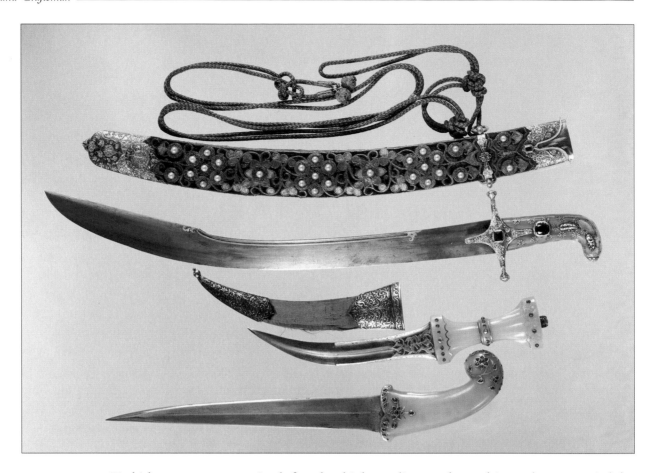

Turkish armour was prized for the high quality workmanship and was copied by European armourers. It was generally of chain mail or metal plates attached to a quilted garment. The finest examples were generally inlaid with gold or silver. Considerable quantities of armour, including masks, were made in Derbend and Daghestan for the Turkish market. 'Turban' helmets, chain mail and other objects were products of these workshops. During the late 19th and early 20th century a fashion in the United States and Western Europe for Islamic inspired decoration created a market for copies of this armour. Yataghans, long incurved swords without a handguard, were common in Turkey. These later versions generally are sketchily incised with gilt inlay. The best early examples are skilfully inlaid with figural and foliate patterns incorporating Islamic script.

(Above). Turkish jade hilted jambiya, mid-19th century and an Indian jade hilted khanjar, Mughal, late 18th century, lengths 11¼in. (28.6cm) and 15½in. (39.4cm).

(Right). Detail. West Indian rifle with silver mounts, possibly Sind or Gujarat, c.1800.

Turkish gilt metal and steel helmet, c.1750, Length 20⅛in. (51cm). The roundels mounted on the helmet contain religious verses and the signature of the maker.

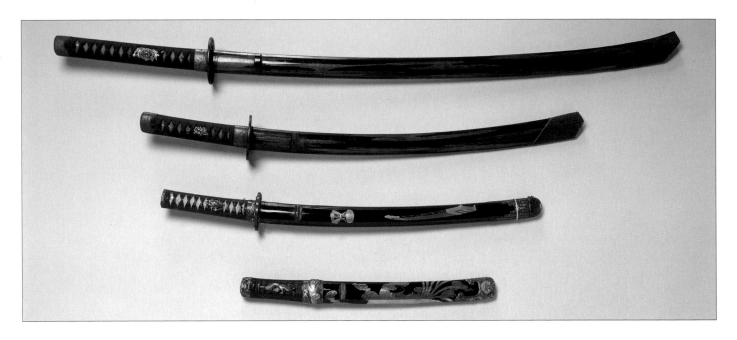

Japanese Swords and the Samurai

(Above). Pair of swords, Wakizashi and Tanto, 18th/19th century mounts.

(Below). Two Katana with mounts removed showing the tang.

The heyday of the samurai was from 1192 to 1868, a period when feudal lords raised armies and obtained loyalty through martial codes, called bushido. Japanese samurai carried a daisho, or two swords. The larger blade is the katana or long sword and the shorter, wakizashi or short sword. The parts of the sword are: the blade including the tang, on which the maker would inscribe his name and often a date; the hilt, usually wrapped in fish skin and tightly bound with cords; the kashira or pommel, cast in metal; the fuchi, a small collar joining the hilt to the blade; the menuki which secures the hilt, and the tsuba or sword guard.

Creating a Japanese Sword

Japanese swords are made of tempered steel with an extremely tough cutting edge backed by softer metal. This is achieved by repeatedly hammering and folding iron slabs together, a process which removes impurities and creates a crystalline pattern in the metal blade which was distinctive to the swordsmith. Once formed, the blade is covered with a light coating of clay or ash, heated, and then submerged in a trough of cool water. After removal the heat-tempered blade edge would be polished and the name of the maker inscribed on the tang. The finest sword blades are by noted, early makers and in superb condition. The shape of the blade and patterned edge are integral to a sword's worth.

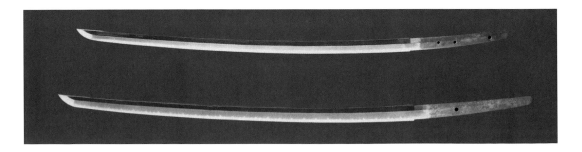

Six tsuba, 18th/19th century.

The Tsuba and Other Fittings

The tsuba is pierced with two apertures to receive a small blade or kozuka and a pronged fork called a kogai. Tsuba are decorated on both sides and are usually made of iron, steel, shakudo (an alloy of gold and copper) and shibuichi (silver and copper). During the Edo period (1615-1868) other metals became popular for tsuba and other sword mounts, ending with the imperial edict by the Meiji emperor outlawing the wearing of swords in 1877.

179

Group of fuchi-kashira by various makers, 18th/19th century. Fine quality gold and other inlays were often employed in the manufacture of sword fittings.

Goto Yujo (1440–1512) was the founder of one of the great families of sword fitting makers, which continued to produce tsuba until the death of his last descendant in 1856. Tsuba and other sword furniture are identified by maker and workshops. Workshops also existed for the manufacture of arrows and metal arrowheads. Different styles of tsuba are associated with specific time periods and schools. Among the finest examples are those worked in multiple metals depicting detailed scenes.

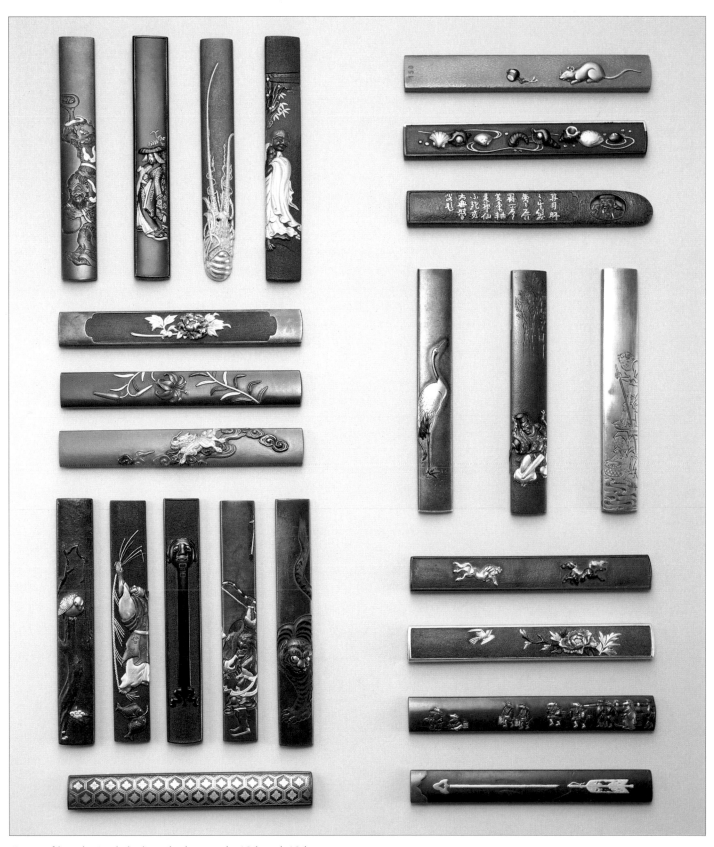

Group of kozuka in shakudo and other metals, 18th and 19th century.

Japanese Armour and Firearms

Japanese armour was created originally of overlapping metal plates which were laced together. Later improvements added additional protection and the division of armour into two basic types: the oyoroi, literally 'great harness' designed for persons of high rank and importance, and the haramaki, intended for the common soldier.

It was during the Kamakura period that armourers rose to greatest importance along with the rise of the samurai and feudal lords. Armour included helmets (kabuto) set with a ridge designed to ward off glancing sword blows and an iron mask (somen) designed in the images of fearsome demons or ferocious animals. The main protective body was formed of laced together lacquered metal or leather plates forming a distinctive pattern. Protective padding also covered the neck and legs. Tied to the back were upright wands (sashimono) used to identify the warrior. Frequently armour is made of associated parts; those which are composed of original examples signed by noted armourers are the most desirable.

Francisco Xavier, a Portuguese priest, arrived in Japan in 1543 bringing with him gifts of a clock and a matchlock rifle. Matchlocks were the most effective firearm for close to two hundred years, developing in the 14th century. They are worked with a lighted fuse which is forced into the touch hole, igniting the powder. Early Japanese matchlocks are usually about four feet in length and have minimal decoration. They differ from other Asian rifles in the shape of the stock, which is usually slender and curves down.

Indonesia, Thailand, and the Philippines

In the 16th century Islam was introduced to Indonesia and gradually supplanted both Buddhism and Hinduism. When the Portuguese, Dutch and English traders reached the archipelago in the 17th century they were astonished by the quantity of gold objects and ceremonial items, including a type of gold handled sword called a kris. The kris has a wavy, watered steel, notched blade. It is often made of meteoric iron, fostering a belief that it had magical properties. Many kris have elaborate, carved wood handles and the finest examples have handles in gold, boldly patterned blades and unusual notched outlines near the grip. Similar to the kris are the bade-bade and golok, both having short curved blades and both widely used throughout Malaysia.

(Opposite). Japanese black lacquer set of armour with haramaki and a lacquer helmet, 18th century. Often Japanese armour is composed of individual elements from different sources.

(Left). Selection of five kris, 19th century or later, each approximately 15in. (38cm) long.

In the Philippines the Moro developed an arsenal of heavy bladed weapons and cannon to fight the Spanish. Many of the short swords are similar in design to those of Indonesia, but are not as refined. The bolo has a short, thick blade. Vietnamese cutting weapons are similar to those from Thailand and owe much to Japanese technology. Japanese mercenaries were in Vietnam and Thailand in the 15th and 16th centuries and their weapons were available to the local swordsmiths. Vietnamese swords are similar to Japanese swords, with a tempered and patterned steel cutting edge. The principal cutting blade of Burma is the dha, with a single cutting edge and slight curved blade. Island tribes fashioned weapons from wood and armour from plaited palm.

BAMBOO AND GOURDS

Bamboo is a species of grass having a hollow interior and strong, pliant body. There are hundreds of varieties and it is noted for its extremely fast growth and long life cycle. Some species flower only once every hundred years. The most common variety is called Mandake or *Phyllostachys bambusoides*.

Bamboo is a versatile plant. Pliant and yet incredibly strong, it can be used to make woven baskets, furniture, small carvings and containers. The surface, also called the skin, can be carved away to leave a design in low relief against a ground of contrasting colour. The roots of the plant, called tubers, form unusual grotesque shapes which can either be enhanced by carving or allow the carving of subjects in the round.

Bamboo Carvings
The majority of Chinese bamboo objects date from the Qing dynasty. Bamboo carving was generally not done in workshops but was an individual art, especially practised by the gentleman scholar.

Chinese bamboo incense cylinder, 17th or 18th century, height 8⅜in. (21.3cm). Bamboo is a versatile material suitable for carving, incising, or veneer.

Bamboo must be aged before it can be carved; if carved while green, it will probably split. The delicate outer surface or skin can be left in relief but is easily bruised and, when cut prior to carving, must be carefully stored.

Some of the more usual bamboo objects are brushpots, wrist rests, small sculptures and incense holders. The finest bamboo carvings are delicately and exquisitely detailed, often depicting extensive landscapes or scenes from popular mythology or literature. Korean brushpots and Japanese netsuke and baskets are often made of bamboo, as are small containers.

The skin of the bamboo plant can be removed and veneered on to other surfaces. Bamboo also provided an excellent surface for carved calligraphic inscriptions with the naturally curving surface fitting neatly around the columns in a building.

The finest bamboo carvings are lively images with a vitality that makes the viewer forget the object is inanimate. Bamboo has a wonderful open surface, when cut against the grain, which absorbs oils and ages into a rich, mellow, brown.

Birdcages

Chinese birdcages are usually constructed of bamboo. The finest examples are delicately formed and supplemented with carved or gilded decoration and elaborate metal mounts. They generally have removable bases, adjustable perches and porcelain feeding and water pots. Metal hooks suspend the cage. These hooks are sometimes made of mixed metals cast in bamboo, dragon or other forms.

The finest bamboo birdcages are not ostentatious. Finely crafted birdcages in unusual shapes with slender members and mixed metal hooks for suspension are highly prized. Subtle decorative carved perches and feeders can add to the overall appearance and not compromise the utility. Many birdcages were created during the 20th century. The majority are roughly constructed and lack the delicate and fine workmanship of earlier examples.

Baskets

The earliest bamboo baskets appeared in Japan during the Jomon period and were utilitarian. Chinese bamboo baskets were imported into Japan throughout the Ming dynasty and earlier. With the popularity and formalisation of the tea ceremony in Japan in the 16th century, a preference for rustic, natively produced baskets developed. These were used to display flowers in alcoves set into the tea ceremony room. Both Chinese and Japanese style baskets were popular in Japan, reflecting different tastes and styles based on differences in the Japanese and Chinese style of tea ceremony.

The baskets made prior to the late 19th century are generally unsigned. In the late 19th century, during the Meiji period, artists led by Hayakawa Shokosai I (1815-1897) began signing baskets. Baskets included in the international Paris Exhibition of 1878 were highly acclaimed, furthering interest in basketmaking in Japan.

Four Japanese woven bamboo baskets, Tanabe Chikuunsai I (1877-1937) and his son Chikuunsai II (b.1910).

A cricket cage, 18th century, height 6½in. (16.5cm). The Chinese kept crickets for both the pleasure of listening to their sound and for fighting. Cricket gourds were often carved and lightly incised with hot needles burning a design into the surface.

Bamboo baskets are crafted from harvested sections of bamboo prepared by drying and cleaning. Once prepared they are carefully and thinly split into strips. Baskets are woven from the base up and created in a variety of weaving techniques. Collectors seek baskets which are expertly woven, of unusual shape, and with an aged, even coloured surface signed by a noted maker. Many baskets were made in Japan during the 20th century. While most are inferior, many are finely constructed and signed by noted craftsmen.

Gourds

Gourds have been moulded or carved in China since antiquity, but the craft was fully explored only in the Ming and Qing dynasties. Gourds were moulded by placing the fruit in a wooden mould, sealed and then removed in the autumn at the end of the growing season. The moulded design appeared in relief and the gourd assumed the shape of the mould.

Snuff bottles, bowls, boxes, vases, brushpots and cricket cages are the most often found forms. Cricket cages generally have wooden or ivory collars with pierced tortoiseshell or ivory covers. Impressed designs include scenes from popular literature, auspicious emblems, landscapes and calligraphy. The finest gourds are those with a warm, mellow surface and moulded, carved or incised designs which complement the overall form. Although many cricket cages were made during the late 19th century, very few quality examples were made during the 20th century.

CLOCKS AND SCIENTIFIC INSTRUMENTS

Islamic Clocks and Scientific Instruments

Islamic scientists were among the earliest Asian creators of many scientific instruments. These instruments grew out of interest in astronomy, a scientific pursuit followed by Islamic scientists from the 9th century and evidenced by over 150 astronomical handbooks published between the 9th and 16th centuries.

Although precision geared instruments had been in use by the Greeks and Romans, it was an Islamic inventor who perfected the astrolabe. These precision instruments were useful for taking exact measurements of all types of astronomical information as well as determining the exact times and orientation for prayers, called the qibla. The earliest examples are beautifully engraved works of art. Other Islamic scientists perfected the armillary sphere, a device used to measure the exact times of the equinox. During the Safavid period, Isfahan became a centre for making these and other instruments. Another centre was in India in Lahore. The finest of these instruments were made up until the 17th century.

The most sought after Islamic scientific instruments date from an early period and are in complete, working condition, with beautifully engraved decorative details. Commonly used astrolabe quadrants were made of wood with printed paper indications. These were used throughout the Islamic world to allow the viewer easily to determine prayer direction and times.

During the 18th and 19th century elaborate clocks and enamel decorated pocket watches were made in large numbers for the Turkish and Persian markets. Many of the pocket watches are extremely elaborate and often set with pearls or other precious stones and embellished with enamel figural or landscape scenes.

Chinese Clocks and Scientific Instruments

Similar advances were made in China at a correspondingly early date. Chinese astronomers had long been active in creating water-powered astronomical clocks. The best known of these early craftsmen was the Chinese scholar Su Sung who completed a water-powered clock tower in the 11th century.

(Opposite). Farruk ibn Abd al-Latif, a candle clock, illustration from a copy of al-Jazari's treatise on automata, Syria 1315, colour and gold on paper, 12⅛ x 8⅝in. (30.8 x 21.9cm).

(Left). Chinese astronomical instruments at the Beijing Observatory, 17th century, created under the direction of Jesuits at the court of the Kangxi emperor.

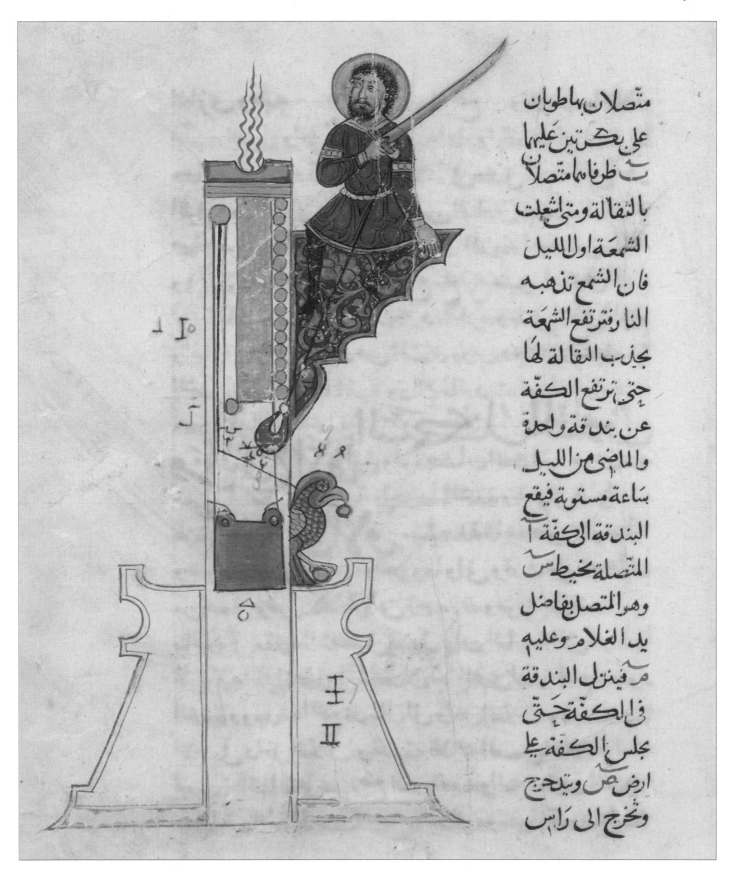

Gilt bronze musical clock, Qianlong Period (1736-1795), English movement signed Jno. Brockbank, London. height 20½in. (52cm). English clockmakers made clocks for the Chinese market beginning in the 18th century. The most elaborate were created for the imperial household. Clock makers in Guangzhou (Canton) also created clocks in a western style, using imported western movements.

During the 17th century European Jesuits at the court of the Kangxi emperor introduced the latest scientific instruments to the Chinese in an attempt to win converts. While they largely failed to convert many to Christianity, the emperor was fascinated by the scientific devices and commissioned the building of an elaborate water-powered clock fountain at the summer palace, the Yuan Ming Yuan. By the late 18th century English entrepreneurs were sending clocks with moving figures and striking mechanisms

Detail Japanese bell-form clock.

Japanese bronze bell-form clock, late 17th century or early 18th century, height 11⅜in. (29cm).

to China. These were gaudily loaded with gilded and enamelled ornamentation. Similar clocks were exported in quantity to India, Turkey and Indonesia.

Many of the clocks exported to China in the late 18th century were made by James Cox of London. Other clockmakers followed and in the 19th century simple bracket-type clocks with spring-wound mechanisms were being exported to Canton and then to other treaty port cities. Clockmaking progressed and Chinese established workshops were set up in most major cities by the end of the 19th century. Pocket sundials and small compasses were regularly made in China throughout the 19th century. Clocks exported from England to China are rare, but even more so are those which are of exceptional quality and in great condition. Those with a gilt bronze surface and 'jewelled' mounts with finely crafted works are the most desirable.

Japanese Clocks and Scientific Instruments

As in China, the Jesuits were active in promoting technology in Japan. The earliest clocks were introduced into Japan in the 16th century and were simple 'lantern style' instruments common in Europe at the time. Japanese clocks were divided into two six hour segments up until 1873 when western style time-keeping was implemented. During the transition to this new system, many old clocks were altered. The most distinctive Japanese clocks are called pillar clocks. Small pocket sundials in the form of small pocket watches were in regular use throughout the 19th century in Japan.

Syrian glass beaker, enamelled and gilded, late 13th century, height 11⅝in. (29.5cm).

GLASS

Central Asian and Islamic Glass

The art of blowing glass into shapes developed around 100 BCE in Syria, a centre for glassmaking in the Middle East under control of the Roman empire. The Romans, Sassanians and Persians were skilled in the art of glass work, developing techniques of cutting, polishing and engraving glass similar to working in hardstone. Although the majority of early Syrian glass articles are uncarved, a few extraordinary objects are deeply undercut, carved or blown into moulds.

Even with the gradual decline of the Byzantine empire, glassmaking centres in Damascus and other cities in the Middle East flourished. Glass centres existed in Persia during the Sassanian period (226-651 CE) and continued in the Islamic period. Islamic glass workers drew on earlier Sassanian designs for inspiration, probably wishing to associate their reigns with the glories of the Sassanian Empire.

Islamic glass was often wheel engraved, lustred, gilded, faceted or enamelled. In the 7th century Islamic glass workers developed a technique to stain glass using metal oxides and glass produced in the Middle East was a prized luxury item, exported to Europe and China. Enamelled glass was well established under the Seljuqs with centres in Syria and Aleppo. A lively tradition of glassmaking continued in Iran through the 19th century with coloured, blown glass vessels inspired from earlier designs.

Group of Ancient Syrian glass vessels, 2nd to 4th century CE. Ancient glass often has an iridescent surface, resulting from the chemical reaction of elements in the soil on the glass.

During the Ottoman period many glass objects were made: bowls, flasks, drinking vessels, lanterns and even stained glass windows. Ottoman glassmakers were centred in Istanbul and other locations during the 18th and 19th centuries. Beykoz is the centre for glass manufacturing in Turkey, producing objects both in western and Asian shapes. The finest of these many types are large enamelled mosque lamps of inverted bell shape, usually embellished with kufic script. Copies of mosque lamps and other forms were made in the 19th and 20th centuries.

The finest Islamic glass is enamelled on a beautifully proportioned vessel or lamp with bold calligraphy in bright, clear colours heightened with gilding. The majority of Islamic glass articles were actually imported into the Ottoman empire from Bohemia during the late 19th and early 20th century. These glass objects are generally not finely made. Islamic style enamelled wares were also made in France during the late 19th and early 20th century.

Chinese Glass

A variety of early small glass objects were made in China prior to the Ming dynasty. Most of these are small beads, jewellery or carvings imitating jade pendants and the majority were made in the Han dynasty and were included as tomb furnishings with the deceased.

Group of Turkish glass vessels, Beykoz Works, 19th century, height of largest 11in. (27.9cm). The blue and white porcelain sprinkler is Chinese, 17th century and typical of export porcelain sent from China to Western Asia.

In the Qing dynasty there was a revival of glass production largely due to the influence of Jesuits who helped establish the imperial glass manufactory in 1696. These early 18th century glass objects are usually minimally decorated with etched designs and are often susceptible to crizzling, a deterioration of the metal due to the presence of too much alkali in the formula. It is assumed that the European glass formula used in the late 17th and early 18th century contained this defect, resulting in Chinese craftsmen unwittingly creating glass objects which became crizzled.

During the mid-18th century cased glass techniques were developed and glass was often carved with figural, landscape and other naturalistic designs. The techniques for carving glass were very similar to those for carving jade and other stones. Chinese glass vessels often have sketchy four-character reign marks on the base. Collectors search for carved Chinese glass objects which are cased with carving that sensitively uses the various colours in the design. Glass with carved landscapes and images from nature are generally the most desirable.

The majority of 20th century Chinese glass is monochromatic and in tones of aubergine, blue or yellow. Late in the century there was a revival in the industry with many finely made copies in earlier styles.

Chinese Enamel Decorated Glass

A parallel tradition to blown and carved glass is enamel decorated glass. Opaque enamel colours were introduced by the Jesuit artisans who oversaw the imperial factories. Notable among these was a brilliant rich yellow and pink.

The earliest reliably dated enamelled glass articles date to 1716. The high quality of those dating from this period indicates that the craft was already well established and it is very probable that earlier examples were made. Enamelled glass was mostly confined to small objects and decorative motifs include landscapes, nature and portraits. Enamelled glass objects almost always include reign marks in painted enamels. Painted enamel glass of the highest quality will be extraordinarily well painted in a bright palette. The painted scene will complement the shape and use of the object. Enamels easily chip and examples which are perfect are the most desirable.

Chinese glass vase, Qianlong Period (1736-1795), height 8in. (20.3cm). Brightly coloured Chinese glass was first manufactured under Jesuit direction in Beijing during the late 17th century. Earlier glass was much less colourful and in ancient times served as an exotic substitute for jade.

IVORY AND HORN CARVINGS

Among the earliest surviving Asian ivory objects are presentation caskets, panels and icons carved in Constantinople between the 6th and 13th centuries. Based on ancient Roman and Greek classical models, these carvings also display motifs found on ivory and other carvings from western and central Asia. These were brought to western European princely houses where they remained long after the destruction of the Byzantine empire in 1453.

China

Elephant, mammoth and walrus ivory, bone, and rhinoceros and oxhorn were often used to embellish objects in Asia. Worked by abrasion and carving, these materials were often decorative, symbolic and thought to be imbued with special properties. Common uses were as inlays in furniture and on weapons, handles for cutting blades, vessels, jewellery, and figural carvings.

Ivory and bone carvings were present in Shang China, where bones with inscriptions, called oracle bones, were used to tell the future. Finely carved ivory figures, wrist rests, table articles, boxes, ceremonial cups made from rhinoceros horn and water buffalo horn carved figures were popular subjects in both the Ming and Qing dynasties. Most 16th century or earlier carved ivory images depict Buddhist subjects. By the 18th century the range of objects and subjects was much expanded.

(Left). Chinese ivory figure of Han Xiangzi, 17th century, height 6in. (15.2cm). Ming ivory carving often combines bold movement with fine detail.

(Opposite). Chinese rhinoceros horn carving, 17th century, height approximately 5½in. (14cm). Rhinoceros horn was believed to protect from poison. Libation cups of rhinoceros horn and of rhinoceros horn shape in Dehua porcelain were popular during the 17th and 18th centuries.

Rhinoceros horn was not only considered a rare and exotic material, it was also believed to offer protection against poisons. Fine quality ivory and horn objects were made for wealthy merchants, aristocrats and the Chinese imperial household. These included fans and small articles for the scholar's table, such as brushpots, table screens and brush rests commissioned from workshops in Beijing and Canton. The finest of these are not only beautifully carved but also have a deep, rich mellow coloured surface.

Pair of Chinese export pagodas, late 18th century, height 25in. (63.5cm). Made of ivory, mica, horn and lacquer, these pagoda and other similar architectural models were exported to the west as emblematic of the exoticism of Asia.

In addition to objects made for the domestic market, a large number of articles were made for export to the west. These objects are often exquisitely carved in minute detail and include boxes to hold tea, pill boxes, calling card cases, fans, letter holders, baskets, architectural models and landscape or figural decorated elephant tusks.

20th century Chinese ivory is abundant and most often poorly carved and in figural subjects or objects based on earlier forms. Few of these objects are well carved. An exception is a group of naturalistically carved ivories in the form of fruits and natural subjects which date to the first half of the 20th century. Of particularly poor quality are the innumerable seated figures of 'emperors and empresses' made in small and large sizes. The largest versions are usually formed over a wooden core and are most often not of ivory but of bone.

India and Sri Lanka

Ivory was also a favourite material of artisans in central Asia and India. Small ivory inlaid wooden articles and furniture were popular in Mughal India. At an earlier date ivory objects carved in India were traded throughout the Roman and Byzantine empires. In the eastern Indian city of Orissa from the 16th to the 19th centuries skilled carvers produced ivory decorative objects as well as large scale furniture. Other ivory centres in India, such as Vishakhapatnam, specialised in ivory inlaid or ivory veneered furniture made for the western market. Much of this furniture is decorated with foliate patterns with blackened details. The finest examples are well designed as furniture and as decorative objects incorporating incised designs.

Indian ivory box, Mughal, 17th century, length 11½in. (29.2cm).

Indian carved ivory throne leg, Orissa, 17th century, height 9¾in. (24.8cm).

Spanish or Portuguese colonial ivory figure, 17th/18th century, height approximately 6⅞in. (17.4cm). Colonial ivory images were made throughout South-east Asia as religious images for the Christian community.

An early group of European subject ivory caskets was made in Sri Lanka during the 16th century and sent to the Portuguese court. The carved panels on these caskets depict some of the earliest European subject images on Asian works of art.

The majority of ivory items dating to the 20th century in India are small decorative painted plaques and carved figures of Hindu deities.

Japan

In Japan ivory netsuke were produced by skilled artisans and ivory inlays and applied elements decorated larger scenes incorporating jade, lacquer, coral and metal foils in a technique called Shibiyama after the family who specialised in this work. In the late 19th century Japanese ivory carvers produced large size figural carvings for export. Okimono, literally 'display things', depict the range of subjects often found in netsuke carvings. As the netsuke carvers lost work during the late 19th century when Japanese dress changed and netsuke were no longer used, the carvers turned to creating okimono.

These prized carvings were proudly displayed in the central alcove of a Japanese reception room, called the tokonoma. The best examples were generally in ivory and by the late 19th century examples were bought and taken abroad to Europe and the United States. Many of these images depict naturalistic subjects, traditional tradesmen or figures from popular mythology. The finest carved figures are extraordinarily detailed and masterworks of technical virtuosity. Lesser examples are pieced of small ivory fragments salvaged from larger jobs.

As in China, Japan has produced huge numbers of carved ivory figures during the 20th century. Generally the Japanese versions are more finely worked than Chinese, particularly those dating to the early 20th century. Ishikawa Komei (b.1852) was one of many highly skilled ivory carvers active in the early Meiji period, receiving commissions from the imperial household as well as wealthy collectors.

Group of Japanese ivory figures, late 19th century. Generally, the finest ivory carvings are composed of only a few separate ivory sections. Large examples, such as this, would by necessity be made of many smaller carved pieces. Small ivory carvings made of pieced together elements are generally of lesser quality.

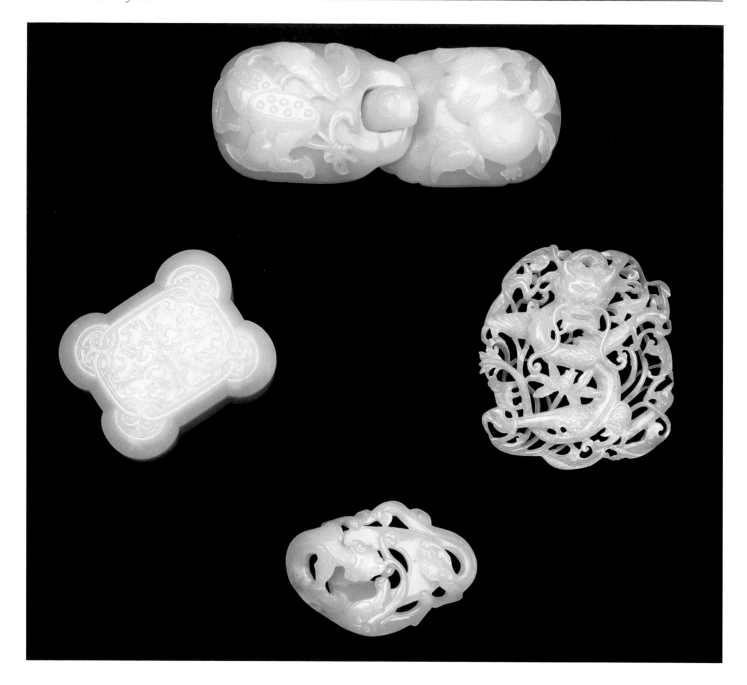

JADE, STONE AND OTHER SMALL CARVINGS

Carved stone cylinder seals were used extensively in the Mesopotamian area beginning around 3500 BCE as a means of recording ownership of property or establishing authorship for documents on clay tablets. These seals would be decorated with mythological figures or other devices which would be unique to the owner. Carved from agate, rock crystal, lapis or other materials, the cylinder seal was the precursor to the signet ring and other types of carved small stone articles commonly found in many Asian cultures.

The most popular of these stones and that most often associated with Asia is jade. There

(Above). Chinese jadeite jar, 18th century, with gilt bronze ring handles, height 9¼in. (23.5cm).

(Right). Chinese Imperial white jade vase, Qianlong mark and Period (1736-1795), height 21½in. (54.6cm). Large jade objects were a favourite of the Qianlong emperor, including vessels of various shapes and boulders carved as miniature mountains.

(Opposite). Selection of Chinese carved jade articles dating from the Ming and Qing Dynasties.

are two types of stone which are commercially referred to as jade: nephrite and jadeite. Nephrite is the more often found material, usually in dark green, white, pale green, brown and occasionally yellow. It is an extremely hard stone, registering 5.5 to 6.5 on the Mohs hardness scale, and cannot be scratched by steel.

Jadeite has a more granular texture and appears in bright emerald and other shades of green, lavender, black, brown and white. The most valuable stones are emerald green and very translucent. Jadeite was not used as a material for carving in China before the 18th century and most examples date from the late 19th or 20th centuries. Other stones and materials used in small carved articles are coral, agate, amber and rock crystal.

visible and polished surface. The object should include a matching stand or base, which is also finely carved or constructed in zitan or another valuable material.

Most mid-20th century Chinese jade and hardstone carvings are made of inferior material and are poorly conceived and executed. Size dominates. In the early and late 20th century, however, schools of jade and hardstone carving flourished and produced exceptionally fine carvings of superb material. During both periods, objects were created which are closely based on earlier prototypes.

Mughal and Ottoman Jade and Stone Carvings

Unlike the Chinese, who carved jade for thousands of years, jade carving came to central Asia at a much later date. Jade carving in the Timrud dynasty (1363-1506 CE) in Turkestan dates to the 15th and 16th centuries, but objects from this period are extremely rare. Most are vessels carved from dark green jade and are based on Islamic metal shapes. The founder of the dynasty, Tammerlane, has his grave marked with a large block of dark green jade. Undoubtedly Chinese jades were brought into this region and dragon-handled vessels attest to the borrowing of Chinese designs. In Turkey many Ottoman vessels are embellished with gold inlay and precious stones.

Chinese jade objects were prized by the Mughal court and helped promote the local market for jade carvings. Many of these Chinese vessels incorporate naturalistic shapes in contrast to the often elegantly simple forms of central Asia. There was much trade between Mughal India and China in jades during the 17th and 18th centuries and the Chinese emperor, Qianlong, extolled the virtues of Mughal workmanship. Mughal jades are often inset with gold and gemstones, but this inlay is flush with the surface rather than in high relief as was the custom in Turkey.

Tobacco entered India through the Portuguese in the 16th century, reaching the Mughal court in 1604. Jade was a favoured medium for carving ovoid water pipe containers called huqqa which would allow the smoke to cool before it was inhaled. Rock crystal was also used for huqqa and other vessels.

Mughal jade vessels of the 18th and 19th century can be exceedingly delicately carved, and often very thin sided. Carving is in crisp, high relief and usually incorporates lotus, leaf or repeating vine and tendril patterns. This delicate tracery was also popular in China and 19th century jade carvings from China and India are often difficult to distinguish. Mughal jades, unlike Chinese examples, do not generally copy archaic bronze forms or have extensive detailed openwork carving. Often the jade used in central Asian carving will have splashes of varying colour or other imperfections. As a consequence, in judging quality, form and decoration are generally more important attributes than material. Fine Mughal jade carvings are distinguished by the deep, lustrous polish. The carved elements stand in crisp contrast to the rounded and worn surface.

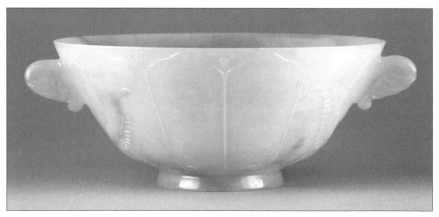

Indian celadon jade bowl, Mughal, 17th century, diameter 5⅞in. (15cm). Celadon refers to a pale greenish white colour, often used to describe jade and ceramic glazes.

Byzantine jewellery section with medallion and coin, Constantinople (?), late fourth century, gold and semi-precious stones, diameter of medallion 3¼in. (8cm). The image is of Constantius II (350-361) mounted by the recipient as an emblem of social status.

Syrian gold bracelet, 11th century, Fatamid Dynasty, width 2¾in. (7cm). The lettering spells out 'Sovereignty belongs to God', in techniques called granulation and filigree.

JEWELLERY

Ancient Jewellery

The ancient cultures of the Mesopotamian river plains and ethnic tribes of island Asia are only tangentially related by geography, but share some commonalities. One of these is jewellery. Ancient gold jewellery from Ur dating from 2600 to 2400 BCE was unearthed by Sir Leonard Woolley, indicating the presence of highly sophisticated metalworking techniques. Simple loop earrings, delicate gold foil headdresses and other items were created with delicate filigree and gold granulated grounds. Jewellery has survived from these ancient sites because of its inclusion in tomb burials. Typical objects include signet rings, cylinder seals of agate and other stones, and agate beaded necklaces and bracelets composed of cylindrical, faceted and oval beads.

Byzantine artisans created striking jewellery designs, the most richly fabricated of which are set with precious stones and pearls in gold mounts. Other examples of Byzantine jewellery are gold, cast with classical images or with Christian references. Small enamel personal icons and gold signet rings were worn by the aristocracy.

The major cultures of Asia all created jewellery and most ancient examples have been excavated from tomb burial sites. While dissimilar in specific design, much ancient jewellery shares common characteristics. Most is composed of gold or gold foils and simple cut and faceted beads made of agate, rock crystal, occasionally glass and, in China, jade.

Indian Jewellery

The most sumptuous of all Asian jewellery was that created for the Mughal rulers in India. Jewellery had been fashionable in India from ancient times as evidenced by the elaborate necklaces and other ornaments carved in stone on female figures. India was also an early major source of precious stones.

Among the finest examples of Mughal jewellery are large engraved rubies and emeralds created for the Mughal rulers in the 17th century. The majority of early jewellery dates from the Mughal period and usually incorporates a combination of gold, enamels and precious stones. The Indian jeweller sought an overall effect and often used stones which, though colourful and large, contained flaws. Gold workmanship is bold and highly visual, but generally not finely executed.

Jewellery was worn by men and women. Men wore pins set in turbans, signet rings and other articles while women wore rings, necklaces, anklets, bracelets and brooches. Most Mughal jewellery designs are of natural forms, depicting flowers or plants. While the wealthy could wear gold, lower castes could not and, in addition to gold, jewellery was made of silver, brass and copper. Much fine Indian jewellery was created during the 20th century, closely based on 18th and 19th century designs. These examples can be difficult to identify from earlier versions.

The Naga tribal cultures created a variety of ornaments incorporating shells, glass beads, animal bones and teeth, and ivory. Although living in India, the Nagas are a distinct cultural minority with racial ties to the Mongolians. Men wore brass neck rings, armlets of ivory and necklaces festooned with miniature skulls emblematic of human heads taken in combat.

Persian and Turkish Jewellery

This bears some similarities to jewellery made in India. Use of gold with precious stones and pearls is common. Qajar jewellery frequently incorporates coins and enamelwork. Turkish jewellery was made not only at the Ottoman court in Istanbul but imported in large quantities from makers in Geneva, creating works especially for the Turkish market. Precious stone-encrusted silver and gold small cups (called zarfs), flywhisks, small boxes and pocket watches were created in addition to lavish personal jewellery.

(Above). Indian table cut diamond bracelet, 18th century, length 6in. (15.2cm).

(Opposite). Indian gold necklace and braided gold ornament, South India, lengths 14¾ (37.5cm) and 16in. (40.6cm).

Group of Central Asian silver and silver gilt jewellery, 19th century.

Turkoman and Central Asian Tribal Jewellery

The nomadic tribes of central Asia value jewellery as a display of status and repository of wealth. A bridal dowry includes large quantities of silver and gold jewellery.

Jewellery from these tribal cultures shares many similarities. Beaded necklaces are often multi-tiered with numerous linked strands of hollow beads, sometimes worked in filigree with granulated grounds. While the majority of nomadic jewellery is silver, gold was also used and both materials often incorporated coral, turquoise and pearls. Silver coins are often included as part of the ornamentation for jewellery suspended from the headdress in long linked chains. Dating jewellery from these regions is extremely difficult and the majority of items available were made during the 20th century based on earlier, traditional forms.

The Jewellery of Tibet, Nepal and Mongolia

Jewellery of the Himalayan kingdoms is boldly fashioned with much use of coral, turquoise and silver. Generally the beads of necklaces are large and irregularly sized and incorporate various materials. Bracelets often have cabochon 'jewels' of turquoise or coral set against a repoussé ground.

Mongolian jewellery is visually similar to that of Tibet and Nepal, but generally is less delicately fashioned with large foliate scroll and geometric patterns worked into the designs. Bold, bright red and turquoise panels set against a silver or silver gilt ground in an unusual setting are the most desirable.

Jewellery from these cultures is extremely difficult to date as it is based on long established patterns and designs. Much of the jewellery available was created during the 20th century.

Thai gold and jewel set crown, Ayuthia, 15th century, height 7½in. (19.1cm).

The most desirable netsuke generally date from the first half of the 19th century or earlier. By the late 19th century traditional Japanese dress was giving way to western fashion and netsuke were made in increasing numbers strictly for the tourist trade. In the 20th century huge numbers were made for the western tourist trade. In the late 20th century restrictions on ivory created a market for netsuke in plastic, often copying earlier designs.

Inro

The inro is a tiered case, usually of three to five compartments, used to hold medicines. It is tied to a silk cord to which it is suspended over the obi, a wide sash tied around the robe. Inro are in a variety of materials. although the majority are lacquer. The earliest examples date to the 16th century, but the form reached a high point in craftsmanship during the 18th century. The cases are finely constructed and thinly sided, fitting snugly together. Inro artists developed a huge variety of decorative motifs and techniques using gold and silver foils, carving, sprinkled shell grounds, simulated metal and other surfaces,

Izuka Toyosai, 18th century, lacquer four case inro with baku and elephant, height 3in. (7.6cm) with an 18th century netsuke. A baku is a mythical animal having the body of a horse, head of an elephant, tail of an ox, and claw feet.

and finely drawn images. The process was laborious with specialised craftsmen creating the wooden case, laquerers putting on the preparatory coats and masters completing the process.

Inro are identified not only by design but also by artist and school. Among the most famous schools of inro makers are the Kajikawa, Koma, Koetsu and Korin, Kanshosai, Toyo and Masanari schools. Great families of inro artists worked in studios producing inro for generations. Other artists worked independently. Beginning in the 19th century artists signed their work. Masterworks were produced by many artists, among whom the most notable is Shibata Zeshin (1807–1891). The finest inro are superbly executed exciting and original designs. Condition is extremely important.

STONE SCULPTURE AND ARCHITECTURAL ELEMENTS

Massive temple complexes such as Angkor Wat of the Khmer or Borobudur in Java are scattered throughout south-east Asia. Remnants of ancient kingdoms with their palaces and fortresses protecting long forgotten geographic boundaries arise from now uninhabited desert plains. The monumental friezes taken from the Assyrian capital are masterworks of the carver's art. The stone carvers who created these magnificent edifices left moving testimony to their skill and their culture.

Stone sculptures created as architectural elements constitute a majority of early carved objects in Asia. Byzantine architecture, with surfaces carved in delicate foliate tracery concealing the bulk of the surface beneath, had a direct influence on later Islamic decoration. The identification of stone sculpture and architectural elements from these cultures is based upon archaeological finds and comparisons with architectural and sculptural remains at the original location. A familiarity with these architectural sites is helpful in identifying stone artefacts.

Large stone carvings were often architectural embellishments, meant to be viewed from a distance and specific perspective, often from below. When evaluating a large stone carving, the stone should be the same variety as the stone used in other carvings from the same period and region. Builders would use only a few sources of stone in an architectural project.

Exterior sculpture should show signs of wear from weathering. A stone figure in sandstone from a wet climate will be dramatically more worn than granite from a dry region, but both will have indications of wear appropriate to their origin. Often sculpture was painted or gilded. Most often this is not evident on stone objects, but very often wooden sculpture will retain some remaining pigments or even more recent pigments retouching original colours. Rot and water damage are often found on wooden sculpture. When the damage is extensive on stone or wood, it will adversely affect the value.

Early Indian Sculpture

The earliest stone sculpture dates to the reign of Ashoka (272–232 BCE), the powerful ruler of the Mauryan empire. Large beautifully polished stone lions atop stone columns commemorating important events and locations were erected in addition to tens of

Indian carved pink sandstone maiden, monkey, and mango tree, c.850 CE. Height 25½in. (64.8cm). Most likely from Rajasthan or Madhya Pradesh, this sculpture would have been an architectural element mounted as a bracket at the top of a roof support inside a temple hall.

Gandharan grey schist image of the Preaching Buddha, 3rd century, height 28in. (71cm). Huge quantities of sculpture in Asia have been destroyed over the centuries. Other examples, such as this torso, which was once a complete figure, survive with missing major elements.

thousands of stupas and other buildings. The Mauryan empire was Buddhist and established Buddhism firmly in India. Buddhist monuments continued to be built during the succeeding Shunga and Andhra periods, creating forms such as the stupa which were to be embraced and reinterpreted by adjoining cultures as pagodas, tiered towers and eventually the magnificent structures in Borobudur and Angkor Wat, each emblematic of the Buddhist cosmos.

Kushan Period

Northern India during the 1st century was a flourishing crossroads with traders from the Roman world transporting goods across the steppes to the Far East. Buddhist pilgrims travelled the same routes and along the way created sculptures which show this diverse mixing of eastern and western culture. Buddhist images were created in the region of Gandhara by Hellenised Roman craftsmen. The westernised figures wear loose diaphanous tunics in a style consistent with that practised in other Roman centres but incorporating the rich, rounded vitality of indigenous Indian sculpture. Huge quantities of sculpture were created in this style using locally available schist, often coated with gypsum. The southern Kushan capital of Mathura created similar images, but without the strong Hellenised influences found in Gandhara.

Gupta Period

The classic Indian style of sculpture developed in central India during the Gupta period (320-647 CE). The Gandharan fashion for thinly draped cloth covering the human figure is emphasised in Gupta sculpture and made even more thin and draping. Gupta figures with snail-like coils of hair (the ushnisha) and the static, majestic pose with heavy lidded large eyes form the basis for all future Buddhist ideal imagery. The best examples emphasise the smooth, open expanse of stone simply covered by a pleated skirt or loose robe. The emphasis is directed towards the pose and serene, benevolent expression.

Around the 5th century during the Gupta and post Gupta periods Buddhism began a gradual decline. Hindu sculpture appears in larger quantities and in south India representations of many Hindu deities were created in red sandstone and granite. The Pallavas and Chola rulers created temple complexes resplendent with numerous carved friezes and reliefs from the 7th to the 12th centuries. By the 15th century Islamic forces overwhelmed south India and the majority of the Hindu kingdoms fell to the Mughals.

Medieval Period

This is a loosely defined term referring to the period between the first incursions of Islam in the 8th century and the gradual decline of Buddhism and ascension of Islam in the 13th century. During this period the Pala state, a Buddhist kingdom in northern India, gradually began to incorporate Hindu elements into the sculpture inherited from the earlier Gupta period. In the 7th century Buddhist and Hindu imagery became increasingly complex due to the influence of Tantric philosophy and Esoteric or Vajrayana Buddhism. The number of bodhisattvas dramatically increased, as did manifestations of Buddha. The name Vajrayana is derived from the main symbol of the vajra or thunderbolt which is usually shown as a stylised group of arrows or, in a more simplified state, as a diamond.

Tantric doctrine asserted the primacy of the female force in the universe and as it emerged so did female representations of counterparts to the principally male Buddhist and Hindu deities. These female sculptures are sensuous, graceful and replete with sexual symbolism evocative of earlier fertility cult figures. The finest examples emphasise the rounded human form accentuated by finely carved facial and other details. With the fading influence of Buddhism, Hindu and Buddhist sculpture began to incorporate Tantric imagery and share many decorative elements. These stylistic influences soon spread throughout south-east Asia.

Mughal Period

During the Mughal period magnificent building complexes were created based on styles brought into India from Persia. These buildings incorporated elaborate inlays of varicolored marbles and other stones in geometric patterns as well as pierced screens called jali which allowed light to penetrate deep into architectural recesses. Jali were made in a great variety of patterns, styles and materials. Geometric and foliate designs are the most common. The finest examples are not flat, pierced surfaces but fully carved and pierced in the round. Architectural panels carved in relief were also created during the Mughal period, often with naturalistic designs of flowering trees or lotus.

*Pala black stone stele of
Syamatara, Eastern India,
Bengal Region, 11th/12th
century, height 40in.
(101.6cm).*

South-east Asian Sculpture

Hindu imagery flowered in Cambodia and the kingdom of Angkor during the 6th to 8th century. This sculpture incorporates the majestic formality of the Gupta style and subtle westernising influences from Gandhara in its depiction of Hindu images.

Pallava and Chola sculpture of south India were also major influences on early Khmer sculpture. The temple complexes built by the Khmer were monuments to honour the god-kings who built them. With the burning and sacking of Angkor in 1177, Buddhist images were introduced along with numerous Buddhist temple complexes embodying the mystical vision of the Buddhist universe in architecture. Enormous building programmes were undertaken incorporating complex carved architectural elements and sculpture mixing Hindu and Buddhist iconography. Succeeding rulers failed to continue the power of the Khmer and by the 16th century Angkor Wat and most of the temple complexes were largely abandoned.

The Champa, a kingdom in southern Vietnam (called Annam by the Chinese), created Hindu temple complexes from the 6th to the 15th century. The finest examples date to before the 12th century and sandstone sculpture created during this period has a majesty similar to that created by the Khmer.

The sculpture of Thailand, Laos and Myanmar was principally Buddhist and based on sculptural types introduced by the Khmer and through direct contact with Buddhists in Sri Lanka and India. The styles adopted in Thailand in Sukhodaya, Chiangmai and Ayuthia continued to evolve slowly based on the Buddhist sectarian belief that the authorised image of the Buddha had been set during his earthly life and no variation from this pattern was acceptable.

By the 12th and 13th centuries Indian sources for early Buddhist images were no longer accessible and the images of Sri Lanka and other sources melded to create various sculptural styles. These Buddhist images share a rounded, languid portrayal of the human form with idealised heavy-lidded eyes, tightly coiled hair, pendulous earlobes and an overall elongation of the body.

Thai sculpture continued to follow this pattern through the 17th century when incursions from Burma eventually forced the relocation of the capital to Bangkok in 1767. Later Thai sculptural forms are based on earlier designs but incorporate inlays of glass and shell on gilded lacquer surfaces. Burma became a dominantly Buddhist kingdom in the 11th century, adopting Buddhism alongside the native Nat religion. Burmese sculpture follows the Thai pattern of adhering to earlier styles.

Crowned Buddha, Burma, 12th-13th century, teak, height 50¼in. (127.7cm).

Cambodian Shiva and Uma, Baphuon style, late 11th century, veined sandstone, height of largest 44in. (110cm).

In Indonesia, Buddhism and Hinduism co-existed with Hindu sculptural types drawn from Pallava and Chola sources. Borobudur, the vast Buddhist temple complex in Java built around 800 CE, was most probably the inspiration and model for the huge complex of Angkor Wat constructed by the Khmer. The entire structure of Borobudur is an architectural visualisation of the Buddhist universe. Built in terraces, large Buddhist sculptures with heavy lidded eyes and squared torsos watch over the numerous terraces which lead the pilgrim through stages approaching enlightenment. The finest Javanese figures have sweetly serene expressions, somewhat idealised forms, and an abundance of decorative detail with elaborate headdresses, necklaces, bracelets, and patterned diaphanous fabric garments. Guardian figures are boldly expressive with deeply carved exaggerated features. With the arrival of Islam in the 15th century, building of Hindu and Buddhist complexes dramatically diminished.

Chinese Sculpture

The early sculptural tradition of China, Japan and Korea differs from that of India and other south-east Asian regions in the use of impermanent wooden structures rather than stone temples. The majority of early Chinese sculpture is Buddhist, with images mostly created in wood or terracotta. Stone guardian figures were created in pairs to guard spirit paths and this tradition continues from the Han through the Qing dynasty. The Ming and Qing imperial tomb guardian animals and figures are generally very formal, massive sculptures and are emulated by many smaller sized examples created for lesser tomb sites throughout China. In addition to these tomb guardian figures, elaborate religious stone sculptures were created based on the type established in Gandhara in the 2nd and 3rd century.

Early stone Buddhist images dating prior to the 5th century survive in numerous cave complexes of which the best known are Yungang and Dunhuang. These caves were frequented by Buddhist pilgrims and contained numerous images set in niches and carved in relief against the stone walls. The figures created during the Northern Wei dynasty are slender, stylised depictions with exaggerated flowing, pleated garments. By the Sui dynasty the garments are much simpler and the figures have more mass. During the Tang dynasty Buddhist images are rounder, more realistic portrayals with characteristic stylised tightly coiled hair, long pendulous earlobes and heavy lidded eyes. The majority of early large sculpture was made of wood or dry lacquer.

The introduction of Mahayana and Vajrayana Buddhism necessitated the depiction of bodhisattvas and a much more complex iconography than had existed under Hinayana Buddhist thought. These figures were often created in wood or bronze and increasingly have long, flowing scarves, elaborate necklaces, and wear garments draped across the torso falling in stylised folds. Over the following centuries sculptural styles vacillated between highly decorative images with elaborate details and relatively simply carved, substantial figures. In

(Opposite). Chinese carved wood figure of Guanyin, 12th/13th century, height 35½in. (90.2cm). This seated position of Guanyin is called 'royal ease'.

(Right). Chinese Buddhist stele, Wei Dynasty, c.500 CE, height 58¼in. (148cm).

(Opposite). Chinese carved limestone torso of a bodhisattva, Tang Dynasty, height 37in. (94cm).

general, the finest Chinese sculpture evokes a sense of solidity and reality with limbs draped in long flowing garments and impassive expressions displaying deep, meditative emotions. Large numbers of stone figures were carved in China during the 20th century. The most popular subjects are Buddhist lions and figures of Guanyin.

Japanese figure of Jizo Bosatsu, 13th century, gesso, kirikane on wood, metal, height 26in. (66cm).

Japanese Sculpture

Very little Japanese sculpture is stone. Most buildings in Japan, as in China, were constructed of wood and sculptures created for temples were most often of bronze, wood or dry lacquer. The earliest wood sculpture dating from the Nara period is closely modelled on Chinese prototypes dating from the northern Wei dynasty with stiff, formalised fabric folds and angularised facial and body features. By the 8th century images of the Buddha are much less stylised with large heavy lidded eyes, full lips and tight coils of hair common in China and other parts of south-east Asia.

During the Heian period (794-1185) two schools of Buddhist thought were founded which introduced a new, complex iconography that moved sculptural representations further from Chinese established models. Grimacing, boldly expressive and aggressively active guardian figures created during the Heian period are masterworks of the carver's art. The height of sculptural naturalism was reached in the late Heian period (897-1185) with a series of sculptures created in Nara. In the succeeding Kamakura and Muromachi Periods (1185-1573) sculptural representations of the Buddha are fuller and more naturalistic, displaying a majestic solemnity in formalised poses. Later sculpture emulates these earlier styles but rarely reaches the success of the originals.

TOBACCO ACCESSORIES AND RELATED MATERIALS

Tobacco entered Asia in the late 16th or early 17th century, but most smoking related paraphernalia dates from the 18th century or later. Chinese snuff bottles constitute one of the largest groups of these wares. Smoking related items were made in Japan as well.

Chinese Snuff Bottles

Snuff, a powdered form of tobacco, was introduced into China in the late 17th or early 18th century. Although its use was officially discouraged, it became immensely popular and small containers were devised to hold the product.

Snuff bottles of various materials were made in China. The most common examples are glass or stone. The best are carved from exemplary material, have expertly and finely carved designs, incorporate natural characteristics of the material into the design and have thin walls with a well-hollowed interior. Snuff bottles were accompanied by mixing dishes, made in as many different materials as the bottles. Snuff bottles can be identified by school and quality of workmanship. For example, the hardstone bottles from the Suzhou area typically display a conscious attempt to use the natural colorations and irregularities in the stone to enhance the carved subject.

(Above). Selection of jade, hardstone and glass snuff bottles made for the Imperial Court, 1720-1820.

(Right). Chinese Imperial enamel on copper snuff bottle, Beijing, Qianlong mark and Period (1736-1795).

Japanese tobacco pipe, case, and netsuke, 19th century. Japanese pipes and tobacco pouches come in a rich variety of shapes and sizes. Most tobacco pouches are of tooled leather.

Snuff bottles are usually made of ivory, bone, silver, bronze, lacquer, amber or glass. Glass snuff bottles can be carved from a single colour or are sometimes made of several cased colours, which are cut through to reveal colours in the carved design. Other glass snuff bottles are applied with patches of different coloured glass, each of which is separately carved into a design.

Inside painted snuff bottles made of hollowed rock crystal or glass are painted on the interior by fine haired brushes. Miniature paintings were signed by artists who depicted popular mythological subjects, landscapes and even portraits of the recipient. Ma Shaoxuan was a noted artist who specialised in the painting of inside painted portrait snuff bottles. The finest painter of the Beijing school of inside painted bottles was Ding Erzhong, working like Ma Shaoxuan during the latter part of the 19th and early 20th centuries.

Perhaps the finest snuff bottles are those made in the imperial palace workshops during the 18th century. These beautifully painted bottles are most often in either painted enamel or painted porcelain. They are identified not only by the quality of the workmanship but also by the imperial reign mark usually written on the base. During the late 20th century glass workshops in China created extremely fine quality copies of early snuff bottles. These are beautifully made and skilfully carved.

Japanese Tobacco Pouches

Tobacco was introduced into Japan in 1605 and within a short time was widely accepted, in spite of governmental edicts issued in 1609 which prohibited its use.

The earliest pipes in Japan were bamboo fitted with metal bowls and mouthpieces. Early 18th century bamboo pipes were often lavishly decorated with lacquer, but later pipes were made of metal. The finest pipe cases are generally either lacquer or carved ivory. Japanese embossed leather tobacco cases, often worked with dragons or other designs, were made throughout the 19th century and were suspended from the sash worn around the waist. Most of these pouches are joined by a metal chain to an ojime; others were attached to a pipe case.

Mughal Water Pipes

Tobacco was introduced into India by the Portuguese in the 16th century and, as elsewhere in Asia, was soon hugely popular. In most of the Islamic world tobacco was smoked in a water pipe. The smoke would travel in a tube through water where it would emerge cool as it was inhaled. The water container is called a huqqa base and is spherical and fitted with small openings into which are inserted tubes. The finest of these huqqa bases are of jade or bidriware and were made in the 17th century.

Tobacco and Opium Pipes and Accessories

In addition to tobacco, the smoking of opium was common in China. Opium had been in use for medicinal purposes in China for hundreds of years, but the smoking of opium is generally believed to have begun in China in the late 17th or 18th century. Chinese merchants requested payment for trade goods in silver, a commodity not in large supply in the west. When American, British and European traders substituted opium for silver in payment, Chinese merchants accepted the change even though the Chinese government protested. When the Chinese imperial government attempted to end the trade, a series of wars erupted, commonly referred to as the Opium Wars, lasting from 1840-1842.

Paraphernalia associated with opium smoking includes pipes of various shapes, glass covered burners, opium containers, trays, scales and small spoons. Opium pipes are long cylinders set with a conical bowl. Many of these are baitong and embellished with enamel decoration. The better quality pipes have ivory or decorated baitong or silver fittings, finely carved glass burners and baitong or silver accessories.

Tobacco pipes of double cylindrical form with slender upright mouthpieces are often erroneously called 'opium pipes'. These were made in large numbers in the late 19th and early 20th century.

Chinese opium pipes, 19th century, length of largest approximately 17in. (43.2cm).

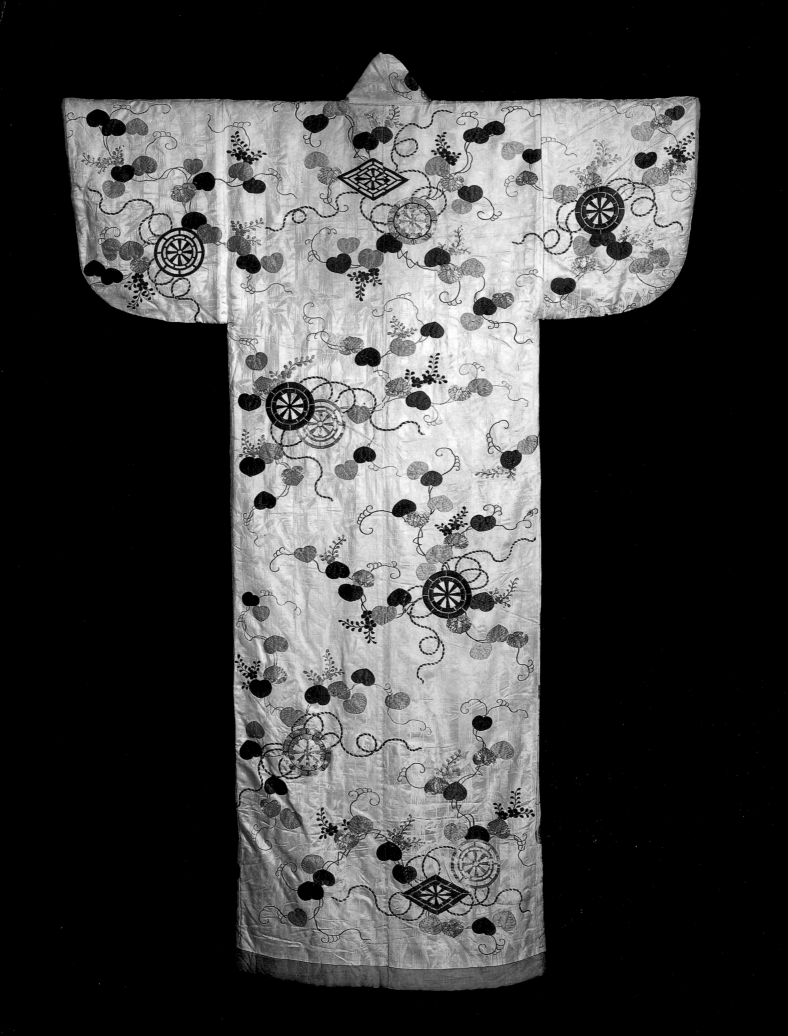

Chapter Five

Textiles

*O*f all fabrics, silk is the most often associated with Asia. It was used for clothing, wrapping special gifts and inclusion in ritual burials. The silk worm larvae begins feeding soon after emerging from the egg and feeds for thirty days, eating as much as twenty times its weight before it is ready to begin spinning its cocoon. Filaments from glands are excreted in long continuous strands around the worm, forming a protective covering until the worm matures into a moth. Once the cocoon is formed the moth is killed, the cocoon harvested and the strands carefully unwrapped. Each cocoon yields about 1,500 feet of silk threads. A huge number of cocoons is required to make a bundle of cloth, approximately 6,000 cocoons for 6 feet of cloth.

Silk cloth was a major trade item from China to the west and the first examples were sent in trade to the Roman world around the 2nd century BCE. In 297 the Roman emperor, Diocletian, secured peace with Persia, the major supplier of silk to Rome. Trade in silk proved to be a mainstay of commerce between China and the west and the trading route became known as the 'Silk Road'. With the conquest of Persia by the Muslims, control of the Silk Road and silk production shifted to central Asia, rivalling the control of the Chinese. Sogdian merchants, a culture in present-day Uzbekistan, controlled much of the silk trade, with weaving centres in Samarkand and Bukara.

Silk was used as a medium of exchange in the ancient world. When defeated by the Tibetan army in 756, the Chinese Tang court sent 50,000 pieces of silk in tribute to Tibet. When payment stopped, Tibetan armies captured the Chinese capital of Changan, now Xian, and payment resumed. In 8th century China four bolts of silk had the value of a fine horse. Much of the early Chinese production of silk centred in Hangzhou and huge quantities of silks and embroideries were sent abroad in trade, as tribute and as gifts. Much of this material was sent to Tibet, where it was received as gifts by the many monasteries.

Silk production was controlled by the Chinese until the 5th century when the secrets of sericulture were discovered by the Syrians. Aleppo, which had been under Byzantine rule, became a major silk weaving and trading centre, made possible by Islamic conquests which removed geographic and political boundaries.

The Byzantine, Ottoman, Safavid and Mughal empires were noted manufacturers of exquisite silks and velvets, with fabrics incorporating rich figured patterns of gold and silver wrapped threads. Cities such as Damascus and Mosul were such noted centres of

---

(Opposite). Woman's Kosode robe, Edo Period, early 19th century, embroidered patterned satin silk, 46 x 67¼in. (117 x 172cm). This sumptuous garment was made for a samurai class woman, identified by the rich embroidery, including the ox wheels, a reference to the novel, A Tale of Ge.

fabric manufacture that fabric names were coined after them: damask for Damascus and muslin for Mosul. Linen was a noted product of Egypt and cotton was woven in Mesopotamia, Yemen, Iran and India.

The nomadic tribes of central Asia are renowned for the weaving and manufacture of rugs and carpets. Turkey and Iran are major centres of knotted pile carpets formed with stretched warp thread between two beams intersected by a weft thread on to which is tied individual knots in dyed wool, cotton or silk thread. The design is formed by the placement and composition of the coloured knots. The tighter and closer the knotted pattern, the more detailed and durable the carpet. Flat-weave carpets called kilims or soumacs are woven and do not have knotted piles.

Resist dyed fabrics called batiks were popular in some parts of Asia, notably Java. These fabrics often combine geometric and stylised foliate patterns.

How to Determine Quality, Condition, and Authenticity

Quality
In judging the quality of fabrics consideration must be given to the overall design and the material. The finest woven or embroidered fabrics have a balanced appearance and careful and consistent workmanship using quality materials. Because fabrics are easily damaged by sun, water, insects and staining, the best preserved examples are very desirable. Central Asian carpets and rugs were made in many centres and differ in types of weaving techniques, knots per inch, pattern and coloration. The finest examples are boldly expressive with a deep, thick pile and strong, fast colours. Clothing should be finely stitched and, if decorated, the embroidered or other designs should be not only detailed but expertly worked. Regional clothing and fabrics are judged by a different standard from those made for the court. Distinctive regional patterns and designs are often marks of a particular culture or tribe.

Condition
Carpets and rugs are extremely susceptible to wear and it is not uncommon to have areas of reweaving. Rewoven areas can be recognised by a subtle difference in colour, texture of the material and knots which are tied in a slightly different manner. Worn areas are occasionally coloured to give an impression of freshness and lack of wear.

When judging clothing, check for stains and fading from sunlight. Ground-in dirt and body oils will eventually cause fabric to rot and decay. Many weavings will begin to split as the cotton warp or weft threads deteriorate. These splits can be repaired but care should be taken that the materials used in the repair will not cause undue stress on the fabric by combining new and old materials.

Cleaning fabrics is a delicate job and one which should be entrusted to a professional. Fabric repair is also best left to an expert. The caustic fluids used in most commercial dry cleaning systems will destroy delicate antique fabrics.

Authenticity

The most elaborate copies are those using bolts of original, early fabric to reconstruct clothing or other objects dating from an early period. Copies of this type are unusual and generally occur with only the most valuable objects. Most copies are fairly easy to detect, either lacking the quality of workmanship when compared to the original or having discrepancies in workmanship.

The majority of rugs and carpets are copied today in China or India and imitate early valuable examples from Persia. These copies can generally be recognised by the inappropriateness of the material, inconsistencies in the design and coloration. Creating a modern version of an early textile is difficult because the silk, wool or cotton material ages and has characteristics of age which can be simulated but not exactly reproduced using modern materials. Working with old materials is difficult because of the fragility of the material. The most successful copies are actually created around an original object, making it difficult to determine the amount of newly rewoven and original material.

A Chinoiserie Tapestry

The Yuan Ming Yuan was the principal summer residence of the Qianlong emperor and the repository of western gifts brought to the Chinese court. Records indicate that these gifts included a set of European 18th century chinoiserie woven tapestries given by a diplomatic mission from Louis XV. In 1860 European troops surrounded, looted and burned the Yuan Ming Yuan and presumably made off with this set of tapestries, which were thereafter 'lost'.

While evaluating a collection in Michigan I happened to see one of these tapestries. There were no photographs proving it had been in Qianlong's collection but an old note attached to the back of the tapestry provided the reference. Although the subject included Chinese figures with pagodas and other exotic structures, the tapestry was clearly not Asian. China and India were both popular and fashionable sources for design from an early period in Europe and it is likely that when it was taken from the Yuan Ming Yuan the looters believed the set to be Chinese. We established the identity by examining auction records from the French auctioneers who had dispersed much of the material in the 1860s and printed a footnote in the auction catalogue documenting the relationship for future reference.

PERSIA AND TURKEY

The powerful Timrud and Safavid dynasties in Persia supported the arts and in particular the weaving of luxurious silk and wool carpets. Many of these woven masterpieces are in museums, but examples dating from the 19th or early 20th century are readily available. Isfahan was the capital of the Safavid empire and it was a cosmopolitan centre open to foreign trade and famous for producing luxurious goods, including textiles.

Velvets were used extensively in both Turkey and Iran for cloth, cushion covers and as tent hangings. These are often decorated with birds, leafy branches, and other naturalistic repeating patterns.

Persian carpets generally have a central design of a medallion bordered by subsidiary patterns, often of geometric or foliate design. In each corner of the main field are spandrels and all are within a large border or a series of smaller and wider borders. These borders usually contain repeating vine or foliate patterns and are finished by an edging called the selvedge. The finest knotted pile carpets have hundreds of knots to the square inch.

After the fall of the Safavid and the rise of the Qajars in the 17th century, carpet weaving dramatically diminished, not to revive until the late 19th century when European and American fashion for the exoticism of the Far East created a demand. Carpets are identified either by the city of production or geographic region. There are hundreds of weaving centres spread throughout Persia. In north-west Persia a major centre is Tabriz, where carpets are noted for the high density of knots per square inch. The region around Hamadan is an important carpet weaving area, with hundreds of small villages which are traditional carpet weaving centres. Other centres are Sarouk, Kashan, and Isfahan, all located within the Arak region. Scattered throughout Iran are numerous nomadic tribal weaving centres.

Tabriz carpets are generally acknowledged to be finely worked. The standard design is a centred medallion with medallions placed in each of the corners in a field of small flowerheads and leafy vines. Tabriz was the centre for the revitalisation of carpet making in Iran during the 19th century and its carpets come in a variety of patterns and sizes and were also made in silk. Heriz carpets usually have a large central medallion but the motifs are executed in a geometric, angular style, often with broad expanses of colour. The borders are usually wide with serrated leaves (herati) in a repeating pattern. Heriz carpets are often woven in very large sizes. Senneh rugs and carpets are distinguished by the repeating rows of teardrop devices (boteh). Sarouks generally have flower-filled fields centred around a large medallion. Many

Isfahan carpet, Central Persia, 16th century, wool on silk, 16ft. 4in. x 6ft. 11in. (498cm x 211cm).

sarouks have grounds that are deep burgundy red. Kashan, Meshed and Kirman carpets often have densely woven flower-filled fields, usually around a central medallion. Kashan carpets are among the most densely knotted of all Persian carpets.

The many tribal weaving centres in Persia produce rugs and carpets which are generally very different in appearance from those made in the cities. These are often small sized, or runners, and have motifs in geometric patterns. Some of these weavings are readily identifiable, others are more difficult to identify because of the nomadic lifestyle of the tribes and close association with other weaving centres. Among the most well known of these tribal rugs are those of Baluchistan, with geometric borders and patterns often in deep red and dark blue.

Unlike the natural, flower-filled patterns of many Persian weavings, rugs from Turkey are much more stylised and coarsely woven. Many Turkish rugs appear in European paintings of the 16th and 17th century, indicating a strong commercial trade at an early date with Europe. Turkish nomadic carpets generally have stylised designs of geometric form and use a looser Ghiordes knot than Persian examples. Turkish rugs are usually lighter in colour and much less detailed than those from Persia. They are also smaller. Small rugs with a central arched panel called a mihrab were made as prayer rugs. Many of these rugs have patterns associated with a particular region and are identified not only by the design but also by the type of weaving and knotting used in the manufacture. Some of the many types and production centres are: Konya, Ladik, Milas, Bergama, Kula and Sivas.

In addition to woven carpets and rugs Turkish weavers excelled at silk and cut velvet garments and hangings. Bursa was both the capital of Ottoman Turkey and centre for fine velvet and textile production during the 16th and 17th centuries. Bursa velvets with recurring patterns were made as yardage for various uses such as cushion covers, wall panels or divan covers. In Ottoman households beds were not permanent structures, mattresses were taken out in the evening and removed during the day. Brightly embroidered quilt covers (yorgan yuzu) decorated these beds. Similarly, thick, stiff cushions (minder) covered in velvet or other materials were set around a room. Boldly woven or embroidered wrapping cloths (bohca) served multiple functions, protecting clothing or bed linens in storage or as table coverings.

One of the holiest sites in Islam is the Kaaba located in the Great Mosque at Mecca. Covering the structure is a large hanging (kriswah), embroidered with verses from the Koran. Each year the covering is removed and cut into small sections as relics for dignitaries and pilgrims.

Cenotaph cover, Turkish, Ottoman Dynasty, 17th-18th century, silk-satin, lampas weave, 74⅝ x 26½in. (189.5 x 67.3cm).

Lakai suzani embroidery, mid-19th century, Uzbekistan, 6ft.4in. x 4ft.6in. (193cm x 137cm).

TURKESTAN AND CENTRAL ASIA

The area referred to as Turkestan extends across the southern boundaries of the old Soviet Union and into the northern reaches of Iran, Afghanistan and as far as western China. Nomadic tribes populate this area and share many similar traits and customs. Fabrics produced by these nomadic peoples differ from region to region but encompass several major categories. The suzani is a wedding or bridal cotton cloth of square shape and embroidered with foliate designs in silk. The brightly embroidered cloths are in colours of red, green, black, blue and bright yellow.

(Above left). Oushak medallion carpet, West Anatolia, early 17th century, wool, 23ft. x 12ft. (701cm x 366cm).

(Above right). Star Kazak, South-west Caucasus, c.1800, wool, 8ft.2in. x 5ft.10in. (249cm x 178cm).

(Right). Tekke bird Asmalyk, Turkestan, early 19th century, wool, 4ft.6in. x 2ft.10in. (137cm x 86cm).

Turkman embroidery robe (cherpi), *silk, length 3ft.6in. (107cm).*

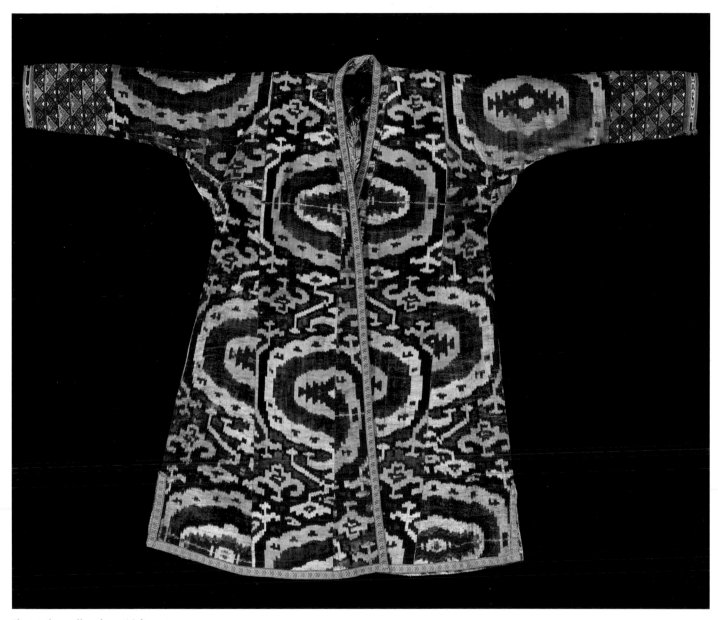

Ikat jacket, silk velvet, 19th century.

Many Turkman tribal rugs and carpets have a rich reddish brown ground centred by rows of polygonal or diamond panels. These include large sized carpets (main) as well as numerous other forms such as saddle blankets, tent bands and door surrounds, which come in a variety of shapes and sizes. Caucasian rugs are generally boldly patterned and coloured in stylised geometric patterns. The best known type from this region is the Kazak. Other tribal rugs are Karabagh, Kuba and Shirvan.

The other major tradition in this region is ikat weaving. This is a resist dying technique similar to batik and is actually surmised to have originated in Indonesia. Ikat are made by dying the threads in bundles or bunching the dyed cloth to produce a distinctive pattern. In addition to pile rugs, the Caucasus produced flat weave rugs called soumacs.

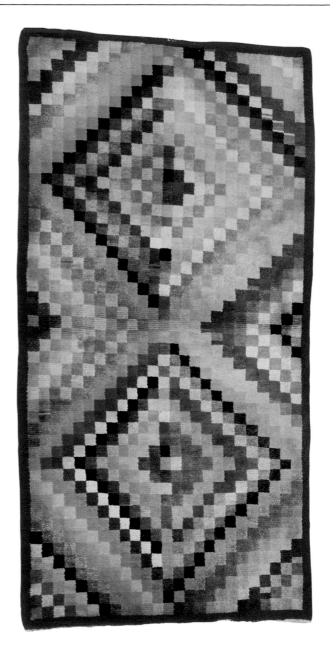

CHINA AND TIBET

Tibetan chequerboard rug,
c.1890-1900, wool, 5ft.8in.
x 2ft.10in. (173cm x 86cm).

Chinese carpets and rugs are knotted in the same manner as those from the Middle East. Generally Chinese carpets are more loosely woven than Middle Eastern carpets and they served a different function. Carpets in China were used for floor coverings but also for covering tables, beds, benches or saddles. Long pillar rugs hang and encircle a column in a building, with the design meeting at the edges to form a continuous pattern.

The motifs on Chinese carpets and rugs are traditional, with images of dragons, Buddhist lions, lotus, phoenix and Chinese characters among a field strewn with clouds or other auspicious emblems. The ground is usually monochromatic within a key-fret or foliate border. Colours are strong and bright. Red, white, blue, yellow and russet brown dominate. 19th and 20th century Chinese carpets often have a pile of differing height

conforming to the outline of the designs. The differing levels are achieved by clipping the pile, which also has the effect of making the looser and shorter knots wear more rapidly. A major centre of manufacture from the 17th century to the end of the 19th century was Ningxia. By the early years of the 20th century production was geared more to the western market and traditional designs were eclipsed.

The Chinese produced a variety of fabrics out of silk. Velvet was first introduced into China in the 16th century through contact with Spanish velvets brought in by European traders. Kesi, or cut silk, is another type of woven fabric in which coloured threads are restricted to the woven design, producing an embroidered effect. Robes, hangings, chair and table covers and rank badges are often kesi weavings. Large hanging figural and

Pair of Ningxia pillar rugs, mid-19th century, 7ft. 7in. x 4ft. 1in. (231cm x 124cm) and 7ft. 9in. x 4ft. (236cm x 122cm).

251

Ningxia carpet, c.1700, wool on cotton, 8ft.5in. x 5ft.9in. (257cm x 175cm).

landscape kesi panels are sometimes woven with gold or metal wrapped threads. Less fine examples will have details painted in. The Chinese man's robe worn for official court functions is called a chao fu. It has a full shirt and wide sleeves.

Huge numbers of textiles were sent to Tibet from China. Silk was considered a medium of exchange and was sent as gifts from the Chinese court to Tibetan monasteries. These silks were worked into large hangings, table covers, altar frontals, ceremonial clothing, banners and other objects. Among the most striking examples are embroidered silk Buddhist hangings created for the monasteries. Simulated tiger and other animal skin rugs were woven in Tibet as part of ritual worship. These symbolised dominance over untamed and negative energy. Other rugs were made in a long narrow format divided into squares and used for prayer mats.

Robes

The court or dragon robe was worn for everyday business. Articles of official clothing were first standardised in the Ming dynasty and further codified in the early Qing dynasty by the Manchus, a minority tribe from the north-west of China. In addition to the use of clouds, dragon robes have a lower edge of boldly coloured striped stylised waves centred by a shaft symbolising a mountain peak. Other decorative elements include auspicious symbols appearing in groups of eight or twelve. Twelve symbol robes were reserved for imperial use. The outer layer of a man's dress was called a pufu. The official rank of the wearer was identified by a rank badge worn on the front of the pufu, represented by different animals. A woman's dress was similar to a man's but less standardised. In addition to a robe, a woman's wardrobe included a skirt and skirt panel along with other undergarments.

Imperial twelve symbol dragon robe, Qianlong Period (1736-1795). Embroidered in a satin stitch with gold wrapped thread. The twelve symbols of imperial authority are: sun, moon, constellation, rock, axe, stripes, golden pheasant, double dragons, water plant, sacrificial cups, flames and millet seed.

Chinese silk civil rank badge, Xianfeng Period (1851-1861). Showing the silver pheasant, the insignia of the 5th civil rank.

Rank Badges

Rank badges developed in the Ming dynasty, but the animals representing the ranks were not codified until the early Qing dynasty. Ming rank badges allowed higher ranking officials to choose which of two animals to wear as insignia. Civil officials could choose one of two kinds of birds, military officials one of two animals. Later clarification dictated that officials could wear only one animal with no choice.

With the advent of the Qing dynasty clarification was sought and the number of animals was reduced from ten to nine and the old Ming order slightly altered. The badges

of the highest rank were reserved for princes; these were dragon badges with either four or five claws, contained within squares or circles. Qing civil official badges were: Crane, first rank; golden pheasant, second rank; peacock, third rank; goose, fourth rank; silver pheasant, fifth rank; egret, sixth rank; mandarin duck, seventh rank; quail, eighth rank; and paradise quail, ninth rank. Military rank badges include both natural and mythical animals, such as lions, leopards and the qilin, a type of combination horned animal with lion and dragon characteristics.

Chinese silk military rank badge, Qianlong Period (1736-1795). Showing the lion, representing the 2nd rank military officers' position.

255

Chinese kesi scroll hanging, 18th century. Kesi is a type of tapestry weaving of extremely fine quality. This example shows the eight immortals and the three gods of happiness welcoming Xi Wangmu, the Queen Mother of the West, to Penglai, the mythical island of the immortals. Lesser quality kesi work is often enhanced by painted details.

The most desirable rank badges are those representing the less common ranks and also those in the finest workmanship. Kesi badges and those worked in gold and silver thread are among the best examples.

Fabrics for Export to Europe

Silk garments and uncut fabrics were a major export item from China to the west. The earliest silks were exported to the west in the late 16th or 17th century for wealthy European

Chinese export silk dress made for the French market, c.1760.

noble families. By the 18th century production had dramatically increased and silk textiles were made specifically to order in designs often supplied by western merchants. Embroidered dresses, shawls, curtains and bed hangings were so desirable that European weavers sought protection from the imports by banning them from the marketplace. Ultimately this failed, and European weavers responded by copying the Chinese designs.

JAPAN

Japanese silk and gold weave campaign coat, Edo Period, mid-19th century, 5ft.5in. x 9ft.2in. (165cm x 279cm). Decorated with poetry in brush and ink in a deliberate archaic style. The poem is about the transient existence of flowers as a metaphor for the short and glorious.

As in China, the Japanese used silk in many garments. Early records indicate that most of the best quality silk was imported from China, and early Japanese silks were almost indistinguishable from Chinese examples. A separate tradition gradually developed and Japanese fabric workers excelled at dyeing techniques first introduced by Chinese but then perfected by Japanese craftsmen.

Kimono

The kimono, worn by both men and women, is an ancient design which has remained relatively unchanged over hundreds of years. The kimono generally is cut from a single width of cloth into seven sections. There are various types of kimono distinguished primarily by the width of the sleeves and length. A man's kimono is shorter than a woman's.

Both are tied with a sash which is secured at the back with a large, formal knot. Over the years the obi, as the sash is called, became more elaborate and noticeably decorative. Because Japanese kimono have no pockets, objects were suspended from a cord looped over the obi and secured by a netsuke. Kimono generally are dyed and have patterns which often have abstract backgrounds with naturalistic dyed or embroidered designs covering the entire surface. There are various techniques of dyeing the fabric, but all early dyes were made of either vegetable or mineral colours. Kosode were worn by commoners and often as everyday garments. These robes developed early and, while most are plain, some are stencilled with designs and even overlaid with gold or silver leaf (see page 240)

Small silk cloths for wrapping presents are called fukusa. These were often sumptuously decorated with embroidery and it was customary to return them once the gift had been received.

Japanese cotton resist dyed fireman's coat, 19th century, 39½ x 48in. (100.3 x 121.9cm). The bold characters proclaim the brigade name. The coats were soaked in water to protect the wearer. Firefighters in Japan enjoyed special status and were considered heroes.

KOREA

Korean embroidered screen, Choson Dynasty, 18th century, embroidery on silk, 55½ x 144in. (141 x 366cm). Much decorative imagery in east Asian art incorporates symbols representing longevity, such as on this screen.

Korean weavers were heavily indebted to Chinese craftsmen. Korea served as a conduit for Chinese design to Japan and was late to develop an indigenous textile industry. Very few early Korean textiles exist and these are closely modelled on Chinese prototypes. Beginning in the 17th century Korean artisans embroidered screens and wall hangings with Chinese subjects executed in a distinctly Korean manner. These screens were often made for festive occasions. In the 19th century wrapping cloths (fabric panels used to wrap precious objects or gifts) were made in many different sizes but were usually square and made of hemp, silk or cotton. The striking abstract patterns were formed from small scraps of cloth sewn together.

MUGHAL INDIA

Richly embroidered silks with foliate and arabesque designs were worn in the Mughal court. These were decorated with all manner of animals, flowers and other natural subjects. The richest and heaviest of the Moghul brocades is called kimkhab. Gold, silver and silk are used to create patterned fabric with sumptuous gold or silver designs. These brocades probably resulted from the Mughal desire to impress the populace and gradually grew to be the costume of the wealthy. Persian weavers were brought to Gujarat and then to Benares which became a major weaving centre. The opulent Mughal court style was emulated in independent kingdoms throughout India. Brocades are identified by the amount of gold and silver used in the fabric. Thinly hammered and drawn gilt silver wire was wrapped around silk threads which were then woven into patterns on a loom. The gilded surface or mixture of gold with the silver prevented tarnishing. The principal costume is called a maghribi and comprises a robe and tunic.

Fabrics for the Western Market

With the British ascendancy, fewer garments were made and by the 19th century weavers were directing their efforts to western market textiles. Indian cotton chintz, a glazed fabric with resist dyed patterns, was far superior to comparable European textiles. The bright coloured dyes were fast and the patterns bold and exotic. Bed coverings with 'tree of life'

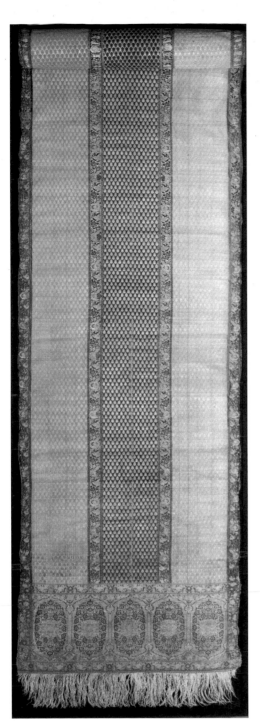

(Left). Indian or Iranian sash, 17th/18th century, gold and silver brocade, 180¾ x 23⅜in. (459 x 59.4cm). Sashes such as this example were worn as clothing accessories, wrapped and folded over the wearer's robe.

(Below). Kashmir paisley shawl, 19th century.

patterns, dresses, waistcoats, curtain hangings, shawls and other cottons were sent abroad in huge numbers. Embroidered cotton was a speciality of Gujarat. In the region of Golconda craftsmen developed a technique for free-hand painted and stencilled cotton fabrics. These often elaborate fabrics were strongly influential on western design in the 18th century.

In the region of Kashmir weavers specialised in shawls made of the fleece of highland mountain goats which were extremely warm and soft. These were decorated in traditional boteh designs in complicated, interwoven patterns in bright colours. The East India Company began exporting Kashmir shawls to Europe in the late 18th century. By the late 19th century these popular shawls had competition from machine-woven examples made in European factories.

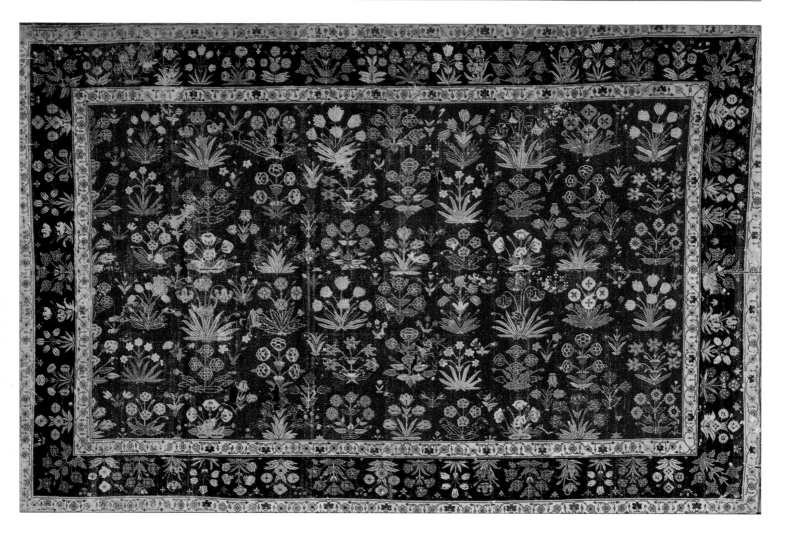

Carpets

Carpet weaving began in earnest in India in the 16th century during the reign of Akbar who sent artisans from the Persian court to establish manufacturing centres in India. Persian artists adopted the Persian illuminated manuscript style for carpet patterns and the earliest carpet designs in India are similar to those in Persia. During the reign of Shah Jahan, flower patterned carpets woven in a high number of knots per square inch were introduced. There are two major types of Indian carpets: those with foliate designs and those with figural scenes. Knotted pile carpets gradually developed a broader range of subjects.

(Above). Mughal flower carpet, North-west India, 17th century, wool on cotton, 9ft. 10in. x 15ft. (300 x 457cm).

(Opposite). Indian painted cotton palampore for the American market, late 18th century, 84 x 124in. (213.4 x 315cm). Palampores were commissioned by the East India Company for import to the U.S. during the late 18th century.

SOUTH-EAST ASIA

Batik cloths with wax resist designs and ikats are made of cotton in Indonesia, Malaysia and Java. Worn as clothing, these cloths are often brightly coloured and strongly patterned. The batik process probably originated in India; Gujarat textiles employ a wax resist technique. The first mention of batik is on a Dutch bill of lading dating from 1680, but the oldest surviving Indonesian batiks date from the late 18th century.

Cotton cloth used in batik must be free from imperfections or it will snag and pull in the dyeing process. Indian and European cottons were generally preferred. Colours are in hues of brown or blue. The process begins as the cloth is soaked in peanut or other oils, adding to the absorbency, and then dyed using a wax resist process. After dyeing, the cloth is boiled and the oils removed.

Early batik designs were hand drawn; later wooden and copper plates stamped the designs on to the cloth. The source of the designs is traditional, based on nature or mythology. Woven Indonesian textiles are created in patterns which have specific meanings and are intended for specific uses: weddings, birth ceremonies, naming ceremonies or other special occasions.

(Opposite). Batik garment. Detail below

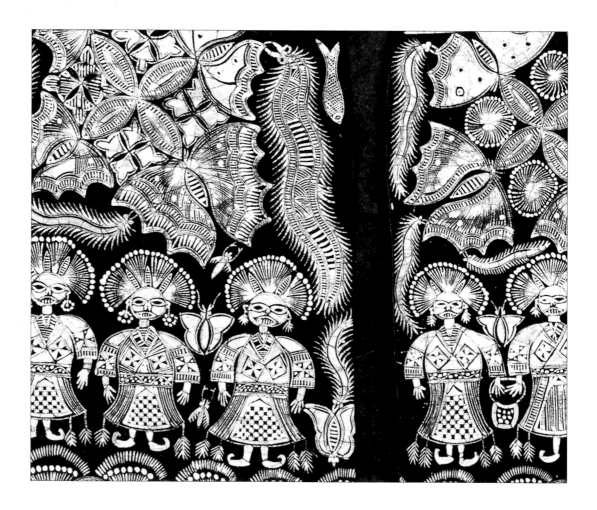

20TH CENTURY ASIAN TEXTILES

The majority of rugs and carpets woven during the 20th century are commercial products in traditional designs. Late in the century many traditional Persian designs were copied and woven in India and China. Nichols Chinese carpets were woven in large numbers during the first half of the 20th century and sold in the United States. These have stiff, deep piles and sculpted surfaces.

While most Asian countries continued to produce clothing in traditional designs in silk or cotton, the majority of these garments, particularly those following World War I, are artistically inferior to the examples which they often imitate. Some notable exceptions are Japanese kimono, traditional Indian garments, Indonesian batik and ethnic minority clothing.

Chapter Six

Paintings and Prints

*P*aintings on silk or paper with coloured ink and water or oil pigments have been made for thousands of years in Asia. Equally ancient are wall paintings in tombs, freely painted ceramic designs and even painted lacquer vessels.

There are two basic types of painted design: calligraphy and narrative or pictorial representations. Both types are found throughout Asia. Whatever the subject, the basic materials of the painter are the same: brushes with fine animal hair bound together and secured in a wooden or bamboo handle, an ink stick, coloured pigments, a water pot for dipping the brush, silk or paper, and an ink stone.

How to Determine Quality, Condition, and Authenticity

The criteria for judging the quality of Asian paintings varies based on the type of technique. Chinese, Japanese or Korean ink paintings on paper or silk are freely executed and much more spontaneous than Islamic, Tibetan or Mughal paintings which document a particular scene or event. The brush is loaded with ink and, as it touches the surface, the stroke is irrevocable. It cannot be erased. The composition is mentally planned in advance and the artist generally works swiftly, with brushes of various sizes dipped in ink according to the intended darkness or heaviness of the line. A skilfully painted scene has the minimum of required strokes necessary to communicate the emotions desired by the artist.

Quality

An artist's style is influenced by the time in which he lives, his homeland and, in short, all those experiences and influences which shape a person. Through observation, a viewer can train the eye to recognise differences in technique and style of painting and detect characteristics of fashion and technique common to a particular geographic region, time period or artist. A mental catalogue can be developed of these characteristics which can be used as a base point against which other works are judged. Signed works are judged in comparison with other signed works by an artist, and the body of work by an artist is judged against other artists from the same period. Anonymous works are judged in the same manner, making comparisons to authored works from the same time period.

(Opposite). Imperial Menologion for January, Byzantine, Constantinople, c.1040, vellum, 11⅝ x 9¼in. (29.7 x 23.6cm). Menologion is taken from the Greek for 'month'. It was created in the imperial scriptorium in Constantinople and represents each month with images of saints. The detailed painting style and presentation presage Islamic miniature paintings and book illustrations.

Ma Yuan (1190-1225 or later), album leaf, landscape. Ma Yuan was one of the great painters of the Southern Song Academy.

Inks were used by painters and calligraphers in stick or cake form. Ink is made from carbon recovered from burning pitch mixed with oils and glue pressed in a mould. Many ink sticks and cakes have moulded decoration and are sometimes dated and inscribed. The most prized ink stones are duanstones from Guangdong province. Others are ceramic.

Landscape Painting

Landscape paintings in China offered a perspective which is entirely different from western scientific perspective. Objects in Chinese paintings are depicted in a flat manner with little regard for depth and distance. Part of this is due to the immediacy of working in ink versus oils. In the west a painter could go back and rework part of an image. Ink paintings do not allow this flexibility. Chinese ink paintings capture the mood of the painter rather than exact representations of the objects or scenes which are depicted.

Shi Tao (1642-1707), landscape, signed, scenes of Yangzhou, album of eight leaves, each 10¾ x 8in. (27.3 x 20.3cm).

Artists in China learned through copying the works of master painters. These copies often include exact reproductions of the original artist's signature and artist's seal. The seal was generally carved from a soft stone and pressed into red or black ink and affixed to the surface of the painting, accompanied by a short inscription by the artist. Other viewers, admirers or artists would often add their commentary to a painting and also affix their seals to their comments.

*Descent of the Amida Trinity,
early 14th century, colour,
silk, and kirikane on silk, 33
x 15½in. (83.8 x 39.4cm).*

Amida Buddha

The earliest artistic centres in Japan were Buddhist monasteries. The largest number were in Nara, a centre of culture and the arts largely inspired by contact with Tang China. Emissaries brought back to Japan models of Chinese civil government, paintings, architectural designs and other works of art. This rich exchange was interrupted during the Fujiwara period when Tang power began to wane. A new religious movement swept Japan around Amida, the Buddha of compassion, welcoming deceased devotees into the western paradise. Images of Amida were painted in compassionate, loving attitudes which the believer would view while on the deathbed.

Yamoto-e

With the absence of many Chinese contacts, Japanese artists began to assert themselves. Calligraphy assumed greater importance during the Fujiwara period, as did narrative scroll paintings. The best known narrative scroll painting subject created during the Fujiwara period is 'The Tale of Genji', decorated in a uniquely Japanese style called Yamato-e, literally translated as 'Japanese painting'. Yamato-e paintings have lightly drawn outlines filled in with bright, thick opaque colours and have no counterpart in Chinese painting traditions.

Pair of screens, Hasegawa School, calligraphy by Tetsuzan Sodan (1532-1617), each 40 x 137in. (101.6 x 348cm).

The Japanese had traditionally passed on poems, stories and folklore verbally and only began to change after regular contact with China and the Chinese written language. In the 5th and 6th centuries Chinese Buddhist texts reached Japan and shortly afterwards the Japanese began adopting the Chinese style of writing. Calligraphy accompanied scroll paintings as poetry or commentaries and styles of calligraphic script developed, practised by noted artists. By the 11th century purposely made papers, mainly in blue or white, were in use for calligraphy.

Zen Buddhism

Chinese contact was again established during the Kamakura period and the greatest influence on Japanese painting styles came again from religious sources. Zen Buddhism was imported to Japan from China and with it a new style of painting. Zen practitioners were not concerned with religious imagery, rather introspection and self-improvement. There was a new emphasis on realism in painting. Zen-inspired gardens emphasising man's interaction with nature were created, as were paintings of nature subjects and portraits of noted Zen master teachers. A Zen practitioner would meditate on a landscape or nature scene as a means of self-improvement.

Emerging from Zen teaching was the Suiboku style of painting, a technique of freely drawn images in black inks. Suiboku was brought to Japan from China, where it was practised by skilled, educated painters who were not part of the official painting academies. These painters' works were brought to Japan where Japanese painters sought to emulate the style. Suiboku scroll paintings were meant to be viewed at special occasions or times of the year and were sumptuously mounted with brocaded silks, a type of mounting called Kakemono. The founder of Suiboku painting was Shuban, a Zen priest in Kyoto, who taught the great painter who followed in his style, Sesshu (1420-1506).

Tosa and Kano Schools

During the Muromachi period, wealthy feudal lords demanded art that displayed their power and influence. Although Suiboku continued as a distinct style, two new schools of painting emerged, based on the Yamato-e type. These were the Tosa and Kano schools. Tosa school painting is precisely drawn and filled in with coloured, muted inks, depicting great historic events and religious imagery. Gradually Tosa declined and was supplanted by a new style created by Kano Masanobu (1434-1530), an aristocrat living in Kyoto. This style of painting combined elements of Yamato-e and Suiboku styles with

Hakuin Ekaku (1685-1768), Hotei juggling a saucer, hanging scroll, ink on paper, 50 x 11¼in. (127 x 28.6cm).

often strong, black ink strokes beautifully filled in with coloured inks on a gold foil background. Created for feudal lords, these sumptuous paintings would illuminate the dark castle interiors with reflected light.

Many folding screens and painted door panels were created in this style during the Momoyama and Tokagawa periods. Some of the great Kano school painters include Kano Takanobu (1571–1618), Kano Mitsunobu (1565–1608), Kano Sanraku (1559–1635) and Kano Sansetsu (1589–1651). It was a member of the Kano family, Kano Tanyu (1602–1674), who became the best known painter of the Edo period.

Tosa School, c.1550, pair of six panel screens, ink colour and gold on paper, 69 x 144in. (175.3 x 365.6cm).

Rimpa School

Paintings during the Edo period were created by exceptional artists, among them, Tawaraya Sotatsu (1589-1651), Honami Koetsu (1558-1637) and Ogata Korin (1658-1716). Korin was not only a talented painter, but also excelled in ceramics and lacquerwork (see pages 169 and 170). Koetsu was also multi-talented and with a grant of land established an artists' colony which eventually led to the founding of the Rimpa school of painting. Koetsu and his fellow artists often collaborated together, creating stunningly beautiful works in ceramics, lacquer, calligraphy and painting. Ogata Korin, who also espoused Rimpa aesthetics, followed in this tradition.

Nanga

The peace and prosperity of the Edo period allowed for greater contacts with China and the influence of Chinese literati style paintings – paintings created by the educated scholar artist as opposed to paintings by professional court painters. Literati style painting, called Nanga school paintings, were immensely influential during the Edo period and continued to inspire Japanese artists into the Meiji restoration. Among the many influential artists who practised in this style were Ikeno Taiga (1723-1776) and Aoki Mokubei (1767-1833). The exposure to western perspective influenced other artists and a lively mixing of artistic styles emerged during the 18th and 19th centuries.

Yoga and Nihonga Styles

Increased western contact furthered the influence of western painting techniques into a style called Yoga. Japanese subjects and scenes were painted in western oil and watercolour techniques. In response to the possible abandonment of traditional painting styles, Dr. Ernest Fenollosa (1853-1908) and Okakura Tenshin (1862-1913) promoted the concept that western perspective could be assimilated into the Japanese artist's repertoire without sacrificing traditional Japanese approaches. The school of painting which developed is called Nihonga. Two early practitioners of this style were Kobayashi Kokei (1883-1967) and Maeda Seison (1885-1977).

Suzuki Kiitsu (1796-1858), 100 Deer, ink and colour on paper, 37 x 13¼in., (93.9 x 33.5cm).

Yosa Buson (1716-1783), Eagle, ink and light colours on paper, 56⅛ x 22⅝in. (142.5 x 57.5cm).

The Printmaking Process

Woodblock printing probably originated in China. A wooden block is carved with a design or characters which are inked and then covered with a paper which would be pressed on to the design. Monochromatic prints required only one block. Colour prints required a separate block for every colour. To make a print the artist would draw the image on paper which would then be traced on to other sheets by assistants. Each of these copies would be on thin, almost transparent sheets which would be attached to a smooth block of wood secured in a frame so it would not warp or split. The design would be cut into the wood through the traced copy with a sharp knife and the negative areas cut away.

Colour prints would have only the colour parts of the design left in relief on the block. A complex print with many colours could require many separate woodblocks. Each time a separate colour was applied the paper would be carefully aligned to ensure the colour was within the lines of the image depicted. Because each print was done by hand, there were very limited runs of each image. Although each print is similar, there are minute differences. As the woodblock was used more and more, the crisp edges and outlines might become dull and would result in an image that would be noticeably different from the prints taken earlier. Sometimes a printer would sharpen these outlines by touching up the carving, which would allow the woodblock to be used longer. Prints taken from these touched up and recarved blocks are generally less desirable than those originally printed.

Subject Matter

Colour printing first began in Japan in the 17th century and was achieved by the use of vegetable or mineral dyes which were mixed to a paste and spread on to the woodblock surface. The major early proponent of woodblock prints was Hishikawa Moronobu (1625-1695).

In the 17th century Tokyo boasted a wealthy middle class and there was a great demand for popular prints. They were made for books, albums or as individual or multiple sheets. Shape and size varied depending on the subject.

The most well-known type of print is called Ukiyo-e, which translates as 'floating world'. These prints depict scenes from everyday life and were popular from the 17th century through the 19th century. Portraits of famous beauties, actors and the latest fashions are common subjects. Among the great masters of Ukiyo-e prints are Isoda Koryusai (active c.1765-1788), Suzuki Harunobu (c.1725-1770), Kitagawa Utamaro (1753-1806) and Katsushika Hokusai (1760-1849). In the 19th century nature, wildlife and

---

(Opposite). Kitagawa Utamaro (1753-1806), Mirror of Courtesans of the Green Houses: Usumizu and Ariwara, 15 x 10⅟₁₆in. (38.2 x 25.5cm).

landscapes are introduced. Most prints include the artist's signature, title of the work, publisher's seal and sometimes even an official seal indicating it had been approved by the government censor. The master of these techniques and subjects was Ando Hiroshige (1797–1858). During the 19th century printmakers explored the triptych format which allowed them greater versatility in portraying images from theatre or other subjects which required more space. By the end of the 19th century Japanese printmaking was in decline and was revived by artists working in traditional techniques but with fresh perspectives.

(Above). Utagawa Hiroshige, White Rain at Shono from the series 53 Stations of Tokaido, coloured ink on paper, 10 x 15⅛in. (25.4 x 38.5cm).

(Opposite). Korean grapevine screen, Choi Sok-hwan, c.1825, Choson Dynasty, ink and colours on paper, 31¾ x 117⅝in. (80.6 x 298.7cm).

KOREAN PAINTINGS

Korean paintings dating earlier than the 14th century are based largely on Chinese examples and are extremely rare. The dominant theme among these religious paintings is the Amitabha Buddha and images of the western paradise. These are called 'pure land' paintings. Centred with images of Amitabha, they were extremely popular during the Koryo period, just as in Japan. Devotees of the Pure Land sect believed that viewing an image of Amitabha immediately before death would insure acceptance into the western paradise. Images are finely drawn and based largely on Chinese examples.

During the Choson dynasty Korea was in the midst of social and political changes which allowed much greater freedom and experimentation in the arts. Landscape paintings were created inspired by Chinese masters of the Northern Song Dynasty. Nature subjects were also popular. These paintings are extremely rare, most having been destroyed by the numerous foreign invasions during the 15th century. Created at the same time are calligraphic sutra manuscripts (sagyong) on deep indigo paper and painted in gold or silver inks. During the Choson period massive Buddhist temple paintings called Taenghwa were created, inspired by similar examples from Tibet. These were brought outside the temple for special occasions.

As in China, Korea had official painting academies where court painters were trained. Painters who operated under bureaucratic oversight were largely called to create images of the royal household and dignitaries. There also existed a tradition of independent scholar painters who operated outside the academy. The scholar painters were not restricted and, in general, paintings created by them are far more lively and spontaneous than those of the academicians. Among the most notable of these is Chong Son (1676-1759) who painted in a Chinese literati style, favouring landscapes which were actual representations of sites in Korea. The importance of establishing native Korean crafts and painting styles during the 18th century led to the use of genre as subject matter. Two of these genre painters are Kim Hong-do and Yun Tu-so (1668-1715). Korean paintings include traditional scroll formats and also painted screens. There is a strong Korean folk art painting tradition.

PERSIAN PAINTINGS AND CALLIGRAPHY

Miniature paintings executed for manuscripts have survived in larger numbers than any other type of Persian painting. Archaeological evidence indicates that magnificent large scale wall paintings of foliate and figural subjects adorned palace walls, but only a few fragmentary examples survive.

Manuscripts have survived in greater numbers because of their portability and the protection afforded by being enclosed within covers. The earliest calligraphic script is kufic, written on vellum and created during the Abbasid dynasty. Kufic was replaced by Naskhi, used for translations of texts from other languages. There were many other regional and specialised calligraphic styles. Among these are muhaqqaq and nastaliq scripts. Kufic was not in general use after 1600. Calligraphy developed as an art form to spread the Islamic message and in the process served a decorative function by using stylised script.

Illuminated Manuscripts

The earliest illuminated manuscripts developed from a tradition established during the 8th and 9th centuries. The style is related closely to painted ceramics, having enamelled figural scenes dating from the 12th and 13th centuries. Early 13th century sketches also display an affinity to Chinese painting techniques.

Shahnama, rear view.

A format developed incorporating illustrations and decorative embellishments in a strict codified pattern. Books were considered precious objects, tangible symbols of education, wealth and power. An illuminated manuscript is carefully organised and compiled with oversight from a master artist or administrator who would select the subjects to be presented and assign court artists and calligraphers to the project. Artists specialised in types of decoration: battle scenes, court subjects or studies of nature. Painting was a means of legitimising power, and one of the most popular of subjects was the book of kings, the Shahnama. The earliest paintings are dominated by the human figure and the landscape and architecture are largely stylised backdrops.

The high point of manuscript illustration was reached in the 15th century, with centres in Baghdad, Shiraz and Herat. Artists in Herat produced an astounding array of magnificent works. One of the many painters of renown from this period was the brilliant Timrud artist Bihzad, of whom little is known and to whom many works have been attributed. An illuminated manuscript could easily take months or years to complete. The finest of these illustrated manuscripts were produced for royalty from the 12th through the 18th centuries and include a limited range of subjects: epic stories, romances and scientific treatises. The miniaturist depicted images in relation to their importance to the action. Distance is indicated by placement, not perspective,

The Shahnama made for Shah Tashmasp (1514-1576) of Persia, 258 illustrations and illuminations executed between 1520-1540. This example shows a scene of Faridun striking Zahhak with an ox-head mace before the angel Aurush, c.1525, 10¾ x 6¹³⁄₁₆in. (27.2 x 17.3cm).

and typically there are several focal points within every painting. The scenes are brilliantly colourful and depicted in fine detail, particularly nature.

Examples painted before the end of the 16th century were strictly governed by spacial regulations and traditional practices, rules which restricted artistic creativity but ensured the continuity of styles and techniques. Most early painted manuscripts were created to illustrate the great works of Persian poetry and literature. Around 1600 a major change took place, divorcing manuscript painting from these established practices and freeing the artist to create works of great imagination and originality. Artists depicted subjects with unabashed realism, even caricature. Individual painted pages were created and numerous artists emerged working in the new style.

During the 16th and 17th centuries painters enjoyed strong patronage and many illustrated books were produced. Among the most famous is the Shahnama of Shah Tahmasp or the Houghton book of kings, consisting of 760 folios and 256 images produced in the 1520s. Renowned 16th and 17th century painters include Riza-i Abbasi, and his student Muin Musavvir (1617-1708). By the end of the 17th century many of the finest painters had left Persia for the Mughal court. Qajar court art continued the pattern established earlier, but introduced western style oil painting. The finest are large portraits, executed in formal poses. Lesser examples are often stylised and naïve. During the late 18th century and into the 19th century, Qajar artists copied many earlier manuscripts.

TURKISH MANUSCRIPTS AND PAINTINGS

Early Turkish miniature paintings can be traced to the Uighurs who emigrated to Turkey in the 9th century. Uighur influence continues into the 15th century. Tughrul Bek, the founder of the Seljuq empire, introduced a realistic style of painting showing scenes of everyday life and combat. Very little of this early work survives, but the style spread to other central Asian areas. The Uighur court painters also influenced Persian miniaturists. The principal difference between Persian and Turkish painting styles is the Turkish preference for realism. After the fall of Constantinople, Italian painters, including the Renaissance master Gentile Bellini, who arrived in 1479, were invited to the Turkish court.

Paintings of astonishing realism were produced for the court of Suleiman the Magnificent, with exacting architectural detail and images taken from real life. Suleiman brought court painters from throughout the Ottoman empire to his court. Among the best known of these artists is Hafiz Osman (1642-1698), active during the reign of Suleiman and noted for his realistic style and colourful palette. Another well-known artist, working with ink sketches, was Sahkulu, specialising in intimate ink drawings. The style of painting established by the early Ottoman artists continued through the 18th century. Western oil techniques became popular in the 18th century and during the 19th many European artists were commissioned to work at the Ottoman court.

Calligraphy was practised in all Islamic countries but it reached a high degree of skill under the Ottoman court. Early calligraphic works by Seyh Hamdullah (1436-1520), Hafiz Osman and others were used as examples by later calligraphers, and their style carefully emulated. Tools of the Islamic calligrapher included scissors, a pen-knife, pen rest and a burnishing tool for preparing the paper.

(Opposite). Portrait of a painter, Turkish, late 15th century, opaque watercolour and gold on paper, 7⅜ x 5in. (18.8 x 12.7cm).

INDIAN PAINTINGS

Battle with Raktavija, India, 1775-1800, pigment on paper, 7⁷⁄₁₆ x 10¹⁄₁₆in. (18.3 x 25.5cm).

Paintings in India have long been used for religious and ethical education. There are several major centres of Indian painting. Mughal miniature painting centred in the court at Delhi. A strong, distinct style of painting emerged in the Deccan sultanates and in Rajasthan and the Punjab Hills.

In addition to geography, Indian art is much influenced by religion. Mughal paintings are often intimate views of court life, historical subjects or nature, while Hindu or Jain imagery is almost entirely religious or emotive. The format also differs. Mughal paintings were almost always bound as books, while Hindu paintings derive from paintings on palm leaves and were loose. Although early examples from the 16th century are distinct, gradually the various influences combine.

Persian artists came to the Mughal court in the 16th century at the behest of Humayun, the son of Babur, the founder of the Mughal dynasty. Humayun's son, Akbar,

(Opposite). Attributed to Jai Ram, Udaipur, c.1736, Mahrana Jagat Singh 1734-1751, watching the Rasila performed in the courtyard of the City Palace, 23¹³⁄₁₆ x 17⁷⁄₁₆in. (60.5 x 44.3cm).

(Above). Indian Company school, c. 1816, Three Recruits, gouache on paper, 9⅜ x 14¹¹⁄₁₆in. (23.8 x 37.3cm).

(Opposite). Northern India (late Mughal style), c. 1750, pleasure palace pavilion, pigments on paper, 13⅛ x 9⅞in. (33.3 x 25.1cm).

greatly expanded the number of artists and established a royal atelier in Delhi. Western concepts of space and shading were introduced in the 16th century and, with the increased popularity of court painting, regional artists working in Rajasthan and the Deccan emulated the style.

The format developed under Akbar became the model for later Mughal painting. Hindu artists were trained in the Persian tradition, depicting scenes from Persian literature and images of the court and noble life. Mughal painting is a mixture of Hindu and Persian traditions. Details were carefully rendered with richly decorated scenes. Akbar's descendants continued the tradition until the reign of Aurangzeb, one of the sons of Shah Jahan. Aurangzeb neglected the artists and many left the court for other patrons. This dispersal further popularised and spread the Mughal style. An exception during the late 17th and 18th centuries was in the Punjab Hills where religious subjects dominate. Although there were periods of revival, the art form gradually declined along with Mughal political power.

During the late 18th and early 19th century paintings created under the sponsorship of schools governed by the British East India Company were active in Bombay and Calcutta, producing finely drawn documentary watercolours and gouaches.

Stupas with Ushnishavijaya, Nepal, dated 1387-88, pigment on cotton, 34 x 25¾in. (86.4 x 65.4cm). The rows of numerous stupa represent the symbolic figure 100,000.

TIBETAN PAINTINGS

Tibetan paintings are generally executed on the walls of temples or are painted banners or hangings called thankas. Both are religious depictions, showing deities surrounded by a retinue and often contained within a mandala, or magic circle. A mandala is a formal representation with a central deity surrounded by subordinate deities, usually with objects representing attributes which are symbolic of ideas or emotions. The earliest thankas date from the 10th century or earlier, but most examples date from the 18th and 19th centuries. Typically figural representations in a thanka are very detailed and brightly coloured. Tibetan iconography dominates the subject matter and most are images based on tantric Buddhist art brought to Tibet from India from the 8th to 11th centuries. Tantric Buddhist art emphasises magic and esoteric symbolism expressed in specific poses

Tara and other deities, Central Tibet, c.1075, pigments on cotton, 48 x 31½in. (122 x 80cm). The goddess Tara offers protection to the believer from various physical dangers. The smaller images represent her ability to offer help under specific circumstances.

Glossary

Abr – Persian term for ikat.

Abumi – Japanese stirrup.

Abura-zara – Japanese dish to catch lantern oil or wax drips.

Adu zatua – Nias carved memorial sculpture for the dead.

Agni – Vedic god of sacrificial fire.

Aikuchi – Japanese type of dagger without a guard.

Ainu – principal native ethnic group of Japan, now residing in Hokkaido.

Ajiro – Japanese wickerwork pattern.

Aka e Kutani – Kutani porcelain with predominantly red overglaze enamels.

Aks – Persian term for gold or stencilled decoration.

Alam – Persian term for a metal standard carried in Shiite processions.

Alang – a building for storing rice in Toraja, Sulawesi.

Album paintings – small paintings contained in a book format.

Alkaline glaze – type of low fired glaze used on stoneware.

Amaterasu – Japanese goddess of the sun.

Amida Buddha – Buddha who has achieved enlightenment and is the embodiment of enlightenment, compassion, and wisdom, presides over the pure land of the west.

Amida-Yakushi – Japanese depiction of the buddha in common priestly robes and partially uncovered upper torso.

Amitabha – Tibetan/Chinese buddha of the western paradise.

Anagama – type of Japanese kiln.

Ananda – pre-eminent disciple of Buddha, who usually appears in monks' robes with another disciple, Kasyapa.

Andon – type of Japanese lamp.

Andon-zara – underplates for Japanese lamps.

Angada – heroic monkey in the epic Ramayana.

Angenan – Balinese ceremonial offerings,

Anhua – Chinese porcelain decorative technique with subtle designs visible only under careful examination.

Animism – ancient belief that every object has a soul or spirit.

Aniruddha – grandson of Krishna.

Annam – Vietnam.

Annealing – process of working heated metal.

Aode Kutani – Kutani porcelain almost completely covered with dark, usually green, enamel ground.

Aogai – Japanese term for a type of iridescent abalone shell used for inlay.

Apsaras – heavenly figures often depicted with billowing scarves.

Arabesque – formalised foliate decoration.

Aratame – Japanese censor's seal found on many prints dating from 1854 to 1871.

Archer's ring – ring with a lip or catch for holding the string of a bow.

Arhat – Buddhist disciple who has attained enlightenment.

Arita – centre for porcelain manufacture in Japan beginning in the 17th century.

Armature – metal interior framework used to support a clay core in bronze casts.

Artemisia – a medicinal herb whose leaf is often depicted as a mark of good fortune on the bases of Chinese porcelain.

Arupadhatu – in Buddhism, a state of the soul in the journey towards nirvana.

Asura – Hindu and Buddhist demon.

Avalokitesvara – the bodhisattva of compassion; in Korea Kwanum, China Guanyin, Japan Kannon.

Avatar – Hindu incarnation of a deity.

Aware – Japanese depiction of beauty that is slightly melancholy.

Badiyeh – Persian wine bowl.

Baghmal – Central Asian silk dyed velvet ikat.

Bagu – linen-like fibres used in textiles.

Baimiao – outline type of Chinese painting style.

Baitong – Chinese metal alloy composed of brass and tin, also called paktong.

Baku – Chinese mythical creature with an elephant trunk, rhinoceros eyes, ox tail and tiger feet.

Balarama – brother of Krishna.

Baldachin – Central Asian term for brocade.

Bamboo – fibrous plant often used in imagery in Asia and as a building and carving material. Bamboo is one of the three friends, with plum blossoms and pine.

Banasura – the demon king father of Usha.

Banko ware – type of Japanese ceramic, often with enamel decoration.

Banten – Balinese sacrifice to the gods.

Bark cloth – type of cloth made from the fine inner fibre between the outer bark and the trunk of varieties of fig (*Ficus*), breadfruit (*Artocarpus*), and mulberry (*Brousometia papyrifera*) trees.

Barong – cutting blade weapon of plantain leaf design of Borneo and Mindaneao.

Bat – Chinese symbol of good fortune.

Batik – wax reserved fabric decorated with painted or printed designs.

Bauphuon style – temple in Angkor Wat constructed in the 11th century.

Beater – frame attached to a loom used to consolidate the weft.

Bell – one of the eight symbols of Buddhism.

Besihung – an iron container used by the Lampung culture to hold soot used in ritual ceremonies.

Betang – in Borneo, the Dayak term for longhouse.

Betel – mild narcotic substance made from betel leaves and lime often used in South-east Asia.

Betel nut containers – containers for holding betel nut, lime, and leaves.

Beykoz – Turkish glass manufacturing centre.

Bhutas – malignant creatures which eat flesh and dwell in cremation sites.

Bi – ancient Chinese jade disc with a central hole commonly included in burials and having ritual significance.

Bichar – Turkish straight bladed knife often with a silver sheath; called a kard in Persia.

Bidriware – Indian metalwork having a high zinc content with copper, inlaid with silver or gold against a dark contrasting ground.

Biscuit – unfired and unglazed ceramic.

Bizen (bisen) ware – type of high-fired stoneware from Bizen Province with a natural ash-glaze in colours of gold, orange or bluish green with reddish streaked patches, often prized as a tea ceremony ware.

Blanc de Chine – white type of porcelain made in the kilns at Dehua in Fujian province.

Bo – Chinese ancient bronze bell.

Bodhi tree – type of fig tree (*Ficus religiosa*) underneath which the historic Buddha, Siddhartha Gautama, achieved enlightenment, literally 'enlightenment'.

Bodhicitta – spirit or will to gain enlightenment.

Bodhisattva – literally 'one who is enlightened', a spiritual being who eschews nirvana in order to remain on earth and assist those who are still on the journey; called posal in Korea.

Bodhisattva Maitreya – Buddha of the Future

Body – term for clay in a ceramic object.

Bohca – in Turkey, wrapping cloths.

Bolo – general name in the Philippines for a long knife.

Bonaspatti – Hindu god whose head often appears on keris sheaths.

Boneless – painting style without outlines.

Bonsai – miniature tree.

Bosatsu – Japanese term for bodhisattva.

Bot – principal room in a Thai temple.

Boteh – flame-like design often found on Persian rugs and carpets.

Brahma – Hindu creator of the universe and a member of the Hindu trinity including Vishnu and Shiva; gods of one of Buddhism's three worlds.

Brahmin – the priestly caste in India.

Brocade – complex multicoloured weaving technique.

Brushpot (bitong) – container used in China and Korea for holding artist brushes.

Buddha – Siddhartha Gautama, the historical buddha lived between 560 and 480 BCE and is also known as Shakyamuni. Literally 'enlightened one', the buddha is the central figure in Buddhism. All who achieve enlightenment can become a buddha.

Buddhism – religion based on the teachings of Buddha.

Bulb bowl – shallow bowl for forcing flower bulbs.

Bunjinga – Japanese term for a type of painting done by scholars.

Burka – Central Asian cloak.

Cakra – ritual wheel or disc.

Calabash – gourd vessel, the attribute of the Chinese immortal Litaigui.

Cameo glass – glass of one or more layers encased with other contrasting colours.

Canopy – one of the eight symbols of Buddhism.

Canton enamel – painted enamelwork made in Canton.

Canton ware – term for blue and white Chinese export porcelain.

Caoshu – type of Chinese calligraphy script.

Celadon – originally a French term now in common usage to refer to a Chinese stoneware with a green glaze in various tones; or a description of a shade of sea green colour in a glaze, as in 'celadon glazed'.

Ceramic – fired clay object.

Chabako – Japanese tea ceremony box.

Chain stitch – embroidery technique with a looped stitch forming a chain pattern.

Cha ire – Japanese tea container.

Chakra – Buddhist wheel or disc; in Korea called the cakra.

Chakram – steel Sikh throwing disc with a sharp cutting edge.

Chalcedony – type of quartz.

Champlevé enamels – enamel technique with the metal surface removed and filled with enamel paste.

Chandra – Hindu god of the moon.

Cha-no-yu – the Japanese tea ceremony.

Chaofu – Chinese court dress.

Chaopao – Chinese full-length robe with fasteners on the side.

Chaozhu – Chinese court beaded necklace.

Chauri – yaks' tail fly whisk held by royal attendants.

Chawan – Japanese tea bowl.

Chiang Mai – Thai city state which emerged as the basis for a distinctive Thai culture.

Chicken cup – Chinese type of finely painted doucai enamel decorated wine cup featuring chickens.

Chinkinbori – Japanese incised lacquer technique heightened with gold or silver foil.

Chinoiserie – decoration derived from Asian sources.

Chobako funa dansu – Japanese storage cabinet.

Chogori – traditional Korean jacket.

Choli – short blouse worn with a sari.

Chongbyong – Korean term for a kudika, a water sprinkler usually of metal.

Choson – Korean era corresponding to 1392-1910 CE and sometimes referred to as the Yi.

Chrysanthemum – flower symbolising the imperial Japanese household.

Chuval – Turkman woven bag.

Cicada – insect symbolising immortality in China.

Cili – Balinese sacrificial gift or image.

Cire perdue – the lost wax process of bronze casting.

Cizhou – Chinese stoneware produced first in the Song dynasty with incised or painted decoration usually in two contrasting colours.

Cloisonné – enamel technique with fine wires called cloisons separating the enamel paste.

Cobalt – mineral used to produce the colour blue, particularly on porcelain.

Coiled body – potters' technique using long strands or coils of clay placed atop each other to build the body of a vessel.

Colophon – a descriptive reference usually at the end of a book, painting or print.

Conch trumpet – in Tibet, a dung, used in offering rituals or calling monks to prayers.

Confucius – common name for the Chinese scholar and philosopher Kong Zi who traditionally lived from 551-479 BCE and who is the founder of Confucianism.

Cong – in ancient China a rectangular stone, usually a jade block pierced with a cylindrical section, often included in tomb burials.

Copper red – type of decorative underglaze colour used most often on stoneware or porcelain and created from copper oxides.

Coromandel lacquer – type of carved and painted lacquer.

Crane – symbol of good fortune and long life in China, Japan and Korea.

Craquelure – a network of cracks in the surface of some oil paintings.

Crazing – fine network of cracks in a glazed surface.

Cricket cage – usually a gourd container with a pierced cover.

Cuerda seca – a glazing technique using an oily substance mixed with manganese to separate colours.

Cushion cover – in Turkish, a minder.

Daimyo – Japanese feudal lord.

Dainichi – Japanese term referring to the image of the buddha wearing a plain priest's robe.

Dakini – spirits of female wrath.

Dalang Wayang – Indonesian puppet master.

Damaru – drum in Tibet.

Damascene – fine overlay of contrasting metal into an iron or steel surface.

Jezail – flintlock rifle in Persia.
Jian ware – Song ceramic type usually of dark brown colour.
Jiao – ancient Chinese bronze wine vessel.
Jichimu – Chinese cabinet wood, literally 'chicken wing wood', because of the distinct feathery grain pattern.
Jiki – Japanese term for porcelain.
Jina – in Jainism a term for one who has attained supreme knowledge.
Jingdezhen – centre of porcelain manufacture in China.
Jiriki – the ability of a skilled Japanese craftsman to create without forethought.
Jue – ancient Chinese bronze ritual wine vessel.
Jumu – Southern Chinese elm.
Jun ware, also **Junyao** – Chinese stoneware produced in the Song dynasty and usually of bright lavender blue.

Kaaba – sacred Islamic shrine located in Mecca.
Kabuki – Japanese popular theatre form which developed in the 17th century.
Kabuto – Japanese helmet.
Kagamibuta – type of netsuke of flat form with a decorative metal plate.
Kago – Japanese baskets.
Kailasa – Hindu mythological mountain which is the home of Shiva.
Kaisho – standard Japanese script.
Kaishu – standard Chinese script, called Haeso in Korean.
Kakemono – Japanese hanging scroll.
Kakiemon – Arita family of potters known for delicate enamel decoration.
Kala – Hindu god of death and time.
Kalas – mythical Hindu monsters which eat time.
Kali – Hindu dark goddess created in a hideous and powerful form to destroy the evil demon Raktabija.
Kama – Hindu god of romantic love.
Kamban – Japanese shop sign.
Kami – Japanese nature deity.
Kamakura – Japanese era coresponding to 1185-1333 CE.
Kamsa – evil uncle of Krishna in Hindu mythology.
Kanji – Japanese term for Chinese characters used in Japanese writing.
Kannon – Japanese term for Guanyin, goddess of mercy, also Avalokitesvara.
Kano – Japanese school of painting based on Chinese Ming styles.
Kaolin – type of clay used in the production of porcelain.
Kapala – Nepalese offering bowl.
Kara-e – Japanese paintings executed in a Chinese style.
Karakusa – literally 'Chinese grasses', a leaf scroll design on Japanese ceramics.
Karashishi – Japanese term for a Buddhistic guardian lion.
Karatsu ware – type of Japanese ceramic.
Kareau – carved protective figure of the Nicobar Islands.
Karma – in Buddhism, the actions on earth which determine the form in which one will be reincarnated.
Kartikeya – six-headed son of Shiva and Parvati.
Kashan – Persian ceramic centre.
Kashibako – Japanese sweetmeat box.
Kashibon – Japanese tray for holding sweets in the tea ceremony.
Kashira – a metal plate on the pommel of the Japanese sword.
Kashkul – Persian term for a begging bowl.
Katabori – Japanese term for carving in the round, usually describes netsuke carving.
Katakana – type of Japanese script.

Katana – type of Japanese sword blade.
Katar – Mughal push dagger.
Kavukluk – Turkish turban stand.
Kendi – ceramic pouring vessel.
Kenzan – Japanese noted Rimpa potter (1663-1743) and family of potters.
Keris – a Malaysian long dagger usually with a patterned steel blade of wavy outline.
Kesi – Chinese fine silk woven tapestry.
Ketoprak – Indonesian folk theatre.
Keyaki – type of Japanese elm.
Khanjar – type of Indian or Persian dagger.
Khmer – South-east Asian ethnic and political group centred principally in Cambodia.
Kiku – Japanese term for chrysanthemum with sixteen petals.
Kilij – Turkish curved sword with a wide blade tip.
Kilim – flat weave carpet.
Kiln – an oven used to heat a substance until it solidifies or fuses.
Kimono – long coat-like Japanese garment tied at the waist with a sash called an obi.
Kinji – Japanese polished gold lacquer ground.
Kinrande – delicately potted porcelain with gilt decoration.
Kinuta – Japanese term for a fine type of longquan celadon.
Kiri – Japanese term for the Paulownia tree or flower.
Kirikane (kirigane) – Japanese gold leaf decoration.
Kirin – Japanese mythological animal with the body of a deer, tail of an ox, horse hooves and a single long horn.
Kiseruzutsu – Japanese pipe case.
Kiwame – Japanese censor's mark for 1791-1842.
Ko-gushibako – Japanese small box to hold women's combs.
Kobako – Japanese incense box.
Kodansu – Japanese small cabinet.
Kodogu – Japanese incense set.
Kogo – Japanese small incense box.
Ko-gushibako – Japanese small box to hold women's combs.
Ko Kutani – old Kutani, generally refers to Japanese Kutani made in the 17th and 18th centuries.
Komai – Japanese metalwork with inlaid silver or gold wire and blackened surface.
Koro – Japanese incense burner.
Korwar – Cendrawash Bay Area tribal figure carved as a spirit receptacle after death.
Koryo – Korean era corresponding to 936-1392 CE.
Ko-Seto – Japanese ceramic from Old Seto.
Kosode kimono – Japanese kimono worn by the highest social classes.
Koto – Japanese plucked musical instrument.
Kozuka – Japanese small utility knife.
Kraak – Dutch term for a Chinese blue and white porcelain made for export during the 17th century.
Kraton – Indonesian palace.
Kris – *see* Keris
Krishna – in the Hindu religion the eighth incarnation of Vishnu.
Kromo – Javanese language.
Ksatriya – warrior hero in Indonesian theatre.
Kubachi – Persian ceramic centre.
Kubi-e – Japanese woodblock printed portrait.
Kufic – angular type of Arabic script.
Kui dragon – also Gui, Chinese dragon appearing in profile on ancient bronze vessels.

Kukri – short curved blade used by the Gurkhas.

Kuku – Sumatran term for a fingernail motif in carving.

Kuku pancanaka – a long curved fingernail with special powers in Indian mythology.

Kumbakarna – Hindu figure in the epic, Ramayana.

Kumihai – Japanese ceremonial sake cup.

Kundika – Indian term for an ovoid vessel with a tall spout.

Kurodana – Japanese lacquer set of shelves.

Kushide – comb design on Nabishima dish foot.

Kutahya – Turkish ceramic factory active from the 18th century.

Kutani – type of Japanese ceramic produced since the 17th century.

Kut – Vietnamese tribal term for figural carved posts at the corners of a mausoleum, placed to ward off evil spirits.

Kyogen – farcical interlude in a No drama.

Kyoyaki – ceramic wares from Kyoto.

Lacquer – sap taken from a variety of trees found in Asia, which produces a durable and decorative surface.

Lakon – Indonesian theatrical performance.

Lakshmana – Rama's younger brother.

Lakshmi – Hindu goddess and wife of Vishnu.

Lama – Buddhist monk of any order.

Lamaism – type of Buddhism in Tibet, Nepal, and Mongolia.

Lambrequin – border decoration of beaded necklaces.

Lampas – type of textile weave with double warps and wefts.

Lao Zi – founder of a Chinese philosophical sect.

Lapis lazuli – light to dark blue stone often flecked with silver.

Laque burgaute – lacquer technique with inlaid mother-of-pearl scenes against a black background.

Laterite – porous rock formed from leached soil.

Lei – archaic Chinese bronze vessel of ovoid outline with a wide mouth.

Leiwen – Chinese decorative motif of spirals usually found on archaic bronze vessels.

Lemba – marsh grass used in making fabric.

Leopard – the third rank of a military official in China.

Linga parvata – the lingam belonging to the spouse of Shiva.

Lingam – erect phallus of Shiva.

Lingzhi fungus – motif usually appearing in Chinese art representing longevity.

Lishu – Chinese clerical script.

Literati – educated scholar class in Ming China who excelled in painting, poetry, and the other arts.

Lohan – *see* Arhat.

Lohan chuang – Chinese daybed

Lokapala – mythological Chinese guardian figures.

Lokeshvara – Buddhist lord of the earth.

Longquan ware – Chinese type of celadon ware made in Zhejiang province.

Lontar fibres – leaf used in tying off ikat.

Lopburi style – Thai style based on Khmer prototypes, called after the city of Lopburi, the Khmer city in Thailand.

Lotus – aquatic plant often depicted in Asian arts.

Lucknow – centre of Indian culture.

Ludruk – form of Javanese folk theatre.

Luk – the curves on a kris blade.

Luohan – the highest level of holy man in Buddhism, usually portrayed in groups of sixteen or eighteen and also called arhat.

Madanika – Hindu term for an attractive woman.

Maebyong – Korean high shouldered vase with a tapered base.

Mahabharata – Indian epic.

Mahakala – angry manifestation of Avalokitesvara.

Mahavidyas – term for the ten Hindu tantric goddesses: Black Kali, Tara, Sodashi, Bhuvaneshvari, Bhairavi, Chinnamasta, Dhumavati, Bagala, Matangi and Kamala.

Mahayana – a major branch of Buddhism which emphasised the role of the bodhisattva Maitreya – Buddha of the future – called Miruk in Korean.

Makara – mythological water creature with features of a crcodile, elephant and serpent.

Makie – Japanese lacquer technique using gold or silver powders on wet lacquer producing a three-dimensional effect.

Mamluk – slave.

Mamuli – Sumba term for horseshoe-shaped forms of gold or silver.

Mandala – diagram used to assist meditation based on the Buddhist view of the universe.

Mandarin – High civil official in Qing Dynasty China.

Mandau – Dayak sword.

Mandorla – An almond-shaped radiance framing the depiction of a figure.

Manju – flat circular netsuke.

Manjusri – bodhisattva of knowledge and wisdom (China Wenshu, Japan Monju), typically riding a lion.

Mara – Buddhist king of demons.

Marananda – Indian monk who introduced Buddhism to Korea.

Martaban – large stoneware storage jars manufactured in China and South-east Asia.

Mashal – Persian broad based candle stand.

Mashrabiya – window or screen covering composed of small turned wood elements in a geometric pattern.

Meiji – Japanese era corresponding to 1868-1912 CE.

Meiping – Chinese vase form with high shoulders and tapered foot.

Menpo – face protector of Japanese armour

Menuki – Japanese sword appliqués which are fixed to the sword hilt.

Metallic oxide – oxides of a metal used to colour glass and enamel pigments.

Mihrab – an arched niche indicating the direction of Mecca.

Mikawachi – location for the manufacture of Hirado ware.

Minai – type of pottery with glazed enamel decoration.

Minbar – pulpit in a mosque.

Mingei – in Chinese art, objects made for inclusion in a tomb; in Japan, a return to the simplicity of traditional crafts.

Mingqi – items made for the funeral and interred within a tomb.

Mino ware – Japanese ceramics made in Mino province and often used in the tea ceremony.

Miroku – Japanese Buddhist depiction of the Buddha wearing a simple priest's garment.

Mirror – in Asia generally mirrors were used not only as practical accessories for cosmetics but also had symbolic significance as an object that would ward off evil and also was a repository for the soul.

Mishima ware – popular type of Japanese ceramic made in the Karatsu kilns.

Mithuna – couple engaged in an erotic embrace.

Mizusashi – Japanese water container.

Mizuya – Japanese kitchen cabinet.

Mogu – Chinese painting style without outlines, sometimes referred to as 'boneless'.

Mokugyo – wooden gong used in Buddhist ceremonies.

Shibayama – Japanese inlay of precious stones and ivory.

Shibuichi – Japanese alloy comprised of one part silver to three of copper.

Shigaraki ware – type of Japanese ceramic originally produced as utilitarian wares and later prized for its natural, rustic appearance.

Shiite – Islamic sect which believes that authority passed directly through descendants of Muhammed's son-in-law, Ali.

Shikishibako – Japanese box for poem papers.

Shino ware – Japanese ceramic ware first made in the 16th century.

Shinto – Japanese religion literally translated as 'way of the gods'; Shinto has a strong emphasis on ancestor worship, belief in nature spirits, and respect for other natural forces.

Shippo – Japanese term for cloisonné enamel or a cash pattern with ribbons.

Shishi – Japanese term for a lion-like mythical creature.

Shiva – the principal god of the Hindu trinity.

Shogun – hereditary title of a military ruler in ancient Japan.

Shoji – sliding doors set with translucent paper in Japanese buildings.

Shou symbol – Chinese character for longevity.

Shufu – type of Chinese ceramic marked with the characters shu and fu.

Shunga – Japanese erotic pictures.

Si Gale Gale – Sumatran funerary puppet used in rituals.

Siam – Thailand.

Silica – silicon dioxide, an essential component of glass.

Silla – Korean kingdom within the Three Kingdoms period and corresponding to 57 BCE-935 CE.

Simurgh – phoenix-like mythical bird.

Singa – Sumatran mythical animal with attributes of the water buffalo, horse, and serpent.

Singha – a stylised guardian lion.

Singhalese – ethnic majority group in Sri Lanka.

Siraha Salawa – Nias carved ancestor portrait.

Slip – a refined clay applied to a ceramic vessel to provide a suitable ground for decoration.

Soapstone – soft stone often used in Asian carvings, also called steatite.

Soft paste – type of porcelain fired to a lower temperature.

Somen – entire mask worn as part of Japanese armour.

Sometsuke – Japanese term for blue and white porcelain.

Song – Chinese term for pine.

Sosho – type of Japanese script.

Soto – form of Japanese Zen Buddhism.

Spur marks – glaze imperfections on ceramics left by a kiln support.

Sri Lanka – Ceylon.

Sri Vijaya – ancient South-east Asian maritime kingdom existing from 8th to 13th centuries.

Stag – Chinese symbol of prosperity and long life.

Steatite – *see* soapstone.

Stele – free-standing inscribed column or panel.

Stoneware – ceramic type which is high fired, non-porous and opaque.

Stupa – a conical mound used to hold Buddhist relics, symbolic of the mind of buddha; in Tibet a chorten.

Sueki ware – early Japanese coil constructed and wheel finished ceramic type first made around the 5th century; while generally undecorated, sometimes embellished with incised patterns.

Sufi – a mystic.

Suibokuga – Japanese colour decorated paintings created by Zen artists during the Muromachi period.

Sukhothai – also Sukhodaya, kingdom in Thailand.

Sumida gawa – type of thick-sided brightly enamelled sculpted porcelain made in Japan from the late 19th century.

Sumi e – Japanese painting in ink only.

Surahi – Persian long-necked flask.

Surimono – privately printed commemorative Japanese prints given as gifts.

Surya – Hindu god of the sun.

Sutra – Buddhist texts.

Suzuribako – Japanese writing box.

Swatow – type of Chinese porcelain made in kilns in Fujian province.

Tabar – Mughal saddle axe.

Taihu – type of decorative rock used in garden sculpture, noted for the fantastic shape usually with many hollows and apertures.

Takamaki-e – Japanese lacquering technique in which the design is built up in high relief.

Takri – type of Indian script.

Tamba ware – Japanese ceramic type first made c.1200, often with a natural ash glaze.

Tansu – Japanese storage cabinet.

Tanto – short Japanese blade.

Tantric – Hindu and Buddhist sects which promote the female elements with esoteric ritual and magic.

Taotie – Chinese mask decoration often appearing on bronze vessels, often called 'monster masks'.

Tara – Buddhist and Hindu goddess.

Tarashikomi – Japanese painting technique applying ink to damp paper.

Tau tau – carved memorial sculpture from Sulawesi.

Tawqi – type of Arabic cursive script.

Teadust – type of Chinese stoneware glaze.

Tebako – Japanese box.

Temmoku – Japanese term for Song Dynasty stoneware with cut-out glazed designs in silhouette.

Tenbu – Hindu guardian deities.

Tenpo – Japanese designation for the period 1830-1843.

Terracotta – Term for earthenware.

Tetsubin – Japanese iron kettle.

Thangka – Tibetan ritual paintings to aid in meditation.

Theravada – conservative form of Buddhism which emphasises the achievement of enlightenment by personal effort, practised principally in Burma, Thailand, Laos, Sri Lanka, and Cambodia.

Three Friends of Winter – Chinese term for the pine, bamboo, and plum.

Thuluth – form of cursive writing often used for headings.

Tianhuang – *see* soapstone.

Tianqi – filled in coloured lacquer, a technique with recesses cut into the lacquer surface filled in with coloured lacquer to form a scene or design.

Tielimu – Chinese cabinet wood of dark brown colour used mostly as a secondary timber.

Tiwah – Dayak ceremony where the soul of the dead leaves the living world.

Tobi Seiji – Japanese term for Chinese celadon wares with iron brown spots made in the longquan kilns.

Tokugawa – the shogun family which ruled during the Edo period in Japan from 1603-1868.

Tokoname – Japanese alcove in a house in which displays of paintings or artworks are shown.

Tokkuri – Japanese narrow neck container.

Tombak – gilded copper.

Torii – entrance gate to a Japanese Shinto shrine.

Transitional wares – Chinese porcelain made during the mid-17th century near the end of the Ming and beginning of the Qing dynasty.

Trimurti – the Hindu trinity of Vishnu, Shiva and Brahma.

Tripitaka – canon of Buddhist scriptures.

Tripurasundari – manifestation of goddess Durga.

Trousse – Asian cutlery set in a carrying case.

Tsampa – thick barley porridge.

Tsa-tsa – Tibetan portable shrine.

Tsuba – hand guard on a Japanese sword.

Tsuishu – Japanese term for cinnabar carved lacquer.

Tsuitate – a Japanese small, one-panel wooden screen.

Tsutsugaki – Japanese dye resist decorative fabric technique.

Tunggal panaluan – carved Sumatran ritual staff.

Tungkot Malechat – Sumatran ritual carved figural staff.

Tun tun – Borneo measuring stick.

Twelve Symbols – Chinese symbols of imperial power: sun, moon, heavenly bodies, mountains, dragon, pheasant, axe, FU character, paired sacrificial vessels, water plant, fire, and rice.

Uchiwa – Japanese rigid fan.

Uki e – Japanese print with western perspective.

Ukiyo – the floating world.

Ukiyo e – pictures of the floating world, refers to woodblock prints from the Edo period.

Umbrella – one of eight symbols of Buddhism.

Urna – small bump between the eyes of Buddha.

Urushi – Japanese term for raw lacquer.

Usha – Hindu goddess of dawn.

Ushnisha – cranial protuberance at the top of Buddha's head representing supreme wisdom.

Vaisravana Vajra – thunderbolt, weapon used by Hindu deity Indra; in Tibet Dorjey.

Vajra – Tibetan ritual object.

Varaha – third incarnation of Vishnu as a boar.

Varna system – Indian caste system.

Vase – one of the eight symbols of Buddhism in China.

Vasudhara Vasuki – Hindu mythological snake who helped churn the sea of milk.

Vibisana – brother of Rahvana in the Ramayana.

Vidyadharas – Hindu mythological flying creatures.

Vihara – Hindu water monster.

Vishnu – one of the major Hindu gods.

Wabi – Japanese ideals associated with Zen Buddhism.

Wadansu – Japanese chest for small objects.

Waka – 31-syllable classical poem.

Wakizashi – Japanese medium size sword.

Warp – length-wise threads on a loom or in a carpet.

Wat – monastery complex in Cambodia and Thailand.

Wayang Golek – type of Indonesian puppet theatre using wooden puppets.

Wayang Klitik – type of Indonesian puppet theatre using leather and wooden puppets.

Wayang Kulit – type of Indonesian puppet theatre using leather puppets.

Wayang Topeng – type of Indonesian theatre with masked dancers.

Weft – horizontal threads in a textile.

Weiqi – Chinese board game played with black and white games pieces.

Wenshu – in China, the Buddhist bodhisattva of wisdom, also called Manjusri in Sanskrit, often depicted on a tiger.

Wheel engraving – engraving by a rotating wheel.

Wheel of Teaching – one of the eight Buddhist symbols, also called the wheel of the law.

Wu – Chinese term for ebony.

Wucai – Chinese term literally meaning five colours, combining underglaze blue with enamels.

Xi Wang Mu – the Chinese Queen Mother of the West who guards the fruit on the peach trees of immortality.

Xingshu – Chinese type of calligraphy, also called 'running script'.

Yab-yum – Tibetan image of sexual union symbolises the joining of wisdom and compassion.

Yaksha – Hindu male nature spirit.

Yakshi – Hindu female nature spirit.

Yama – Hindu god of death.

Yamantaka – Buddhist deity, the ferocious emanation of Manjusri, the god of wisdom.

Yamato-e – Japanese painting with Japanese themes.

Yangban – Korean aristocratic official.

Yashoda – foster mother of Krishna.

Yatate – Japanese portable case for writing implements.

Yayoi ware – early Japanese earthenware dating approximately to 250 BCE-250 CE, built by hand coiling the clay and with simple painted patterns.

Yen yen vase – vase form with an incurvate neck and baluster lower body.

Yin and Yang – complementary and dualist concept of the universe espoused by the Chinese philosopher Lao Tze.

Yingqing – Chinese type of porcelain with a pale bluish tinged glaze.

Yixing – type of Chinese unglazed brown or yellow toned ceramic often used for teawares.

Yoga – Japanese term for western painting, first popular in Japan after the beginning of the Meiji period in 1868.

Yogini – Hindu fertility goddess.

Yokthe-pwe – Burmese puppet theatre.

Yoni – Hindu symbol of the female principal.

Yorgan yuzu – in Turkey, a quilt cover.

You – archaic Chinese bronze ritual wine vessel with a handle and cover.

Yue – type of Chinese greenware.

Yumu – Chinese cabinetwood, a variety of elm.

Zarf – Turkish small size cup with shaped lip.

Zen – Japanese Buddhist sect; Chan in China, Son in Korea.

Zhang – Chinese term for camphor.

Zitan – Chinese cabinetwood of the rosewood family of dark reddish-black colour, popular during the 18th century.

Zodiac – the Chinese animals of the zodiac correspond to each of the twelve months: rat, ox, tiger, rabbit, dragon, snake, horse, goat, monkey, rooster, dog and pig.

Zun – Chinese archaic bronze vessel with flared wide mouth and tapered foot.

Zuo – Chinese term for oak.

Zushi – portable shrine.

Appendix 1

Chronological Tables

Afghanistan
Safavid Rule	1501-1736 CE
Durrani Empire	1747-1773 CE
Disunity	1809-1837 CE
British involvement	1839-1919 CE

Bhutan
State of Monyul	500 BCE-600 CE
Independent Monarchies	810 CE
Mongolian/Tibetan Occupation	11th century
Portuguese Visit	1629 CE
Tibetan Invasion	1629-1647 CE
British East India Occupation	1772-1773 CE
British Invasion	1834-1835 CE
End of theocracy and establishment of hereditary monarchy	1907 CE
Independence	1947 CE

Brunei
Islamic Sultanates	1515-1838 CE
European involvement	1839-1906 CE
British Administration	1906-1984 CE
Independent	1984-

Burma (Myanmar)
Early Pyu settlements	500-200 BCE
Formative stage of Pyu Society	200 BCE-850 CE
Burman incursions	850-1044 CE
First Burmese Empire at Pagan	1044-1287 CE
Period of fragmentation	1287-1531 CE
Second Burmese Empire	1531-1752 CE
Konbaung Dynasty	1752-1885 CE
British Crown Colony	1886-1948 CE
Independent	1948-

Byzantine Empire
Constantinople dedicated	330 CE
Roman Empire divided	395 CE
Muslim Conquest of Holy Land	639 CE
Great Schism	1054 CE
Saladin captures Jerusalem	1187 CE
Fourth Crusade sacks Constantinople	1204 CE
Constantinople falls to Ottoman Turks	1453 CE

Cambodia
Funan Period	150-550 CE
Chenla Period	550-802 CE
Khmer Empire	802-1431 CE
Sack of Angkor	1437 CE
Contested Period	1431-1863 CE
French Protectorate	1863-1953 CE
Independent	1954-

China
Xia Dynasty	2205-1766 BCE
Shang Dynasty	1766-1045 BCE
Zhou Dynasty	1045-256 BCE
W. Zhou	1045-771 BCE
E. Zhou	771-256 BCE
Spring and Autumn Period	772-481 BCE
Warring States Period	481-221 BCE
Qin Dynasty	221-206 BCE
Han Dynasty	206 BCE-220 CE
Three Kingdoms	221-280 CE
Six Dynasties	265-589 CE
Northern Dynasties	386-581 CE
Northern Wei	386-535 CE
Eastern Wei	534-550 CE
Western Wei	535-557 CE
Northern Qi	550-577 CE
Northern Zhou	557-581 CE
Sui Dynasty	589-618 CE
Tang Dynasty	618-906 CE
Five Dynasties	907-960 CE
Liao Dynasty	907-1125 CE
Song Dynasty	
Northern Song	960-1126 CE
Southern Song	1127-1279 CE
Jin Dynasty	1115-1234 CE
Yuan Dynasty	1279-1368 CE
Ming Dynasty	1368-1644 CE
Hongwu	1368-1398 CE
Jianwen	1399-1402 CE
Yongle	1403-1425 CE
Hongxi	1425 CE
Xuande	1426-1435 CE
Zhengtong	1436-1449 CE
Jingtai	1450-1457 CE
Tianshun	1457-1464 CE
Chenghua	1465-1487 CE
Hongzhi	1488-1505 CE
Zhengde	1506-1521 CE
Jiajing	1522-1566 CE
Longqing	1567-1572 CE
Wanli	1573-1620 CE
Taichang	1620 CE
Tianqi	1621-1627 CE
Chongzhen	1628-1644 CE
Qing Dynasty	1644-1911 CE
Shunzhi	1644-1662 CE
Kangxi	1662-1723 CE
Yongzheng	1723-1735 CE
Qianlong	1736-1795 CE
Jiaqing	1796-1820 CE
Daoquang	1821-1850 CE

Xianfeng	1851-1861 CE
Tongzhi	1862-1874 CE
Guangxu	1875-1908 CE
Xiantong	1908-1911 CE

Cyprus

Hittite	1500-1450 BCE
Egyptian domination	1450-1000 BCE
Phoenician dominance	850-750 BCE
Assyrian rule	750-612 BCE
Persian rule	525-333 BCE
Alexander and Heirs	333-58 BCE
Roman rule	58 BCE-395 CE
Byzantine rule	395-1191 CE
Richard Lionheart, England	1191-1192 CE
Frankish rule	1192-1489 CE
Ottoman Empire	1571-1878 CE
British Administration	1878-1925 CE
British Crown Colony	1925-1960 CE
Independent	1960-

India

Indus Valley Civilisations	2500-1500 BCE
Aryan Invasions	2000-1500 BCE
Shaishunaga Nanda Period	642-322 BCE
Maurya Period	322-185 BCE
Shunga Period	185-72 BCE
Andhra Period	70 BCE-300 CE
Kushan Period	100-300 CE
Gupta Period	320-647 CE
Medieval Period	600-1200 CE
Pala Period	730-1197 CE
Chola Period	897-1200 CE
Sultanate of Delhi	1216-1526 CE
Vijayanagar Period	1300-1565 CE
Madura Period	1646-1900 CE
Mughal Dynasty	1526-1857 CE
Babur	1526-1530 CE
Humayun	1530-1540 CE
Akbar	1556-1605 CE
Jahangir	1605-1627 CE
Shah Jahan	1627-1658 CE
Aurangajeb	1658-1707 CE
Rajput	1500-1900 CE
British East India Company	1803-1857 CE
British Crown Colony	1858-1947 CE
Independent	1947-

Indonesia

Early kingdoms	500-1377 CE
Islamic kingdoms	1290-1682 CE
European involvement	1511-1942 CE
Independence	1945-

Iran

Achaemenian Dynasty	559-330 BCE
Seleucid Dynasty	312-247 BCE
Parthian Dynasty	247 BCE-226 CE
Sassanid Dynasty	226-651 CE

Umayyad Caliphate	642-750 CE
Abbasid Caliphate	750-1258 CE
Tahirid Dynasty	821-873 CE
Saffarid Dynasty	867-1163 CE
Samanid Dynasty	829-999 CE
Buyid Dynasty	945-1055 CE
Ghaznavid Dynasty	977-1186 CE
Seljuq Dynasty	1040-1220 CE
Ilkhanid Dynasty	1256-1336 CE
Timurid Dynasty	1405-1500 CE
Safavid Dynasty	1500-1722 CE
Zand Dynasty	1747-1787 CE
Qajar Dynasty	1787-1925 CE
Pahlavi Dynasty	1925-1979 CE

Iraq

Sumerians	3500-1900 BCE
Babylonians and Assyrians	1900-500 BCE
Chaldeans	612-539 BCE
Umayyad Dynasty	661-750 CE
Abbasid Caliphate	750-1258 CE
Seljuq Dynasty	1055-1256 CE
Ilkhanids	1256-1335 CE
Safavids	1501-1638 CE
Ottoman Empire	1534-1918 CE
British Mandate	1920-1932 CE
Independent	1932-

Islamic Dynasties

Abbasids (Baghdad)	750-1258 CE
Afsharids (Persia)	1736-1796 CE
Anatolian Seljuks (Anatolia)	1077-1308 CE
Aq Qoyunha (Turkoman)	1467-1502 CE
Artuqids (Turkey)	1098-1232 CE
	1104-1408 CE
Assassins (Iran and Syria)	1090-1270 CE
Ayyubids (Iraq)	1171-1260 CE
Bahmanids (Afghan)	1347-1526 CE
Barakzai (Afghan)	1826-1973 CE
Bengallis (India)	202-1576 CE
Buyids (Iran)	932-1062 CE
Danishmends (Turkey)	1085-1173 CE
Delhi (India)	1206-1556 CE
Durrani (Afghan)	1747-1826 CE
Fatamids (Syria)	909-1171 CE
Ghaznavids (Afghan/N.India)	977-1150 CE
Ghurids (Afghan)	1150-1212 CE
Golconda (India)	1512-1687 CE
Hamdanids (Iraq/Syria)	904-1003 CE
Hashimites (Iraq/Jordan)	1916-1958 CE
Ilkhanids ((Iran/Iraq/Syria)	1252-1335 CE
Jalayirids (Iraq/Iran)	1336-1442 CE
Janids (Transoxiana)	1599-1785 CE
Khans of Khiva (C.Asia)	1511-1919 CE
Khans of Kokand (Uzbekistan)	1700-1876 CE
Khwarazm Shahs (Transoxiana)	1077-1231 CE
Mamluks (Syria/Iraq)	1250-1517 CE
Mangits (C.Asia)	1785-1921 CE
Mughals (India)	1526-1857 CE

Muzaffarids (Iran/Kurdistan)	1314-1393 CE
Ottomans (Turkey)	1280-1922 CE
Pahlavi (Iran)	1925-1979 CE
Qajars (Iran)	1779-1925 CE
Qarakhanids (Transoxiana)	840-1212 CE
Qara Qoyunlu (C. Asia)	1380-1469 CE
Qaramita (Bahrain)	899-1030 CE
Safavids (Iran)	1501-1736 CE
Saffarids (Iran)	861-903 CE
Samanids (Iran/Transoxiana)	819-999 CE
Al Saud (Arabia)	1735-
Seljuks (Afghan/Persia/Iraq)	1038-1194 CE
Shaybanids (Afghan/Transoxiana)	1500-1599 CE
Tahirids (Turkestan)	820-873 CE
Timurids (C. and W. Asia)	1363-1506 CE
Tulunids (Syria/Palestine)	868-905 CE
Umayyads (Syria)	661-750 CE
Uqaylids (Syria/Iraq)	990-1096 CE
Zangids (N.Syria/Iraq)	1127-1174 CE
Zayanids	1236-1554 CE

Israel

Canaanites and Amorites	3000 BCE
Kingdom of Israel	1023-922 BCE
Assyrian Conquest of Israel	722-539 BCE
Persian Period	538-333 BCE
Conquest by Alexander	323 BCE
Ptolemies and Selucids	320-168 BCE
Independence	142-63 BCE
Roman / Byzantine Rule	63 BCE-636 CE
Umayyad Caliphate	661-750 CE
Abbasid Caliphate	750-910 CE
Fatamid Caliphate	910-1171 CE
Crusaders	1099-1291 CE
Mamluk	1291-1516 CE
Ottoman Empire	1516-1918 CE
Independent	1948-

Japan

Jomon Period	10,500-646 BCE
Yayoi Period	300 BCE-300 CE
Kofun Period	248-646 CE
Asuka Period	552-645 CE
Nara Period	645-794 CE
Heian Period	794-1185 CE
Kamakura Period	1185-1333 CE
Nambokucho Period	1333-1392 CE
Muromachi Period	1392-1573 CE
Momoyama Period	1573-1615 CE
Edo Period	1615-1868 CE
Meiji Period	1868-1912 CE

Java

Central Java	600-900 CE
Sumatran Dominance	750-850 CE
Hindu Central Java	850-930 CE
East Javanese Period	930-1478 CE
Muslim Conquest	1400-1600 CE
Wayang Style	1400-

Jordan

Canaanites and Amorites	3000 BCE
Kingdom of Israel	1023-922 BCE
Assyrian Conquest of Israel	722-539 BCE
Conquest by Alexander	322 BCE
Maccabean Revolt	168 BCE
Roman/Byzantine Rule	63 BCE-614 CE
Destruction of Temple in Jerusalem	70 CE
Muslim Conquest	638 CE
Crusader Wars	1099-1291 CE
Creation of Jordan	1948 CE

Korea

Neolithic	6000-300 BCE
Chinese Dominion	108 BCE-313 CE
Three Kingdoms	57 BCE-668 CE
Koguryo	37 BCE-668 CE
Paekche	18 BCE-663 CE
Old Silla	57 BCE-668 CE
Unified Silla Kingdom	668-935 CE
Koryo Period	936-1392 CE
Choson Period	1392-1910 CE

Kuwait

Al-Sabah Dynasty	1760-
Independence	1961 CE

Laos

Kingdom of Lan Xang	1353-1707 CE
Internal conflict	1707-1893 CE
French Protectorate	1893-1953 CE
Independent	1953-

Lebanon

Phoenicia	2500-323 BCE
Conquest by Alexander	323 BCE
Roman/Byzantine Rule	63 BCE-661 CE
Umayyad Caliphate	661-750 CE
Abbasid Caliphate	750-910 CE
Fatamid Caliphate	910-1171 CE
Crusaders	1110-1291 CE
Mamluk	1291-1516 CE
Ottoman Empire	1516-1918 CE
French Mandate	1920-1953 CE

Malaysia

Early Kingdoms	200-1400 CE
Malay States	1400-1824 CE
European involvement	1824-1957 CE
Independent	1957-

Mongolia

Mongol Conquests	1125-1264 CE
Mongol Empire	1264-1368 CE
Tammerlane	1369-1405 CE
Period of Disunity	1369-1691 CE
Chinese Rule	1691-1911 CE
Independent Mongolia	1911-

Nepal

Birth of Buddha in Lumbini	563 BCE
Licchavi Kingdom	400-750 CE
Transitional Kingdoms	750-1200 CE
Khasa Malla Kings	1100-1484 CE
Malla Kingdom Divided	1484 CE
Gorkha Kingdom	1559-
Shah Dynasty	1768-

Oman

Umayyad Caliphate	661-750 CE
Portuguese Occupation	1508-1650 CE
Ottoman Empire	1659-1741 CE
Sultan Said bin Sultan	1804-1856 CE

Philippines

Chinese and Arab trading centres established	750-1521 CE
Spanish Colonisation	1521-1898 CE
American Colonisation	1898-1946 CE

Qatar

Al-Thani Dynasty	1850-

Saudi Arabia

Mohammed	570-632 CE
Four Rightly Guided Caliphs	632-661 CE
Umayyad Caliphate	661-750 CE
Abbasid Caliphate	750-1171 CE
Ayyubids	1171-1260 CE
Mamluks	1250-1517 CE
Ottoman Empire	1536-1634 CE
Wahhabis	1746-1932 CE
Independent	1932-

Singapore

Established as trading centre	13th century CE
British Possession	1819-1867 CE
British Crown Colony	1867-1959 CE

Sri Lanka

Early Buddhist Influences	543 BCE-161 CE
Duttha Gamani to Kassapa of Sigiriya	161-479 CE
Anuradhapura Period	500 BCE-993 CE
Chola Occupation	993-1070 CE
Polonnaruwa Kings	1070-1215 CE
Dambadeniya and Gampola Kings	1215-1411 CE
Kotte Dynasty	1412-1550 CE
Portuguese Domination	1550-1658 CE
Dutch Domination	1656-1796 CE
British Administration	1796-1948 CE
Independent	1948-

Syria

Phoencia	2500-323 BCE
Conquest by Alexander	323 BCE

Roman/Byzantine Rule	63 BCE-661 CE
Umayyad Caliphate	661-750 CE
Abbasid Caliphate	750-910 CE
Fatamid Caliphate	910-1171 CE
Crusaders	1110-1291 CE
Mamluk	1291-1516 CE
Ottoman Empire	1516-1918 CE
Independent	1918-1920 CE
Insurrection	1925-1926 CE
Independent	1946-

Thailand

Ban Chiang Culture	3500-600 BCE
Dvaravati Period	600-1000 CE
Hindu Javanese Influence	700-1000 CE
Cambodian Dominance	1022-1250 CE
Sukhothai Period	1250-1378 CE
Ayuthia Period	1351-1767 CE
Bangkok Era	1767-1932 CE

Tibet

Emperor Trisong Dezen	755-797 CE
Sakya Dynasty	1270-1358 CE
Mongolian Control	1642-1720 CE
Chinese Rule	1720-1795 CE
Independent Rule	1795-1906 CE
Chinese Rule	1906-1911 CE
Independent Rule	1918-1950 CE
Chinese Rule	1950-

United Arab Emirates

Kingdom of Hormuz	1200-1507 CE
Portuguese Control	1498-1633 CE
British Protectorate	1892-1971 CE
Independent	1971-

Vietnam

Chinese Domination	43-939 CE
Independent Rule	939-1009 CE
Ly Dynasty	1009-1225 CE
Tran Dynasty	1225-1400 CE
Le Dynasty	1428-1787 CE
Nguyen and Trinh Conflict	1626-1673 CE
Nguyen Dynasty	1802-1945 CE
French Rule	1883-1954 CE

Yemen

Umayyad Caliphate	661-750 CE
Abbasid Caliphate	750-1171 CE
Zayyid Dynasty	9th c.-1517 CE
Ottoman Empire	1517-1635 CE
British capture Aden	1839 CE
British control	1882-1918 CE
Independence of N. Yemen	1918 CE
British conflict	1918-1934 CE
United Republic of Yemen	1990-

Appendix 2

Major marks on Chinese and Japanese works of art

Xuande mark 1426-1435.

Xuande mark 1426-1435.

Xuande mark on an 18th century bronze censer.

Chenghua mark 1465-1487.

Hongzhi mark 1488-1505.

Zhengde mark 1506-1521.

Jiajing mark 1522-1566.

Jiajing mark 1522-1566.

Longqing mark 1567-1572.

Wanli mark 1573-1620.

Kangxi mark 1662-1723.

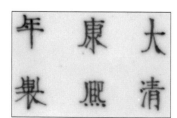

Kangxi mark 1662-1723.

Kangxi mark 1662-1723.

Yongzheng mark 1723-1735.

Yongzheng mark 1723-1735.

314

Qianlong mark 1736-1795.

Daoguang mark 1821-1850.

Guangxu mark 1875-1908.

Kai.

Jiaqing mark 1796-1820.

Tongzhi mark 1862-1874.

Hu Wen Ming Zuo.

Miyao and Ei (Eisuke).

Jiaqing mark 1796-1820.

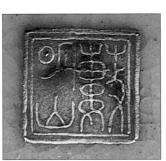

Yabu Meizan.

Fuku.

Appendix 3

Religions

All of the world's major religions originated in Asia: Christianity, Islam, Buddhism, Hinduism and Judaism. With the exception of Christianity and Judaism, the adherents of each are primarily Asian peoples. There is a strong tradition of animistic and shamanistic belief among minority tribes and peoples in Asia which is often incorporated into a major belief system. Religion has had an enormous impact on the culture and arts of Asia. The majority of figural sculpture in Asia is based on either Hindu or Buddhist images. The finest architecture is religious. The transmission of religious thought was often accomplished by representative means: calligraphy, painting and sculpture. The distinctions which arise in how these thoughts are represented and transmitted is the basis for our understanding of many of the Asian art forms.

Animism

Most Asian cultures have a belief system deeply rooted in a respect for the spirits of nature. Animate and inanimate objects are believed to possess a spiritual force which can be beneficial to humans or not, depending upon the manner in which human interaction occurs. The Nat culture in Burma is an example, with a belief in numerous nature spirits. Amulets, ritual and charms offer protection and control over demons, deities and spiritual forces, allowing the human and spirit world to coexist.

Buddhism

Buddhism was founded in 563 BCE by Siddhartha Gautama in Nepal, who after years of study reached enlightenment and assumed the title of Buddha, literally translated as 'one who has awakened'. Buddhists believe in reincarnation, cycles of birth, death and rebirth, and the possibility of reaching a state of perfection called Nirvana.

Buddhism is divided into two main sects: Hinayana, dominant in Nepal, Kashmir, Thailand, Java, Sri Lanka, and Burma; and Mahayana, found in China, Tibet, Central Asia, Korea, Japan, and Mongolia. They share the doctrines of: the Four Noble Truths and The Eight Fold Path to attaining Nirvana. The Four Noble Truths are: 1. All things are subject to the laws of cause and effect and undergo suffering; 2. Suffering is caused by self-centred desires; 3. Suffering can be made to cease; 4. Suffering can cease by following the Eight Fold Path. The Eight Fold Path is composed of: 1. Right views; 2. Right resolve; 3. Right speech; 4. Right action; 5. Right work; 6. Right effort; 7. Right mindfulness; 8. Right concentration. The Noble Truths and The Eight Fold Path together are the Dharma or Buddhist law, which will if followed allow the believer to reach a state of non-suffering or Nirvana and attain buddhahood.

There are many Buddhas of the past, present, and future and these are assisted by bodhisattvas, selfless guardians who, in order to assist mankind, voluntarily choose not to enter Nirvana and act as intermediaries between the corporal and spirit worlds. One of the most influential of the bodhisattvas is Avalokitesvara, who rules the world between the passing of the historical buddha and the arrival of the buddha of the future Maitreya. The Buddha is identified by a cranial knot or bump called the ushnisha, a mark of super human wisdom. Buddhist doctrine is taught in visual and textual form. Paintings often are organised into mandalas, a representation of the ordered Buddhist universe. The mandala shows the relationship between matter and spirit with the Buddha at the centre and with manifestations of various bodhisattvas in the cosmos. Esoteric Buddhism refers to a Buddhist branch which emphasises many manifestations of the Buddha, bodhisattvas and other beings identified by a complex iconography, stance, and gestures. Tibetan Buddhism establishes five celestial Buddhas, one for each direction and one for the earth, called Akshobhya, the Buddha of the western paradise.

Christianity

A monotheistic religion with roots in Judaism. Christians believe in the resurrection of the dead and an afterlife. A doctrine of belief is centred in the Bible, a series of letters and books drawn from Jewish texts and writings of followers of Jesus Christ, God's son and an agent of salvation for believers. Christian communities are scattered throughout all of Asia, but are mostly small minorities of the population. The first Christian state was Armenia in 301 CE, followed by the eastern branch of the Roman empire, centred in Byzantium. The declining fortunes of the Byzantine empire reduced the presence of Christians in Asia, particularly after the emergence of Islam and the conquest of Constantinople in 1453. Christians fall into many divisions; the largest is the Catholic church, followed by Orthodox and Protestant branches.

Confucianism

Founded in the 6th century BCE in China by the philosopher Kung Fu Tzu, Confucianism is primarily concerned with individual morality, ethical behaviour and the proper exercise of power by those in government. It is an ethical system of living to which rituals have been added to recognise important occasions.

Confucian belief incorporates elements of Daoism and Buddhism. There is an order in nature and human society mirrors that order. All human relationships require nurturing, mutual respect and obedience. Individuals are responsible for their actions for either good or ill. Chinese civil government is rooted in Confucian ideals.

Daoism

Founded by Lao Tze (604-531 BCE), a contemporary of Confucius, Daoism began as a set of philosophical teachings, evolving into a set of religious beliefs in the 5th century. Daoism, Buddhism and Confucianism are the principal religions of China. The Dao is an all encompassing force which permeates all matter and the goal of a believer is to achieve oneness with the Dao. Daoist divinities are manifestations of aspects of the Dao. Daoists believe in diversity in all things, good and evil, light and dark, male and female, expressed in the balance of the yin and yang. The natural balance of the cosmos was upset by human intervention. It is man's responsibility to try to restore this harmony, to nurture the essence of life, called the qi, which envelopes us all. Daoists seek solutions to problems through contemplation and meditation, see virtue in compassion, avoid excess and practise humility. Daoism is principally practised in China and was regarded as the state religion. The main guide is the I Ching, or Book of Changes which is used to suggest the right course of action through a practised reading of the eight trigrams: symbols which represent elemental forces.

Hinduism

A system of belief arising from ancient Aryan Vedic religion. Hinduism includes beliefs in local gods and spirits as well as a supreme deity who appears with many manifestations and guises. Among the Hindu deities are Brahma (the creator), Shiva, Parvati and Ganesha. Hindu worship is expressed in devotional ritual offerings to the deities. Hindus believe in the transmigration of the soul, a process by which the soul leaves the body after death and enters another body. Actions dictate whether the soul enters life at a higher or lower level. Reincarnation can include animals or plants. The inequalities of life are a direct result of the actions taken in a previous existence.

Islam

A monotheistic religion which shares common roots with Christianity and Judaism. Founded by the prophet Mohammed in 622, Islam rapidly spread throughout Asia and into Europe. The Koran is the principal religious text, believed by Muslims to be God's word. There are five pillars of Islamic teaching: 1. To recite the creed 'There is no God but God and Mohammed is his Prophet'; 2. To pray five times daily facing the holy city of Mecca; 3; To tithe regularly; 4. To fast during the holy month of Ramadan; 5. To make at least one pilgrimage (hajj) to Mecca

during one's lifetime. There are two major divisions of Islam: Shiites and Sunni. Most Muslims are Sunni. Shiite Muslims are strict traditionalists who believe in an unbroken line of leaders from Mohammed.

Jainism

Jainism contains many elements taken from both Hinduism and Buddhism. It originated in eastern India and is founded on the belief in a successive line of twenty-four Jina, miraculous beings who have overcome great trials to obtain enlightenment. The universe is layered and home to celestial beings as well as organic life. The essence of a person is his accumulation of good and evil acts, called karma. A person is reincarnated into a higher or lower state depending upon his actions. Escape from continual reincarnation is only possible through asceticism.

Judaism

A monotheistic religion with adherents worldwide and in western and central Asia. The Diaspora of the Jews began in the 6th century with the capture of Jerusalem by the Babylonians. Jewish law is enumerated in divinely inspired texts which include regulations concerning acceptable behaviour and ritual surrounding worship. The centre of worship was the temple in Jerusalem, destroyed first by the Babylonians and then the Romans in 70 CE. Following the destruction of the second temple, Jews established centres of learning and communities in most countries in western and central Asia. Judaism shares a common background with both Islam and Christianity.

Shintoism

The indigenous religion of Japan, based on worship of the Kami, a nature deity. The Kami represents all that is noble and good and permeates all matter. Shintoism recognises other spirits which are not part of the Kami and which can act for either good or ill. All things which act in harmony with each other are manifestations of the Kami. Shinto belief is non-exclusive and deeply ingrained in Japanese culture. Many Shinto believers are also Buddhists.

Zoroastrianism

An ancient religion based on the teachings of Zarathustra (c.13th century BCE). It flourished in Iran under the Sassanians but diminished in importance under Islam, with adherents eventually moving to India where they are called Parsees. Good and evil are in conflict, although ultimately good triumphs. The one created god, Ahura Mazda, assists good through emanations of himself called Yazatas. The sacred scriptures, called the Avesta, and hymns called the Gathas, express the sanctity of the creations of Ahura Mazda and the importance of protecting the purity of the four elements: fire, water, air and earth. Worship involves ritual cleansing and constant maintenance of a holy purifying fire.

Robinson, B.W. *The Baur Collection,* Geneva, 1980

Rogers, J.M. *Islamic Art and Design 1500-1700,* London, 1983
The Spread of Islam, Oxford, 1976
The Topkapi Saray Museum: The Treasury, Boston, 1987

Rosenfield, John et al. *The Courtly Tradition in Japanese Art & Literature,* Fogg Art Museum, Harvard University, Cambridge, 1973

Rowland, B. *The Art and Architecture of India,* London, 1977
The Evolution of the Budda Image, New York, 1963

Scarce, Jennifer. *Domestic Culture in the Middle East,* Edinburgh, 1996

Schaap, Robert (editor). *Meiji: Japanese Art in Transition,* Society for Japanese Arts and Crafts, Leiden, 1987

Selected Masterpieces of Asian Art, Museum of Fine Arts, Boston, 1992

Selected Treasures of National Museums of Korea, National Museum of Korea, Seoul, 1985

Sickman, L. and A. Soper. *The Art and Architecture of China,* New York, 1978

Singer, Jane Casey and Philip Denwood. *Tibetan Art: Towards a Definition of Style,* London, 1997

Singer, Robert T. (editor). *Edo: Art in Japan: 1615-1868,* National Gallery of Art, Washington, D.C., 1998

Singh, M. *Himalayan Art,* New York, 1968

Siribhadra, Smitthi and Moore, Elizabeth. *Palaces of the Gods: Khmer Art and Architecture in Thailand,* Asia Books, Bangkok, 1997

Sivaramamurti, Calambur. *The Art of India,* New York, 1974

Skelton, Robert and Francis Mark (editors). *Arts of Bengal: The Heritage of Bangladesh and Eastern India,* exhibition catalogue, Whitechapel Art Gallery, 1979

Skelton, Robert (editor). *The Indian Heritage: Court Life and Arts under Mughal Rule,* exhibition catalogue, Victoria & Albert Museum, London, 1982

Skelton, R. et al *Treasures from India: The Clive Collection at Powis Castle,* The National Trust, London, 1987

Smith, Judith. *Arts of Korea,* New York, 1998

Smith, Lawrence et al. *Japanese Art: Masterpieces in the British Museum,* London, 1990

Snellgrove, D. (editor). *The Image of the Buddha,* London, 1978

Snellgrove, D. and H.E. Richardson. *A Cultural History of Tibet,* London, 1968

Stanley-Baker, Joan. *Japanese Art,* London, 1984 and 1991

Strachan, Paul. *Imperial Pagan: Art and Architecture of Old Burma,* Honolulu, 1990

Stratton, Carol and Miriam M. Scott. *The Art of Sukhotay: Thailand's Golden Age,* Kuala Lumpur, 1981

Swallow, D. and J.Guy. *Arts of India 1550-1900,* Victoria & Albert Museum, London, 1985

The Asian Art Museum of San Francisco: Selected Works, Seattle, 1994

The Indian Heritage: Court Life and Art Under Mughal Rule, exhibition catalogue, Victoria and Albert Museum, London, 1982

The Victoria and Albert Museum, Catalogue of the Collection, New York, 1983

Thorp, Robert L. *Son of Heaven: Imperial Arts of China,* Seattle, 1988

Thurman, Robert and David Weldon. *Sacred Symbols,* exhibition catalogue, Sotheby's and Rossi and Rossi, New York, 1999

Tokugawa Art Museum, *The Shogun Age Exhibition,* Tokyo, 1983

Transactions of the Oriental Ceramic Society, Journal, London

Treasures of Islam, exhibition catalogue, Geneva and London, 1985

Tucci, G. *The Religions of Tibet,* London, 1970

Uhlig, Helmut. *On the Path to Enlightenment: The Berti Asscchmann Foundation of Tibetan Art at the Museum Reitberg,* Zurich, 1995

Victoria and Albert Museum, *Indian Art,* London, 1969

Victoria and Albert Museum. *The Indian Heritage: Court Life and Arts Under Mughal Rule,* exhbition catalogue, London, 1982

Vollmer, John E. et al. *Silk Roads, China Ships,* exhibition catalogue, Royal Ontario Museum, 1983

Von Folsach, Kjeld. *Islamic Art, The David Collection,* Copenhagen, 1990

Welch, Anthony. *Calligraphy in the Arts of the Muslim World,* Austin, 1979
Shah Abbas & The Arts of Isfahan, New York, 1973

Welch, Stuart Cary. *India: Art and Culture 1300-1900,* exhibition catalogue, Metropolitan Museum of Art, New York, 1988

Whitfield, Roderick and Pak Youngsook (editors). *Korean Art Treasures,* Seoul, 1986

Williams, Joanna. *The Art of Gupta India,* Princeton, 1982

Worlds Columbian Exposition of 1893 Revisited, Tokyo National Museum, Tokyo, 1997

Zhongguo Wenwu Jinghua (Masterpieces of Chinese Cultural Heritage), Beijing, 1997

Zimmer, Heinrich. *The Art of Indian Asia,* New York, 1955

Zwalf, W. (editor). *Buddhism: Art and Faith,* exhibition catalogue, British Museum, 1985
The Heritage of Tibet, British Museum, exhibition catalogue, London, 1982
The Shrines of Gandhara, British Museum, London, 1979

5000 Years of Korean Arts, Tokyo National Museum, Tokyo, 1976

CERAMICS

Akaboshi, Goro and Heichiro Nakamaru. *Five Centuries of Korean Ceramics,* Tokyo, 1975

Allen, James W. *Islamic Ceramics,* Oxford, 1991
Eastern Ceramics and other Works of Art from the Collection of Gerald Reitlinger, Ashmolean Museum, Oxford, 1981

Arts, P.L.W. *Japanese Porcelain,* 1983

Aslanapa, Oktay. *The Iznik Tile Kiln Excavations, Istanbul, 1984*

Atasoy, Nurhan and Raby, Julian. *Iznik: The Pottery of Ottoman Turkey,* London, 1989

Atil, Esin. *Ceramics from the World of Islam,* Freer Gallery of Art, Washington, D.C., 1975

Audsley, G.A. and J.L. Bowes. *Keramic Art of Japan,* Liverpool and London, 1975

Ayers, J. *The Baur Collection: Japanese Ceramics,* Geneva, 1982
Far Eastern Ceramics in the Victoria and Albert Museum, London, 1980
'Porcelain for Palaces, the Fashion for Japan in Europe, 1650-1758', *Oriental Ceramic Society,* London, 1990
Blanc de Chine, exhibition catalogue, China Institute., New York, 2002

Butler, Sir Michael, Medley, Margaret and Stephen Little. *Seventeenth Century Chinese Porcelain from the Butler Family Collection,* Alexandria, Virginia, 1990

Caiger-Smith, Alan. *Lustre Pottery Technique, Tradition and Innovation in Islam and the Western World,* London, 1985

Carswell, John. *Blue and White Chinese Porcelain and its Impact on the Western World,* exhibition catalogue, Chicago, 1985
Kutahya Tiles and Pottery from the Armenian Cathedral of St. James, Jerusalem, 2 vols., Oxford, 1972
'Chinese Ceramics from Allaippidy in Sri Lanka', *A Ceramic Legacy of Asia's Maritime Trade,* Oxford University Press, Singapore, 1985
Chinese Porcelain and its Impact on the Western World, exhibition catalogue, Chicago, 1985

Chinese Ceramics from Japanese Collections, exhibition catalogue, Asia House Gallery, New York, 1974

Cort, Lousie, Farhad, Massumeh and Gunter, Ann C. *Asian Tradtions in Clay: The Hague Gifts,* Smithsonian Institution, Washington, D.C. ,2000

Du Boulay, Anthony. *The Taft Collection of Chinese Porcelains,* catalogue, New York, 1995

Fehervari, Geza. *Islamic Pottery, A Comprehensive Study based on the Barlow Collection,* London, 1973

Fujioka, Ryouichi. *Shino and Oribe Ceramics,* Tokyo, New York, and San Francisco, 1977
Tea Ceremony Utensils, Tokyo, 1973

Garner, Harry. *Oriental Blue and White,* London, 1954

Godden, Geoffrey A. *Oriental Export Market Porcelain and its influence on European Wares,* London, 1979

Gompertz, G. St. G.M. *Korean Pottery and Porcelain of the Yi Period,* London, 1968

Grube, Ernst J. *Islamic Pottery of the Eighth to the Fifteenth Century in the Keir Collection,* London, 1976

Howard, David S. *A Tale of Three Cities: Canton, Shanghai & Hong Kong,* exhibition catalogue, 1997

Howard, David S. *Chinese Armorial Porcelain,* London, 1974

Howard, David and Ayers, John. *Masterpieces of Chinese Export Porcelain from the Mottahedeh Collection in the Virginia Museum,* London, 1980

Impey, Oliver R. 'Soba Cups and Other Folk Porcelains of Japan', *Transactions of the Oriental Ceramic Society 43* (1979), pp.47-65
Meiji no Takara Treasures of Imperial Japan: Porcelain I & II, London, 1995

Islamic Pottery, 800-1400 AD, Islamic Art Circle Exhibition Catalogue, Victoria & Albert Museum, London, 1969

Itoh, Ikutaro and Yutaka Mino. *The Radiance of Jade and the Clarity of Water: Korean Ceramics from the Ataka Collection,* exhibition catalogue, New York, 1991

Jenkins, Marilyn. *Islamic Pottery, A Brief History,* The Metropolitan Museum of Art, New York, 1983

Jenyns, Soame. *Later Chinese Porcelain,* Glasgow, 1971
Japanese Pottery, London, 1971
Japanese Porcelain, London, 1965

Kerr, Rose. *Chinese Ceramics: Porcelain of the Qing Dynasty 1644-1911,* Victoria and Albert Museum, 1986

Kidder, J. Edward. *Jomon Pottery,* Tokyo and Palo Alto

Ko-Shigaraki – Jars from Shigarakios Medieval Kilns, Shiga, Miho Museum, 1999

Koyama, Fujio. *The Heritage of Japanese Ceramics,* New York, Tokyo, and Kyoto

Krahl, Regina. *Chinese Ceramics in the Topkapi Saray Museum, Istanbul,* London, 1986
Chinese Ceramics in the Topkapi Saray Museum, London, 1986

Lane, Arthur. *Early Islamic Pottery,* London, 1947
Later Islamic Pottery: Persia, Syria, Egypt, Turkey, London 1957

Lawrence, Louis, *Satsuma,* London, 1991

Little, Stephen. *Chinese Ceramics of the Transitional Period: 1620-1683,* China Institute in America, exhibition catalogue, 1984

Medley, Margaret. *The Chinese Potter,* London, 1976
Yuan Porcelain and Stoneware, London, 1974
Korean and Chinese Ceramics, Fitzwilliam Museum, Cambridge, 1975

Mikami, Tsugio. *The Art of Japanese Ceramics,* New York and Tokyo, 1972

Nakagawa, Sensaku. *Kutani Ware,* Tokyo and New York, 1979

Philon, Helen. *Early Islamic Ceramics,* Benaki Museum, Athens, 1980

Pinder-Wilson, Ralph. *Islamic Pottery, 800-1400 AD,* exhibition catalogue, The Victoria and Albert Museum, London, 1969

Pope, Arthur U. *Fourteenth Century Blue and White: A Group of Chinese Porcelains in the Topkapi Sarayi Muzesi Istanbul,* Washington, D.C., 1970

Pope, John A. *Chinese Porcelains from the Ardebil Shrine,* Washington, D.C., 1981

Porter, Venetia. *Islamic Tiles,* New York, 1995
Medieval Syrian Pottery (Raqqa Ware), Ashmolean Museum, Oxford, 1981

Poster, Amy G. *From Indian Earth: 4000 Years of Terracotta,* exhibition catalogue, Brooklyn Museum, 1986

Rhodes, Daniel. *Tamba Pottery: The Timeless Art of a Japanese Village,* Tokyo, New York, and San Francisco, 1970

Rinaldi, M. *Kraak Porcelain: A Moment in the History of Trade,* London, 1989

Scanlon, George. 'Mamluk Pottery: More Evidence from Fustat', *Muqarnas 2,* 1984, pp.115-126

Scarce, Jennifer. 'Ali Mahammad Isfahani, Tile Maker of Tehran', *Oriental Art 22,* 1976, pp.278-288
'The Arts of the Eighteenth to Twentieth Centuries: Architecture, Ceramics, Metalwork, Textiles From Nadir Shah to the Islamic Republic', Peter Avery (editor), *Cambridge History of Iran,* Vol. 7, Cambridge, 1991, pp.890-958

Schiffer, Nancy N. *Japanese Porcelain 1800-1950,* Westchester, 1986

Schwaab, Dean J. *Osaka Prints,* New York, 1989

Scott, Rosemary. *Imperial Taste: Chinese Ceramics from the Percival David Foundation,* 1989

Shibata Collection, Part V, Kyushu Ceramic Museum, 1992

Smith, Lawrence. 'Japanese Porcelain in the First Half of the 19th Century', *Transactions of the Oriental Ceramic Society 39* (1974), pp.43-82

Tanaka, Migaku and Shouzou Tanabe. *Sue Ware, Nippon Toji Zehnshu,* vol.4, Tokyo, 1977

Tregear, Mary. *Song Ceramics,* Fribourg, 1982

Valenstein, Suzanne G. *A Handbook of Chinese Ceramics,* New York, 1989

Various authors, *Nihon Toji Zenshu* (A Pageant of Japanese Ceramics), 30 vol., Tokyo, 1975 and later

Watson, Oliver. *Persian Lustre Ware,* London, 1985

Watson, Oliver. 'Ceramics', *Treasures of Islam,* London, 1985

White, Joyce C. *Discovery of a Lost Bronze Age: Ban Chiang,* exhibition catalogue, Pennsylvania, 1982

Wilkinson, Charles W. *Nishapur: Pottery of the Early Islamic Period,* The Metropolitan Museum of Art, New York, 1973

Wilson, Richard L. *Inside Japanese Ceramics,* New York and Tokyo, 1995

Wood, Donald et al. *Echizen: Eight Hundred Years of Japanese Stoneware,* Birmingham Museum of Art, Birmingham, 1994

Yabe, Yoshiaki. *Kakiemon Nihon no Toki 20,* Tokyo, 1989

Yamashita, Sakuro. *Koimari to Kokutani,* Tokyo, 1968

METALWORK

Al-Jadir, Saad. *Arab and Islamic Silver,* London, 1981

Allan, James W. *Islamic Metalwork: The Nuhad Es-Said Collection,* London, 1982, 1999
Metalwork of the Islamic World, The Aron Collection, London, 1986
Nishapur Metalwork of the Early Islamic Period, New York, 1982

Atil, Esin. *Renaissance of Islam: Art of the Mamluks,* Washington, D.C., 1981
Islamic Metalwork in the Freer Gallery of Art, exhibition catalogue, Washington, D.C., 1987

Bagley, R. *Shang Ritual Bronzes in the Arthur M. Sackler Collections,* Washington, D.C., and Cambridge, Massachusetts, 1987

Barett, Douglas, *Islamic Metalwork in the British Museum,* London, 1949

Brown, Claudia. *Chinese Cloisonné: The Clague Collection,* Phoenix Museum of Art, 1980

Chase, W.T., *Ancient Chinese Bronze Art: Casting the Precious Sacred Vessel,* New York, 1991

Cohen, Lawrence A. and Dorothy C. Ferster. *Japanese Cloisonné,* New York and Tokyo, 1982

Dodds, Jerrilyn editor, *Al-Andalus: The Art of Islamic Spain,* New York, 1992

Earle, Joe. *Flower Bronzes of Japan,* Michael Goedhuis Publications, London, 1995

Fairley, Malcolm. *Japanese Enamels of the Meiji,* London, 1998

Fehervari, Geza. *Islamic Metalwork of the Eighth Century to the Fifteenth Century in the Kier Collection,* London, 1976

Fong, Wen (editor). *The Great Bronze Age of China,* Metropolitan Museum of Art, exhibition catalogue, New York, 1981

Garner, Sir Harry. *Chinese and Japanese Cloisonné Enamels,* London, 1972

Goke, Tadaomi. *Shibata Zeshin Meihinshu,* Tokyo, 1981
    Shibata Zeshin ten, Tokyo, 1980

Hillenbrand, Robert (editor). T*he Art of the Saljuqs in Iran and Anatolia,* Costa Mesa, 1994

Impey, Oliver et al. *Meiji no Takara Treasures of Imperial Japan: Metalwork I & II,* London, 1995

Kernan, John D. *The Chait Collection of Chinese Export Silver,* New York, 1985

Kerr, R. *Later Chinese Bronzes,* London, 1990

Komaroff, Linda. *The Golden Disk of Heaven: Metalwork of Timrud Iran,* Costa Mesa and New York, 1992

Lawton, Thomas. *Chinese Bronzes of the Warring States Period,* Freer Gallery of Art, Smithsonian Institution, 1982

Lester, Gerd. 'Japanese Cloisonné: Its Craftsmanship and Artistry', *Arts of Asia,* September/October, 1986, pp.96–105

Mehta, R.J. *Masterpieces of Indian Bronzes and Metal Sculptures,* Bombay, 1971

Melikian-Chirvani, A.S. *Islamic Metalwork from the Iranian World, 8th-18th Centuries,* London, 1982

Nagaswamy, R. *Masterpieces of Early South Indian Bronzes,* New Delhi, 1983

Owyoung, Steve. *Ancient Chinese Bronzes in the Saint Louis Art Museum,* 1997

Pal, Pratapaditya and Stephen Little. *A Collecting Oddysey: Indian, Himalayan, and Southeast Asian Art from the James and Marilyn Alsdorf Collection,* Chicago, 1997
    Bronzes of Kashmir, New York , 1975

Pinn, Keith. *Paktong: The Chinese Alloy in Europe 1680-1820,* Woodbridge, 1999

Pope, John Alexander et al. *The Freer Chinese Bronzes,* Vols. I, II, Washington, D.C., 1967

Rawson, Jessica. *Chinese Bronzes: Art and Ritual,* London, 1987
    The Ornament on Chinese Silver of the Tang Dynasty, London, 1982

Reedy, Chandra L. *Himalayan Bronzes: Technology, Style, and Choices,* Newark, 1997

Rogers, J. Michael and Ward, Rachel M. *Suleyman the Magnificent,* London, 1988

Scarce, Jennifer. 'The Arts of the Eigthteenth to Twentieth Centuries: Architecture, Ceramics, Metalwork, Textiles From Nadir Shah to the Islamic Republic, Peter Avery (editor), *Cambridge History of Iran,* vol. 7, Cambridge, 1991, pp.890–958

Schroeder, U. Von. *Indo-Tibetan Bronzes,* Hong Kong, 1981

Sivaramamurti, C. *South Indian Bronzes,* Lalit Kala Akademi, Bombay, 1963/1981

Stronge, Susan. *Bidri Ware: Inlaid Metalwork from India,* London, 1985

Von Schroeder, Ulrich. *Indo-Tibetan Bronzes,* Hong Kong, 1981
    The Golden Age of Sculpture in Sri Lanka, Hong Kong, 1992

Watson, W. *Ancient Chinese Bronzes,* London, London, 1977

THE ARTISAN AND CRAFTSMAN

Arms and Armour

Alexander, David. *The Art of War, Arms and Armour of the 7th to 19th Centuries,* Oxford, 1992

Blackmore, Howard L. *Guns and Rifles of the World,* New York, 1965

Bottomly, Ian and A.P. Hopson. *Arms and Armor of the Samurai,* New York, 1988

Draeger, D. F. *The Weapons and Fighting Arts of Indonesia,* Rutland, 1972, 1992

Elgood, Robert (editor). *Islamic Arms and Armour,* London, 1979
    The Arms and Armour of Arabia in the Eighteenth, Ninteenth Centuries, London, 1994
    Firearms of the Islamic World in the Tareq Rajeb Museum, Kuwait, London, 1995

Laking, G.F. *Oriental Arms & Armour,* Wallace Collection Catalogues, London, 1964

Leth, André. *Islamic Arms and Armour from Private Danish Collections,* Copenhagen, 1982

Mayer, L.A. *Islamic Armouries and other Works,* Geneva, 1962

Missillier, P. and H. Ricketts (editors). *Splendeur des Armes Orientales,* exhibition catalogue, Paris, 1988

Nicolle, David. *Arms and Armour of the Crusading Era 1050-1350, Vol. 1 Western Europe and the Crusading States, Vol. 2 Islam, Eastern Europe and Asia,* London, 1999

North, Anthony. *An Introduction to Islamic Arms,* Victoria & Albert Museum, London, 1985

Rawson, P. *The Indian Sword,* New York, 1968

Robinson, B.W. *The Arts of the Japanese Sword,* London and Boston, 1970
    The Baur Collection: Sword Fittings, Geneva, 1980

Sato, Kanzan. *The Japanese Sword,* Tokyo and New York, 1989

Spectacular Helmets of Japan, 16th-19th Century, Japan House Gallery, Japan Society, New York, 1985

Stone, George Cameron. *A Glossary of the Construction, Decoration and Use of Arms and Armor,* New York, 1961

Tavareilli, Andrew (editor). *Protection, Power, and Display: Shields of Island Southeast Asia and Melanesia,* Chestnut Hill, 1995

Yumoto, John M. *The Samurai Sword,* Tokyo, 1958

Bamboo

Masterworks of Japanese Bamboo Baskets of Form & Texture from the Collection of Lloyd Cotsen, Los Angeles, 1999

Wang, Shixiang and Wan-go, Weng. *Bamboo Carving of China,* China House Gallery, New York, exhibition catalogue, 1983

Clocks and Scientific Instruments

Mody, N.H.N. *Japanese Clocks,* Rutland and Tokyo, 1967

Nasr, Seyyed Hossein. *Islamic Science, an Illustrated Study,* Westerham, 1976

Scientific and Technical Instruments of the Qing Dynasty, The Complete Collection of the Palace Museum, Hong Kong, 1998

Glass

Barrington Haynes, E. *Glass Through the Ages,* London, 1966

Bayramoglu, Fuat. *Turkish Glass Art and Beykoz Ware,* Istanbul, 1976

Brown, Claudia and Rabiner, Donald. *Clear as Crystal Red as Flame: Later Chinese Glass,* China House Gallery, exhibition catalogue, New York, 1990

Carboni, Stefano and David Whitehouse. *Glass of the Sultans,* exhibition catalogue, Corning Museum of Glass, New York, 2001

Charleston, R.J. *Masterpieces of Glass: A World History from the Corning Museum,* New York, 1980

Clairmont, Christopher W. *Benaki Museum,* Catalogue of Ancient and Islamic Glass, Athens, 1977

Dikshit, M.G. *History of Indian Glass,* Bombay, 1969

Glass from the Ancient World, the Roy Winfield Smith Collection, The Corning Museum of Glass, Corning, New York, 1957

Hasson, R. *Early Islamic Glass,* Jerusalem, 1979

Jenkins, Marilyn. *Islamic Glass: A Brief History,* The Metropolitan Museum of Art Bulletin 44:2, 1986

Lamm, C.J. *Glass from Iran in the National Museum, Stockholm,* London, 1935

Rice, D.S. 'Early Signed Islamic Glass', *Journal of the Royal Asiatic Society,* April, 1958

Von Saldern, A. *Glass 500 BC to AD 1900: The Hans Cohn Collection,* Mainz, 1980

Gourds

Wang Shixiang. *The Charms of the Gourd,* Hong Kong, 1993

Ivory

Fabri, Charles. *History of the Art of Orissa,* New Delhi, 1977

History of Japanese Ivory Carving, The Shoto Museum of Art, Tokyo, 1996

Kramrisch, Stella. 'Early Indian Ivory Carving', *Philadelphia Museum of Art Bulletin 54* (1959), pp.55-66

Pal, Pratapaditya. *Elephants and Ivories in South Asia,* exhibition catalogue, Los Angeles County Museum of Art

St. Aubyn, F. (editor). *Ivory: A History and Collectors Guide,* London, 1987

Hardstone and Jade Carvings

Bishop, Peter Reginald. *The Bishop Collection,* Vol. 1, 2, New York, 1906

Catalogue of a Special Exhibition of Hindustan Jade in the National Palace Museum, exhibition catalogue, Taipei, 1983

Childs-Johnston, E. *Ritual and Power: Jades of Ancient China,* China Institute in America, New York, 1988

Chinese Jade Throughout the Ages, Victoria and Albert Museum, London, 1974

Chinese Jades, Archaic and Modern from the Minneapolis Institute of Art, Tokyo, 1974

DoArgence, Rene-Yvon Lefebvre. *Chinese Jades in the Avery Brundage Collection,* Asian Art Museum of San Francisco, 1972

Dohrenwend, Doris. *Chinese Jades in the Royal Ontario Museum,* Toronto, 1971

Forsyth, Angus and Brian McElney. *Jades from China,* Museum of East Asian Art, Bath, 1994

Hanford, S. Howard. *Chinese Carved Jades,* London, 1968

Hung, Wu and Brian Morgan. *Chinese Jade from the Mu-Fei Collection,* London, 1990

Keverne, Roger (editor). *Jade,* London, 1991

Kleiner, Robert. *Chinese Jades from the Collection of Alan and Simone Hartman,* Hong Kong, 1996

Lawton, Thomas et al. *Chinese Art in the Arthur M. Sackler Gallery,* Smithsonian Institution, Washington, D.C., 1987

Lohr, M. *Ancient Chinese Jades from the Grenville L. Winthrop Collection in the Fogg Art Museum,* Harvard University, Cambridge, Massachusetts, 1975

Morgan, Brian. *Dr. Newton's Zoo: Post Archaic Small Jade Animal Carvings,* Bluett and Sons, London, 1981

Moss, Hugh and Gerard Tsang. *Arts from the Scholar's Studio,* Hong Kong, exhibition catalogue, 1986

Na Zhiliang. *Chinese Jades: Archaic and Modern from the Minneapolis Institute of Arts, Rutland,* Vermont and London, 1977

Dictionary of Chinese Jades, Taipei, 1982

National Palace Museum. *Illustrated Catalogue of Ancient Jade Artefacts in the National Palace Museum,* Taipei, 1982

Nott, Stanley Charles. *Chinese Jade throughout the Ages,* Tokyo, 1972

Pinder-Wilson, R. 'Some Rock Crystals of the Islamic Period', *The British Museum Quarterly,* 19, pp.84-87, London, 1954

Rawson, Jessica. *Chinese Jade from the Neolithic to the Qing,* British Museum, London, 1980

Rawson, Jessica and Ayers, John. *Victoria and Albert Museum: Chinese Jade throughout the Ages,* London, 1975

Schneeberger, Pierre. *The Baur Collection: Jades,* Geneva, 1972

Skelton, Robert. 'The Relations Between the Chinese and Indian Jade Carving Traditions', *The Western Influence of the Chinese Arts from the 14th to the 18th Century, Colloquies on Art and Archaeology in Asia,* no. 3, London, 1972

'The Shah Jahan Jade Cup', *Victoria and Albert Museum Bulletin 2* (1966), pp.109-110

Teng Shu-ping. *Hindustan Jades in the National Palace Museum,* exhibiton catalogue, Taipei, 1983

Watt, J.C.Y. *Chinese Jades from the Collection of the Seattle Art Museum,* Seattle, 1989

Chinese Jades from Han to Ching, Asia Society, 1980

Zhongguo Meishu. *Zhongguo Meishu Quanji (Treasures of Chinese Arts and Crafts), Vol. 9, Jade,* Beijing, 1986

Jewellery

Brunel, Francis. *Jewelry of India: Five Thousand Years of Tradition,* New Delhi, 1972

Caplan, A. 'An Important Carved Emerald from the Mogul Period of India', *Lapidary Journal 22,* 1968, pp.1336-37

Colyer Ross, Heather. *Bedouin Jewelry in Saudi Arabia,* London, 1978

Content, Derek J. *Islamic Rings & Gems,* The Zucker Collection, London, 1987

Gerlach, Martin. *Primitive and Folk Jewelry,* New York, 1971

Hasson, Rachel. *Early Islamic Jewelry,* Jerusalem, 1987

Later Islamic Jewelry, Jerusalem, 1987

Islamic Jewellery, Spink and Son Ltd., London, 1986

Islamic and Hindu Jewellery, Spink and Son Ltd., London, 1988

Jenkins, Marilyn and Manuel Keene. *Islamic Jewelry in the Metropolitan Museum of Art,* New York

Markevitch, Elizabeth (editor). *Indian Jewelry,* London, 1987

Stronge, Susan et al. *A Golden Treasury: Jewellery from the Indian Subcontinent,* Victoria and Albert Museum, London, 1988

Masks, Puppets, Dolls

Clara van Groenendael, Victoria. *Wayang Theatre in Indonesia: An Annotated Bibliography,* Dordrecht, 1987

Hatley, Barbara. *Ketoprak Theatre and the Wayang Tradition,* Melbourne, 1979

Leiter, Samuel (editor). *Japanese Theater in the World,* Japan Society, New York, 1997

323

Nunley, John W. and McCarty, Cara. *Masks: Faces of Culture,* exhibition catalogue, St. Louis Art Museum, New York, 2000

Inro and Netsuke

Arakawa, Hirokazu. *The Go Collection of Netsuke,* New York, 1983
'Inro and Netsuke', *Nihon no Bijutsu (Arts of Japan),* Nara National Museums, August, 1981

Baker, Richard and Lawrence Smith, *Netsuke: The Miniature Sculpture of Japan,* London, 1976

Bushell, Raymond. *The Netsuke Handbook,* Rutland and Tokyo, 1985
Collector's Netsuke, New York, 1971
The Inro Handbook: Studies of Netsuke, Inro, and Lacquer, New York, 1979
Netsuke Familiar and Unfamiliar, New York, 1975
Netsuke Masks, Tokyo, 1985
The Wonderful World of Netsuke, Rutland and Tokyo, 1964
The Netsuke Handbook of Ueda Reikichi, Tokyo and Vermont, 1961

Contemporary Netsuke: Selected Ojime and Related Arts, Michael Spindel Ltd., 1993

Davey, Neil. *Netsuke: A Comprehensive Study Based on the M.T. Hindson Collection of Netsuke,* London, 1982

Davey, Neil and Susan G. Tripp. *The Garrett Collection of Lacquer, Inro, Netsuke,* Baltimore, 1993

Ducros, Alain. *Netsuke et Sagemono,* 1987

Edwards, Lisa A. and Margie M. Krebs. *Netsuke: The Collection of the Peabody Museum of Salem,* 1980.

Harris, Victor. *Netsuke: The Hull Grundy Collection in the British Museum,* British Museum, London, 1987

Hurtig, Bernard. *Masterpieces of Netsuke Art,* New York, 1973

Hutt, Julia. *Japanese Inro,* London, 1997

Ishizawa Masao and Barbra Teri Okada. *Netsuke* Exhibition, 1981

Kinsey, Miriam. *Contemporary Netsuke,* Rutland, 1977

Lazarnick, George. *The Signature Book of Netsuke, Inro, and Ojime Artists in Photographs,* Honolulu, 1976
Netsuke and Inro Artists and How to Read their Signatures, Honolulu, 1982

Meinertzhagen, Frederick and George Lazarnick (editors). *The Meinertzhagen Card Index on Netsuke in the Archives of the British Museum, Parts A and B,* New York, 1986

Stern, Harold P. *The Magnificent Three, Lacquer, Netsuke, and Tsuba: Selections from the Collection of Charles A. Greenfield,* Japan House Gallery, New York, 1972

Wrangham, E.A. *The Index of Inro Artists,* Northumberland, 1995

Rocks

Mowry, Robert D. *Worlds Within Worlds: The Richard Rosenblum Collection of Chinese Scholars' Rocks,* exhibition catalogue, Harvard University, Cambridge, Massachusetts, 1997

Sculpture

Czuma, S. *Kushan Sculpture: Images from Early India,* exhibition catalogue, Cleveland Museum of Art, 1985

Fontein, Jan. *The Sculpture of Indonesia,* exhibition catalogue, Washington, D.C., 1990

Frederic, Louis. *Indian Temples and Sculpture,* London, 1959

Gupta, S.P. *Kushana Sculptures from Sanghol: A Recent Discovery,* New Delhi, 1985

Knox, Robert. *Amaravati: Buddhist Sculptures from the Great Stupa,* Trustees of the British Museum, London, 1992

Kramrisch, Stella. *Indian Sculpture in the Philadelphia Museum of Art,* Philadelphia, 1960

Lippe, Aschwin de. *The Freer Indian Sculptures,* Washington, D.C., 1970

Marshall, Sir J. *The Buddhist Art of Gandhara,* Cambridge, 1960

Nishikawa, Kyotaro and Emily J. Sano. *The Great Age of Japanese Buddhist Sculpture AD 600-1300,* Japan Society, New York, 1982

Pal, Pratapaditya. *The Sensuous Immortals, A Selection of Sculptures from the Pan-Asian Collection,* exhibition catalogue, Los Angeles County Museum of Art, Los Angeles, 1977

Russek, R. *Buddha Zwishen Ost & West: Skulputuren aus Gandhara/Pakistan,* exhibition catalogue, Rietberg Museum, Zurich, 1986

Saunders, E. Dale. *Mudra: A Study of Symbolic Gestures in Japanese Buddhist Sculpture,* New York, 1960

Singer, Jane Casey and David Weldon. *The Sculptural Heritage of Tibet, Buddhist Art in the Nyingjei Lam Collection,* London, 1999

Tomii, Reiko and Kathleen M. Friello (editors) *Enlightenment Embodied: The Art of the Japanese Buddhist Sculptor (7th-14th Centuries),* Japan Society, New York, 1997

Zwalf, W. *A Catalogue of Gandharan Sculpture in the British Museum,* Vol. I, London, 1985

Seals, Inkstones, Inkcakes, etc.

Contag, Victoria and Wang Chi-Chien. *Seals of the Chinese Painters and Collectors of the Ming and Ching Periods,* Hong Kong, 1968

Tobacco, Snuff Bottles

Bushell, Raymond. 'Kiseruzutsu: The Japanese Pipe Case', *Arts of Asia,* November/December, 1980, pp 86-95.

Hall, Robert. *Chinese Snuff Bottles I-IV,* London, 1987-1991

Hui, Humphrey K.F. et al. *Hidden Treasures of the Dragon: Chinese Snuff Bottles from the Collections of Humphrey K.F. Hui, Margaret Polak, and Christopher C.H. Sin,* Hong Kong, 1991

Kleiner, Robert. *Precious Playthings: Important Snuff Bottles from the Mack Collection,* exhibition catalogue, London, 2000
Chinese Snuff Bottles from the Collection of John Ault, London, 1990

Moss, Hugh et al. *The Art of the Chinese Snuff Bottle,* New York and Toyko, 1993

Stevens, Bob C. *The Collectors Book of Snuff Bottles,* New York, 1980

Tribal Art

Barbier, Jean-Paul. *The Art of Nagaland,* exhibition catalogue, Los Angeles County Museum of Art, 1984

Barbier, Jean Paul and Douglas Newton (editors). *Islands and Ancestors: Indigenous Styles of Southeast,* New York, 1988

Kramrisch, Stella. *Unknown India: Ritual Art in Tribe and Village,* exhibition catalogue, Philadelphia Museum of Art, 1968

Sather, Clifford. *Posts, Hearths, and Thresholds: 'The Iban Longhouse as a Ritual Structure', Inside Austronesian Houses,* Canberra, 1993, pp.64-115

Taylor, Paul and Lorraine V. Aragon. *Beyond the Java Sea: Art of Indonesia's Outer Islands,* New York, 1991

FURNITURE, LACQUER, WOODWORK

Berliner, Nancy et al. *Beyond the Screen: Chinese Furniture of the 16th and 17th Centuries,* Museum of Fine Arts, Boston, 1996

Clunas, Craig. *Chinese Furniture,* Victoria and Albert Museum, London, 1988

Ecke, Gustav. *Chinese Domestic Furniture,* Rutland, Tokyo, and Hong Kong, 1962

Ellsworth, Robert Hatfield. *Chinese Furniture: One Hundred Examples from the Mimi and Raymond Hung Collection,* New York, 1996
Chinese Hardwood Furniture in Hawaiian Collections, Honolulu Academy of Arts, 1982

Handler, Sarah. *The Austere Luminosity of Chinese Classical Furniture,* Berkeley, California, 2001

Jacobsen, Robert D. *Classical Chinese Furniture in the Minneapolis Institute of Arts,* Chicago, 1999

Koizumi, Kazuko. *Traditional Japanese Furniture,* Tokyo, 1986

Tian Jiaqing. *Classic Chinese Furniture of the Qing Dynasty,* Hong Kong, 1996

Veenendaal, Jan. *Furniture from Indonesia, Sri Lanka, and India during the Dutch Period,* Delft, 1985

Wang Shi Xiang. *Connoisseurship of Chinese Furniture,* Hong Kong, 1990

Wang Shi Xiang et al. *Classical and Vernacular Chinese Furniture in the Living Environment,* Hong Kong, 1996

Weldon, David. *Early Tibetan Manuscript Covers, 12th - 15th Century,* exhibition catalogue, Barbara Mathes Gallery, Anna Maria Rossi and Fabio Rossi, 1996

Wickmann, Michael. *Korean Chests: Treasures of the Yi Dynasty,* Seoul, 1978

Wright, Edward Reynolds and Pai, Man Sill. *Traditional Korean Furniture,* Tokyo, 2000

Lacquer

Boyer, Martha. *Catalogue of Japanese Lacquers,* The Walters Art Gallery, Baltimore, 1970

Dean, Michael. *Japanese Lacquer,* Kyoto, 1984

Fraser-Lu, Sylvia. *Burmese Crafts: Past and Present,* Singapore, 1994
Burmese Lacquerware, Bangkok, 1985

Garner, Sir Harry. *Chinese Lacquer,* London, 1979

Herberts, K. *Oriental Lacquer,* New York, 1949

Jahss, Melvin and Betty. *Inro and other miniature forms of Japanese Lacquer Art,* Rutland Vermont and Tokyo, 1981

Kuwayama, George. *Far Eastern Lacquer,* exhibition catalogue, Los Angeles County Museum of Art, 1982

Lacquer Art, Metropolitan Museum of Art, New York, 1992

Lam, Peter Y.K. (editor). *2000 Years of Chinese Lacquer,* exhibition catalogue, The Chinese University of Hong Kong, 1993

Okada, Barbra Teri. *A Sprinkling of Gold: The Lacquer Box Collection of Elaine Ehrenkranz,* The Newark Museum, Newark, 1983

Pekarik, Andrew. *Japanese Lacquer 1600-1900.* The Metropolitan Museum of Art, New York, 1980

Phillips, Phoebe. *Lacquer: An International History and Illustrated Survey,* New York, 1984

Rague, Beatrix Von. *A History of Japanese Lacquerwork,* Toronto, 1976

Watt, James C.Y. and Ford, Barbara Brennan. *East Asian Lacquer,* New York, 1991

Yonemura, Ann. *Japanese Lacquer,* Freer Gallery of Art, Washington, D.C., 1979

Yu-Kuan, Lee. *Oriental Lacquer Art,* New York and Tokyo, 1972

TEXTILES

Adams, Marie Jeanne. *System and Meaning in East Sumba Textile Design: A Study in Traditional Indonesian Art,* Southeast Asia Studies Cultural Report Series 16, New Haven, 1969

Baker, Patricia L. *Islamic Textiles,* London, 1995

Beattie, May H. *Carpets of Central Persia,* Westerham, 1976

Bennett, Ian. *Rugs and Carpets of the World,* London, 1977

Bier, Carol (editor). *Woven from the Soul, Spun from the Heart: Textile Arts of Safavid and Qajar Iran 16th-19th Centuries,* Washington, D.C., 1987

Black, David. *The Macmillan Atlas of Rugs & Carpets,* New York, 1985

Bode, W. and E. Kuhnel. *Antique Rugs from the Near East,* Germany, 1958

Dimand, M.S. and Jean Mailey. *Oriental Rugs in the Metropolitan Museum of Art,* New York, 1973

Eiland, Jr., Murray L. and Murray Eiland III. *Oriental Carpets: A complete guide,* New York, 1998

Eiland, M. *Chinese and Exotic Rugs,* London, 1979

Ellis, Charles Grant. Oriental *Carpets in the Philadelphia Museum of Art,* Philadelphia, 1988

Erdmann, Kurt. *Seven Hundred Years of Oriental Carpets,* Berkely, Los Angeles and London, 1970
The History of the Early Turkish Carpet, London, 1977

Fiske, Patricia L., W. Russell Pickering, and Ralph S. Yohe (editors). *From the Far West: Carpets and Textiles of Morocco,* exhibition catalogue, Washington, D.C., 1980

Folsach, Kjeld von and Keblow Bernsted, Anne Marie. *Woven Treasures – Textiles from the World of Islam,* Copenhagen, 1993

Franses, Michael. 'Early Ningsia Carpets', *Hali,* vol.5, no. 2, London, 1982

Gillow, John. *Traditonal Indonesian Textiles,* London, 1993

Gittinger, Mattiebelle. *Splendid Symbols: Textiles and Tradition in Indonesia,* The Textile Museum of Washington, 1979
Indonesian Textiles, Irene Emery Roundtable on Museums Textiles, 1979
To Speak with Cloth, Studies in Indonesian Textiles, Museum of Cultural History, Los Angeles, 1989
Master Dyer to the World: Technique and Trade in Early Indian Dyed Cotton Textiles, Washington, D.C., 1982

Holmgren, Robert J. and Anita E. Spertus. *Early Indonesian Textiles from three Island Cultures: Sumba, Toraja, Lampung,* The Metropolitan Museum of Art, New York, 1989

Imperial Ottoman Textiles, exhibition catalogue, Colnaghi Gallery, 1980

Irwin, John and Katherine B. Brett. *Origins of Chintz,* London, 1970

Irwin, John. *The Kashmir Shawl,* London, 1973

Irwin, John and Margaret Hall. *Indian Painted and Printed Fabrics,* Ahmedabad, 1971
Indian Embroideries, Ahmedabad, 1973

Kahlenberg, Mary Hunt (editor). *Textile Traditions of Indonesia,* Los Angeles County Museum of Art, Los Angeles, 1977

Kuman, Rita. *Costumes and Textiles of Royal India,* London, 1999

Mackie, Louise W. *The Splendor of Turkish Weaving: an exhition of silks and carpets of the 13th-18th centuries,* Washington, D.C., 1973

Maxwell, Robyn. *Textiles of Southeast Asia: Tradition, Trade, and Transformation,* Australian National Gallery, Melbourne, 1990

Milanesi, Enza. *The Bulfinch Guide to Carpets,* New York, 1993

O'Connor, Deryn. *Miao Costumes from Guizhou Province, South West China,* Farnham, 1994

Oriental Carpets and Textiles, Bernheimer Fine Arts, London, 1987

Pinner, Robert and Michael Franses. 'East Mediterannean Carpets in the Victoria and Albert Museum: The East Mediterranean Collection', *Hali,* Vol. 4, No. 1, London, 1981

Raby, Julian. 'Court and Export: Part 1 Market Demands in Ottoman Carpets 1450-1550', *Oriental Carpet and Textile Studies II: Carpets of the Mediterranean Countries 1400-1600,* London, 1986, pps 29-38

Scarce, Jennifer. 'The Arts of the Eigthteenth to Twentieth Centuries: Architecture, Ceramics, Metalwork, Textiles' From Nadir Shah to the Islamic Republic, Peter Avery (editor), *Cambridge History of Iran,* vol. 7, Cambridge, 1991, pps 890-958

Simcox, J. *Chinese Textiles,* London, 1994

Spuhler, Fredrich. *Oriental Carpets in the Museum of Islamic Art,* Bulletin, London, 1988
  Islamic Carpets and Textiles in the Keir Collection, London, 1978

Stead, Rexford. *The Ardabil Carpets,* Malibu, 1974

Warming, Wanda and Michael Gaworski. *The World of Indonesian Textiles,* London, 1981

Watt, J. and A. Wardwell. *When Silk was Gold,* Cleveland, 1997

Weir, Shelagh. *Palestinian Costumes,* London, 1989

Wrentz, H.A. *A View of Chinese Rugs, from the 17th to the 20th Century,* London, 1972

PAINTINGS AND PRINTS

All the Woodblock Prints by Shinsui Ito, Tokyo, 1992

Arberry, A. et al. (editor). *The Chester Beatty Library: A Catalogue of the Persian Manuscripts and Miniatures,* 3 vols., Dublin, 1959-1962

Archer, Mildred. *Between Battles: The Album of Colonel James Skinner,* London, 1982
  Indian Paintings from the Punjab Hills, Vol.I, London, 1973
  Visions of Courtly India, London, 1976
  Indian Popular Painting in the India Office Library, London, 1977
  India and British Portraiture 1770-1825, London, 1979
  Early Views of India, London, 1980

Archer, William G. and Edwin Binney, 3rd. *Rajput Miniatures from the Collection of Edwin Binney, 3rd,* exhibition catalogue, Portland, 1968

Arnold, Thomas. *The Library of A. Chester Beatty: A Catalogue of the Indian Miniatures,* 3 vols., London, 1936

Art of the Orient, Vol. II. *Handbook of the Collections in the William Rockhill Nelson Gallery of Art and Mary Atkins Museum of Fine Arts,* Kansas City, 1973

Arts from the Scholar's Studio, The Oriental Ceramic Society of Hong Kong and the Fung Ping Shan Museum, University of Hong Kong, 1986

Ashrafi, M.M. *Persian-Tajik Poetry in XIV-XVII Centuries Miniatures,* Dushanbe, 1974

Asiatic Art in the Rijksmuseum, Amsterdam. Amsterdam, 1985

Aslanapa, Oktay. 'The Art of Bookbinding', *Arts of the Book in Central Asia,* Basil Gray (editor), pp.59-91

Atasoy, Nurhan and Filiz Cagman. *Turkish Miniature Painting,* Istanbul, 1974

Atil, Esin. *The Brush of the Masters: Drawings from Iran and India,* Washington, D.C., 1978
  'Mamluk Painting in the Late Fifteenth century', *Muqarnas,* 1984, pp.163-169
  'Ottoman Miniature Painting Under Sultan Mehmed 11', *Ars Orientalis 9,* 1973, pps 103-120

Barnhart, Richard M. *Peach Blossom Spring,* New York, 1983
  Painters of the Great Ming: The Imperial Court and the Zhe School, Dallas, 1993

Bartholomew, Therese Tse. 'Thangkas of the Qianlong Period', *Tibetan Art: Towards a Definition of Style,* London, 1997

Beach, Milo. *The Imperial Image: Paintings for the Mughal Court,* Smithsonian Institution, 1981
  The Grand Mogul: Imperial Painting in India 1600-1660, exhibition catalogue, Williamstown, 1978
  Mughal and Rajput Painting, New Cambridge History of India, Cambridge, 1992

Bickford, M., *Bones of Jade, Souls of Ice: The flowering Plum in Chinese Art,* New Haven, 1985

Binney, 3rd, Edwin. *Indian Miniature Painting from the Collection of Edwin Binney, 3rd: Mughal and Deccani Schools,* Portland, 1973

Binyon, Laurence, J.V.S. Wilkinson, and Basil Gray. *Persian Miniature Painting,* New York, 1971

Blair, Sheila S. 'The Development of the Illustrated Book in Iran', *Muqarnas 10,* 1993, pp.266-274

Bosch, Gulnar, John Carswell, and Guy Petherbridge. *Islamic Bindings and Bookmaking,* exhibition catalogue, Chicago, 1981

Brauen, M. *The Mandala Sacred Circle in Tibetan Buddhism,* London, 1997

Brijbhushan, Jamila. *The World of Indian Miniatures,* New York, 1979

Brinker, Helmut and Eberhard Fischer. *Treasures from the Rietbert Museum,* New York, 1980

Brown, Kendall H. and Hollis Goodall-Cristante. *Shin Hanga, New Prints in Modern Japan,* Los Angeles County Museum of Art, Los Angeles, 1996

Cagman, Filiz and Zeren Tanindi. *The Topkapi Saray Museum: The Albums and Illustrated Manuscripts,* Boston, 1986

Cahill, J., *Chinese Painting,* Lausanne, 1960
  Fantastics and Eccentrics in Chinese Painting, New York, 1967
  The Restless Landscape: Chinese Painting of the Late Ming Period, University Art Museum, Berkeley, 1971
  Hills Beyond a River: Chinese Painting of the Yuan Dynasty, 1279-1368, New York and Tokyo, 1976
  Parting at the Shore: Chinese Painting of the Early and Middle Ming Dynasty, 1368-1580, New York and Tokyo, 1978
  The Compelling Image: Nature and Style in Seventeenth Century Chinese Painting, Cambridge, Massachusetts, 1982
  An Index of Early Chinese Painters and Painting, Tang, Sung, and Yuan, Berkeley, Los Angeles, London, 1980
  The Distant Mountains: Chinese Painting of the late Ming Dynasty 1570-1644, New York, 1982

Canby, Sheila. *Persian Painting,* London and New York, 1993
  Princes, Poets, and Paladins: Islamic and Indian Paintings from the Collection of Prince and Princess Sadruddin Aga Khan, London, 1998

Chang, Leon Long-Yien and Peter Miller. *Four Thousand Years of Chinese Calligraphy,* Chicago and London, 1990

Clark, Timothy T. and Osamu Ueda. *The Actor's Image: Print Makers of the Katsukawa School,* The Art Institute of Chicago, Princeton University Press, 1994

Cohen, J. Lebold, *The New Chinese Painting 1949-1986,* New York, 1987

Collection of Woodblock Prints by Hiroshi Yoshida, Tokyo, 1976

Cowen, Jill Sanchia. *Kalila wa Dimna: an Animal Allegory of the Mongul Court,* New York and Oxford, 1989

Crighton, R.A. *The Floating World,* Victoria & Albert Museum, London, 1973

Das, Asok Kumar. *Mughal Painting During Jahangir's Time,* Calcutta, 1978

Dawes, Leonard G. *Japanese Illustrated Books,* Victoria & Albert Museum, London, 1972

Diba, L. *Royal Persian Paintings: The Qajar Epoch 1725-1925,* Brooklyn, 1998

Dickson, Martin B. and Stuart Cary Welch. *The Houghton Shahnama,* 2 vols., Cambridge, 1982

Ecke, Tseng Yu-Ho. *Chinese Calligraphy,* Philadelphia, 1971

Eight Hundred Years of Japanese Print Making, Museum of Art, Carnegie Institute, Pittsburgh, 1976-1977

Ellsworth, R.H. *Later Chinese Painting and Calligraphy, 1800-1950,* 3 Vols., New York, 1987

Ettinghausen, Richard. *Arab Painting,* Geneva, 1962
  Paintings of the Sultans and Emperors of India in American Collections, Delhi, 1961
Exquisite Visions: Rimpa Paintings from Japan, Honolulu Academy of Arts in association with Japan House Gallery, Honolulu, 1980
Falk, Toby (editor). *Treasures of Islam,* Geneva, 1985
  Indian Miniatures in the India Office Library, London, 1981
Farrer, A. *The Brush Dances and the Ink Sings: Chinese Paintings and Calligraphy from the British Museum,* exhibition catalogue, London, 1990
Fisher, Carol G. (editor). *Brocade of the Pen: The Art of Islamic Writing,* exhibition catalogue, East Lansing, 1991
Fong, Wen C. *Images of the Mind,* Princeton, 1984
Forrer, Marthi. *Hokusai,* Munich, 1991
Fu Shen and Stuart, J. *Challenging the Past Galerkina, Olympiada. Mawarannahr Book Painting,* Leningrad, 1980
Ghosh, D.P. *Medieval Indian Painting: Eastern School,* Delhi, 1982
Giacalone, Vito (editor). T*he Eccentric Painters of Yangzhou,* New York, 1990
Grabar. Oleg. *The Illustrations of the Maqamat,* Chicago, 1984
Grabar, Oleg and Sheila Blair. *Epic Images and Contemporary History: The Illustration of the Great Mongol Shah-nama,* Chicago, 1980
Gray, Basil. *Persian Painting,* Geneva, 1961
Grube, Ernst. *The Classical Style in Islamic Painting: The Early School of Herat and Its Impact on Islamic Painting of the 15th, the 16th and 17th Centuries,* Geneva, 1968
Grube, E.J. *Persian Painting in the Fourteenth Century: A Research Report* Supplement no. 17, Institute Orientale di Napoli, 38, 1978
  The Classical Style in Islamic Painting, The Early School of Herat and its Impact of Islamic Painting of the Later 15th, 16th, and 17th Centuries, Some Examples in American Collections, New York, 1968
Gugong Bowuyuan Can Lidi Fashu Xuanji (Chinese Calligraphy from all Ages from the Palace Museum), Beijing, 1963
Gugong Fashu (Chinese Calligraphy from the National Palace Museum), 21 vols., Taipei, 1962-1968
Gugong Fashu Xuan Cui (Masterworks of Chinese Calligraphy from the National Palace Museum, 2 vols., Taipei, 1970
Gugong Shuhualu (Catalogue of Paintings and Calligraphy in the Palace Museum), 4 vols., Taipei, 1965
Guy, J. *Palm-leaf and Paper: Illustrated Manuscripts of India and South-East Asia,* exhibition catalogue, National Gallery of Victoria, Melbourne, 1982
Haldane, Duncan. *Islamic Bookbindings in the Victoria and Albert Museum,* London, 1983
Heeramaneck, Alice. *Masterpieces of Indian Painting in the Nasli M. Heermaneck Collection,* New York, 1985
Hillenbrand, Robert. *Imperial Images in Persian Paintings,* Edinburgh, 1977
Hillier, Jack. *Japanese Prints & Drawings from the Vever Collection,* New Jersey, 1976
  The Art of the Japanese Book, Volume one, London, 1987
Hillier, J. and Lawrence Smith. *Japanese Prints: 300 Years of Albums and Books,* London, 1980
Hiroshige and the Utagawa School, 1810-1860, exhibition catalogue, Amsterdam, 1984
Ho, Wai-kam et al. *Eight Dynasties of Chinese Painting: The Collection of the Nelson Gallery,* Atkins Museum, and the Museum of Art, Cleveland, 1980
  The Century of Dong Qichang 1555-1635, Seattle, 1992
Huntington, Susan L. and John C. Huntington. *Leaves from the Bodhi Tree: The Art of Pala India (8th-12th Centuries) and in International Legacy,* exhibition catalogue, Dayton Art Institute, 1990

Illing, Richard. *The Art of Japanese Prints,* London, 1980
Ismailova, A.M. *Oriental Miniatures,* Tashkent, 1980
Izzard, Sebastian. *Hiroshige: an Exhibition of Selected Prints and Illustrated Books,* New York, 1983
Jackson, D. *A History of Tibetan Painting,* Vienna, 1996
James, David. *After Timur: Quroans of the 15th and 16th Centuries,* London, 1992
  The Master Scribes: Quroans of the 10th to 14th Centuries, London, 1992
Japanese Art and Design, Victoria and Albert Museum, London, 1986
Kanazawa, Hiroshi. *Japanese Ink Painting: Early Zen Masterpieces,* Tokyo, 1979
Kandalavala, Karl and Kalpana Desai. *Indian Illustrated Manuscripts of the Kalilah wa Dimnah, A Mirror for Princes from India,* Bombay, 1991
Keyes, Roger S. *Courage and Silence: A Study of the Life and Color Woodblock Prints of Tsukioka Yoshitoshi, 1839-1892.* Ann Arbor, 1982
Keyes, Roger S. and Keiko Mizushima. *The Theatrical World of Osaka Prints,* Philadelphia, 1973
Kondo, Ichitaro. *Japanese Genre Painting: The Lively Art of Renaissance Japan,* Rutland, 1961
Kossak, Steven M. and Jane Casey Singer. *Sacred Visions: Early Paintings from Central Tibet,* exhibition catalogue, The Metropolitan Museum of Art, New York, 1998
Kramrisch, S. *Painted Delight,* Philadelphia Museum of Art, Philadelphia, 1986
Lane, Richard. *Images from the Floating World,* Oxford, 1978
Lauf, D.I. *Secret Revelations of Tibetan Thang-kas: The John Gilmore Ford Collection,* Freiburg, 1976
Leach, Linda York. *Indian Miniature Paintings and Drawings,* exhibition catalogue, The Cleveland Museum of Art, 1986
Lee, Sherman. *Rajput Painting,* exhibition catalogue, Asia House Gallery, New York, 1960
Lentz, Thomas and Lowery, Glenn, *Timur and the Princely Vision: Persian Art and Culture in the Fifteenth Century,* Los Angeles, 1989
Lings, Martin. *The Quroanic Art of Calligraphy and Illumination,* London, 1976
Lings, Martin and Yasin Safadi. *The Quroan,* London, 1976
Loehr, Max. *The Great Painters of China,* Oxford, 1980
Losty, J.P. *The Art of the Book in India,* exhibition catalogue, British Library, London, 1982
Lowery, Glenn D. and Susan Nemazee. *A Jeweler's Eye: Islamic Arts of the Book from the Vever Collection,* Washington, D.C., 1988
Meech-Pekarik, Julia. *The World of the Meiji Print,* New York and Tokyo, 1987
Merritt, Helen and Nanako Yamada. *Guide to Modern Japanese Woodblock Prints: 1900-1975,* Honolulu, 1992
Michener, James A. *The Modern Japanese Print,* Rutland and Tokyo, 1970
Miles, Richard. *The Prints of Paul Jacoulet,* London, 1982
Millstein, Rachel. *Islamic Painting in the Israel Museum,* Jerusalem, 1984
  Miniature Painting in Ottoman Baghdad, Costa Mesa, 1990
Miyajima, Shinchi and Yasuhiro Satoh. *Japanese Ink Painting,* Los Angeles County Museum, Los Angeles, 1986
Moes, Robert. *Auspicious Spirits: Korean Folk Paintings and Related Objects,* exhibition catalogue, Washington, D.C., 1983
Murase, Miyeko. *Japanese Screens from New York Collections,* exhibition catalogue, Asia Society, New York, 1971
  Japanese Art: Selections from the Mary and Jackson Burke Collection, New York, 1975

Murashige, Yasushi (editor). *Rimpa Painting,* Vol. 5, Kyoto, 1991

National Palace Museum. *Masterpieces of Chinese Calligraphy in the National Palace Museum,* Taipei, 1970

National Palace Museum. *Masterpieces of Chinese Portrait Painting in the National Palace Museum,* Taipei, 1971

Newland, Amy and Chris Uhlenbeck. *Ukiyo e to Shin hanga,* New York, 1990

Pal, Pratapaditya. *The Classical Tradition in Rajput Paintings from the Paul F. Walter Collection,* exhibition catalogue, AFA, New York, 1979

Pal, Pratapaditya and Vidja Dehajia. *From Merchants to Emperors: British Artists and India 1757-1930,* Ithaca, 1986

Pedersen, Johannes. *The Arabic Book,* Princeton, 1984

Pinar, S. (editor). *A History of Ottoman Painting,* Seattle and London, 1989

Raby, Julian. 'East and West in Mehmed the conqueror's Library', *Bulletin de Bibliophile* 3, 1987, pp.297-321

Renda, Gunsel et al. *A History of Turkish Painting,* Seattle and London, 1988

Ri-cho Minga. *Folk Painting of the Yi Dynasty of Korea,* Odakyu and Tokyo, 1979

Robinson, B.W. *A Descriptive Catalogue of the Persian Paintings in the Bodleian Library,* Oxford, 1958
Islamic Paintings and the Arts of the Book, catalogue of the Keir Collection, London, 1976
Persian Paintings in the India Office Library, A Descriptive Catalogue, London, 1976
Persian Paintings in the John Rylands Library: A Descriptive Catalogue, London, 1980
Kuniyoshi, Victoria & Albert Museum, London, 1961
Kuniyoshi: The Warrior Prints, Oxford, 1982

Rohatgi, P. *Portraits in the India Office Library & Records,* London, 1983

Rohani, Nasrin. *A Bibliography of Persian Miniature Painting,* Cambridge, 1982

Rosenfield, John (editor). *Song of the Brush, Japanese Paintings from the Sano Collection,* Seattle Art Museum, Seattle, 1979

Ruitenbeek, Claas. *Discarding the Brush,* Amsterdam, 1992

Safadi, Yasin H. *Islamic Calligraphy,* London, 1978

Schimmel, Annemarie. *Islamic Calligraphy,* Leiden, 1970
Calligraphy and Islamic Culture, New York and London, 1984

Schmitz, Barbara et al. *Islamic Manuscripts in the New York Public Library,* New York and Oxford, 1992

Segi, Shinichi. *Yoshitoshi: The Splendid Decadent,* Tokyo, 1985

Shanghai Bowuyuan Cang Lidai Fashu Xuanji (Selections of Calligraphy from the Shanghai Museum), 20 vols., Beijing, 1964

Shimizu, Yoshiaki and John Rosenfield. *Masters of Japanese Calligraphy 8th-19th Century,* Japan House Gallery & The Asia Society Galleries, New York, 1984-1985

Siren, Osvald. *The Chinese on the Art of Painting,* New York, 1962

Sivaramamurti, Calambur. *South Indian Painting,* New York, 1968

Skelton, R. *Ragasthani Temple Hangings of the Krishna Cult,* exhibition catalogue, New York, 1973

Smith, Henry D. *Kiyochika: Artist of Meiji Japan,* Santa Barbara Museum of Art, 1988

Smith, Lawrence. *The Japanese Print Since 1900: Old Dreams and New Visions,* New York, 1983

Sogen, Omori and Terayama Katsujo. *Zen and the Art of Calligraphy,* London, 1981

Stephens, Amy Reigle. *The New Wave,* London and Leiden, 1993

Stevenson, John. *Yoshitoshios Thirty Six Ghosts,* New York and Tokyo, 1983

Stuart, Jan and Rawski, Evelyn S. *Worshiping the Ancestors,* Smithsonian Institution, Washington, D.C, 2001

Sullivan, Michael. *The Birth of Landscape Painting in China,* Berkeley and Los Angeles, 1962
Chinese Landscape Painting in the Sui and Tang Dynasties, Berkeley, 1980

Suzuki, Kei (editor). *Comprehensive Illustrated Catalogue of Chinese Paintings,* 5 vols., Tokyo, 1982

Tai, Susan et al. *Carved Paper: The Art of the Japanese Stencil,* New York and Tokyo, 1998

The Age of Harunobu: Early Japanese Prints c.1700-1780, exhibition catalogue, The Rijksmuseum, Amsterdam, 1977

Topsfield, Andrew. *Paintings from Rajasthan in the National Gallery of Victoria,* Melbourne, 1980
The City Palace Museum, Udaipur: Paintings of Mewar Court Life, Ahmedabad, 1990
An Introduction to Indian Court Painting, London, 1984

Tradition in Transition: Print Masters of the Meiji and Taisho Periods, Los Angeles, 1983

Ukiyo-e Taikei (Outline of Ukiyo-e) 17 Vols., Tokyo, 1975

Von Leyden, R. and M. Dummett. *Ganifa, The Playing Cards of India: A General Survey with a Catalogue of the Victoria and Albert Museum Collection,* London, 1982

Watanabe, Tadashi (editor). *Kawase Hasui Mokuhangashu (Complete Collection of Woodblock Color Prints by Hasui Kawase,* Tokyo and Osaka, 1979

Welch, Anthony. *Calligraphy in the Arts of the Muslim World,* Austin, 1979

Welch, Stuart C. *Royal Persian Manuscripts,* London and New York, 1976
Room for Wonder: Indian Painting during the British Period 1760-1880, New York, 1978
Indian Drawings and Painted Sketches, New York, 1976
Imperial Mughal Painting, New York, 1978

Welch, Stuart Cary and Anthony Welch. *Arts of the Islamic Book: The Collection of Prince Sadruddin Aga Khan,* exhibition catalogue, Asia Society, New York, 1982

Welch, Stuart Cary and Milo Beach. *Gods, Thrones, and Peacocks: Northern Indian Painting from Two Traditions, Fifteenth to Nineteenth Centuries,* exhibition catalogue, Asia House Gallery, New York, 1965

Zhongguo Gudai Shuhua Tumu (Catalogue of Chinese Paintings and Calligraphy), 24 vols., Beijing, 1987

Zhongguo Meishu Quanji: Huihua Bian (Encyclopedia of Chinese Art: Painting), 21 vols., Beijing, 1988

Photographic Acknowledgements

The Asian Art Museum of San Francisco, The Avery Brundage Collection, Chong-Moon Center for Asian Art and Culture – **161, 162**; B60P1949 – **50**; B60P1233 – **54**; B60P17# – **63**; B62P60, B62P61 – **80**; B60 S22+ – **116**; B65 B64 – **118**; B60 B14+ – **119**; B60 B339 – **120**; B60 M286 – **135**; B60 M427 – **156**; B66 S2, B66 S3 – **231**; F2000.39.1 – **222**. Gift of the Asian Art Museum Foundation, B68-Pl – **34**, Gift of the Connoisseur's Council, 1990.201 – **113**. Gift of Raymond G. and Milla L. Handley B86 S7 – **230**. On loan from the Christensen Fund, BL 77 M46 ab – **164**

The Birmingham Museum of Art, Alabama, 1981.171, 1977.208, and 1980.448 – **38**; AF13 .2000 – **167**

Collection of Robert H. Blumenfield – **74, 128, 196, 269**

Collection of James Callahan – **176**

The Denver Art Museum – **265**; Funds from the Dora Porter Mason bequest, 1947.2 – **107**

The Detroit Institute of Arts, Founders Society Purchase, Sarah Bacon Hill Fund, 62.266 – **103**; Robert Hensleigh, photographer copyright 1987 D.I.A. – **145**; City of Detroit Purchase, 26.7 – **150**; Founders Society Purchase, Stoddard Fund for Asian Art, and funds from the Gerald R. Chamberlin Foundation, Inc., 80.25 – **155**; Founders Society purchase with funds from an anonymous donor, 1983.5 – **171**; Founders Society Purchase, 1985.14 – **264**, 1988.62 – **287**

Flying Cranes Antiques, New York – **77, 83, 86, 87, 88, 121, 122, 130, 170, 186**

The Freer Gallery of Art, Smithsonian Institution, Washington, D.C; Purchase, F1956.1 – **44**; Purchase, F1957.24 – **45**; Purchase, F1928.2 – **46**; Gift of Charles Lang Freer, F1903.226 – **47**, F1902.52 – **61**; Anonymous Gift, F1978.47 – **47**; Purchase, Friends of Asian Arts, F1998.25 – **60**; Purchase, F1930.54a-b – **90**; Purchase, F1955.22 – **104**; Purchase F1930.71 – **189**; Purchase F1948.14 – **192**; Purchase F1932.28 – **291**

Cora Ginsburg, New York – **257, 263**

Martyn Gregory Gallery, London – **277**

Nicholas Grindley, London – **141**

Alan and Simone Hartman – **31, 32** (photographs by Jerry Fetzger), **205**

Gerard Hawthorn, Ltd. London – **43, 99, 145, 158, 184**

The Indianapolis Museum of Art, Gift of the Alliance of the Indianapolis Museum of Art, 1983.1 – **62**; Gift of Mr. and Mrs. Eli Lilly – **55**; 60.82 – **68**; IMA60.116 – **73**

Ben Janssens Oriental Art, London – **214**

Kaikodo, New York, photograph by John Bigelow Taylor, New York City – **30**

Roger Keverne, London – **41, 100, 101, 127, 204, 208**

Robert Kleiner, London – **237**

Leighton and Rosemary Longhi – **278, 279, 280** (photograph by John Bigelow Taylor, New York City), **281, 282, 283**

The Minneapolis Institute of Arts, 98.190.5 – **216**; 62.65.1 – **261**; John R. Vanderlip Fund and gift of the Directors Tour, 87.62 – **28**, 83.130 – **36**; Gift of the Asian Arts Council, 98. 69a,b – **40**; Gift of Clifford and Suzanne Roberts, 89. 119a,b – **64**; Gift of Bruce B. Dayton, 79.4 – **58**; Gift of Ruth and Bruce Dayton, 97.81 – **97**, 98.78.5 – **141**, 96.71 ab – **160**, 96.69. lab – **187**; Gift of Mrs. Charles S. Pillsbury, Mary Stinson Pillsbury Lord, Katherine Stevens Pillsbury McKee, and Helen Winston Pillsbury Becker in memory of Charles S. Pillsbury, 51.28.3 – **101**; Margaret McMillan Weber Fund, 65.36.2 – **104**; Gift of the Katherine Kittridge Memorial Fund, 82.10.4 – **109**; bequest of Alfred F. Pillsbury, 50.46.15 – **175**; Gift of Anne de Uribe Echebarria 86.7a-c – **236**; The Ethel Morrison Vanderlip Fund, 91.2a-c – **249**

The Philadelphia Museum of Art, 1928-114-2ab, photograph by Graydon Wood – **98**; photograph by Graydon Wood, 1995, Far Eastern Art Restricted Fund, 1982.105-1 – **213**

The Phoenix Art Museum, Phoenix, Arizona – **76**

Priestley and Ferraro, London – **39**

Private Collection – **137, 142, 151, 271, 272, 273, 275**

Private Collection, photograph by Richard Goodbody, courtesy of The Chinese Porcelain Company – **75, 198**

Private Collection, Jiyoung Koo, New York – **65, 78**

Private Collection, New York – **212**

Private Mid-western Collection, Andrew Kahane, Ltd., New York – **52**

The Richard Rosenblum Family Collection, **202, 203**

Arthur M. Sackler Gallery, Smithsonian Institution, Washington, D.C., Purchase 51996.62.1 – **245**; Gift of Joan and Frank Mount, 51996.104 – **43**

Samina, London – **131**

Scholten Japanese Art, New York – **144, 146, 147, 165, 169, 224, 285, 286**

The Taft Museum of Art, Cincinnati, Ohio, Bequest of Charles Phelps and Anna Sinton Taft, 1931.142 – **72**

Deon Viljoen, Capetown – **143, 149**

The Walters Art Museum, Baltimore, 71.324 – **200**; 42.293, **205**; Bequest of Henry Walters, 1931; 21.8 – **12**, 48.1288 – **48**, 57.527ab – **209**, 1931;83.14 – **261**, MS W.521 Folio 36 – **266**. Collection of John and Berthe Ford – **117, 199, 226, 227, 295, 296, 297, 299**. Museum Purchase, 1941;42.562 – **172**; Gift of Mrs. Roscoe B. Jackson, 26.15 – **209**

Collection of John C. Weber – **240, 258, 259**

Collection of Dora Wong – **239, 274**

Linda Wrigglesworth, Ltd., London – **253, 254, 255, 256**

Index

Page numbers in bold type refer to illustrations and captions